WITHDRAWN
NDSU

FDR
THE OTHER SIDE OF THE COIN

BOOKS BY HAMILTON FISH, LL.D.

The Challenge of World Communism
The Red Plotters
*An American Manifesto of Freedom in Answer to the
    Manifesto on Communism (1848)*
*The American People Are Living on Top of a
    Nuclear Volcano*
FDR: The Other Side of the Coin
*Lafayette in America During and After the
    Revolutionary War*
*New York State: The Battleground of the
    Revolutionary War*

Churchill, Roosevelt, Stalin at the Yalta Conference.

FDR
THE OTHER SIDE OF THE COIN

*How We Were Tricked
into World War II*

Hamilton Fish, LL.D.

VANTAGE PRESS
New York   Washington   Atlanta   Hollywood

Excerpt from *The Cardinal Spellman Story* by Robert I. Gannon, S.J. Copyright © 1962 by Fordham University. Reprinted by permission of Doubleday & Company, Inc.

D
753
F5

FIRST EDITION

All rights reserved, including the right
of reproduction in whole or in part in any form.

Copyright © 1976 by Hamilton Fish, LL.D.

Published by Vantage Press, Inc.
516 West 34th Street, New York, New York 10001

Manufactured in the United States of America
Standard Book Number 533-02220-7

DEDICATION

This book is dedicated to 115 million Americans, the 85 percent who wanted to keep out of another European war, unless attacked, during the latter part of the Roosevelt administration; and to the memory of the nearly 300,000 Americans in our armed forces who were killed in World War II, and 700,000 who were wounded fighting for the preservation of freedom, democracy and peace. They helped to win the victory, but at Yalta the principles they fought for were turned into ashes and Stalin and communism emerged as the victors.

Ten percent of the net proceeds from the sale of this book will go to Operation Freedom, Inc., to carry the truths of freedom into our schools and colleges and eventually behind the iron curtain of all Communist-dominated nations.

CONTENTS

Author's Introduction

1. The Indispensable President and His
   Personality Cult 1
2. The March to War 15
3. "I Have Said This Before and I Shall Say It Again,
   and Again, and Again . . ." 29
4. FDR Surrounded by Radical Appeasers 37
5. How Roosevelt Prodded and Goaded
   the British Government into War 45
6. The Great British Firster, Winston Churchill,
   Who Hated and Feared Communism 48
7. FDR's Implied Promises in 1939 of
   Military Support to France 59
8. FDR's Proposed Betrayal of France and
   Freedom 64
9. Ambassador Joseph Patrick Kennedy 72
10. My Interview with the German Foreign Minister
    Joachim von Ribbentrop on August 14, 1939 79
11. The Famous Interparliamentary Union
    Conference 91
12. Peaceful Arbitration of Danzig or War? 100
13. The Crucifixion of Poland 113
14. The Atlantic Charter 125
15. How the United States Became Involved
    in World War II 131

16. The Tragedy of Pearl Harbor	143
17. General of the Army Douglas MacArthur	163
18. My Reception for Winston Churchill	174
19. The Deplorable Deception During 1944 about the Health of a Mentally and Physically Sick President	181
20. The Tragic Betrayal of Freedom at Yalta	193
21. FDR and Palestine	208
22. A Friendly China Becomes a Communist Empire	216
23. FDR's Attempts to Usurp the Power of Congress to Declare War	224
Conclusion	230
Appendix I. Roosevelt's Foreign Policies, 1933–1941	233
Appendix II. The Forrestal Diaries	235
Appendix III. Interview Between Curtis B. Dall and Former Governor George Earl of Pennsylvania Regarding Secret Efforts of High German Officers and Officials to Surrender Eighteen Months Before the End of the War	237
Appendix IV. Tributes to General Douglas MacArthur, A Great American	242
Appendix V. Statement by Herman H. Dinsmore	245
Bibliography	247
Index	253

AUTHOR'S INTRODUCTION

This book is an agonizing reappraisal written by the author, the Honorable Hamilton Fish, a member of Congress for twenty-five years, ranking Republican member of the Foreign Affairs Committee 1933–43, and ranking member of the Rules Committee 1940–45.

The author is one of the very few former members alive who participated actively in the Congressional foreign policy debates between 1937 and 1945. I made the first speech advocating war with Japan on December 8, 1941 (the first speech ever made in Congress over the radio). This speech was heard by over 20 million Americans and it upheld President Roosevelt's theme of the "Day of Infamy." I now publicly disavow that speech as a result of subsequent historical evidence. I believe that not only the American people but everyone interested in the truths of history is entitled to know the naked truth: that Roosevelt incited and provoked Japan into war by the issuance of an all-out secret war ultimatum in defiance of the Congress, the American people, and the Constitution of the United States, *ten days before Pearl Harbor.*

Even now, every Pearl Harbor Day, December 7, American newspapers editorially denounce Japan for provoking and causing the war in the midst of peace negotiations. This is entirely contrary to the historical facts. The Honorable Clare Boothe Luce was right when she said that President Roosevelt lied us into war by the back door in order to get into war with Germany. Sir Oliver Lyttleton, British Minister of Productions in Churchill's cabinet, speaking before the American Chamber of Commerce in London in 1944, let the cat out of the bag: "Japan was provoked into attacking the Americans at Pearl Harbor. . . . It is a travesty on history to ever say America was forced into the war."*

Emperor Hirohito has been falsely attacked for being responsible for the war. In fact, he consistently urged peace by diplomacy and offered unprecedented concessions, including withdrawal of Japanese troops from China and Vietnam.

What right has anyone, particularly historians, to try to brush under the rug the basic reasons for the unwanted and unnecessary war between Japan and the United States? Those valiant soldiers on both sides who made the supreme sacrifice in that war will have died in vain fighting for their own country unless the truth of history prevails and enables oncoming generations to avoid the pitfalls of another such tragic war.

To hold, after 33 years, that the truth should not be known about the origin of America's participation in World War II, would be a repudiation of history. There is an old Latin proverb, *Veritas magna est et pravelibit*. The truth is mighty and will prevail.

There never was in all history a more deadly and disastrous ultimatum or war. Two months after we became involved in war with Japan, Germany, and Italy through the back door, Winston Churchill on February 15, 1942, made a radio broadcast in which he said, "When I survey and compute the power of the United States and its vast resources and feel that they are now in with us, with the British Commonwealth of Nations, however long it lasts till death or victory, I cannot believe that there is any other fact in the whole world which can compare with that. *That*

---

*United Press International report, June 5, 1944.

*is what I have dreamed of, aimed at and worked for, and now it has come to pass."**

Roosevelt and Churchill were responsible for getting the United States into what Churchill later called "the unnecessary war." The fatal and infamous war ultimatum to Japan of November 26, 1941, opened the U.S. Treasury Department's doors, and an avalanche of 35 billion American dollars kept the British ship of state afloat for the next four years. To Churchill and England it was the realization of a dream; to Americans it is still part of our national debt, costing our taxpayers more than a billion dollars a year. Lend-Lease was only a small part of our total war expenditures. World War II cost the United States 355 billion dollars, a large part of its national debt today. And owing to a sick and dying president's surrender of eastern Europe and Manchuria at Yalta to Stalin and communism, the U.S. has spent in excess of one trillion dollars in defense of freedom against the menace of world communism since 1945.

The United States cabinet is appointed by the president. FDR dismissed from his cabinet Harry Woodring, secretary of war, and arranged to get rid of Charles Edison, secretary of the navy, and substitute Henry T. Stimson and Frank Knox, the two most outstanding war advocates in the Republican party or in the nation. By including them, FDR gathered a group of militant internationalists and interventionists within the cabinet that would go to almost any lengths to involve the U.S. in war with Germany or Japan. It is doubtful that Roosevelt could have picked a more aggressive prowar cabinet. For want of another name, they were the most active warmongers on the political horizon at that time, headed by FDR, Secretaries Hull, Stimson, Knox, Morgenthau and Ickes. The rest of the cabinet, including Frances Perkins, secretary of labor, Jesse Jones, secretary of commerce, Henry Wallace, the vice-president, and Harry Hopkins, the assistant to the president, were all

*Winston S. Churchill, *The End of the Beginning: War Speeches*, 1945, p. 66.

confirmed prowar advocates. In the entire cabinet, there was not one single noninterventionist. At times for political expediency, peace was on their lips but they all rallied around the warlike acts of FDR.

Roosevelt's war cabinet had a great deal of cooperation from the powerful Eastern press, largely for war, such as the *New York Times, Herald Tribune, Washington Post, Baltimore Sun, Boston Herald, Boston Globe*, and the Philadelphia papers. The vast prowar propaganda was heavily financed by the international bankers, armament makers and big business, numerically few in number but exceedingly powerful in financial resources and control over vast publicity and propaganda.

Most members of FDR's cabinet including General Marshall would at the president's suggestion have favored war against Patagonia if it would have involved the United States in war with Germany. Senator Ferguson before a Senate investigating committee asked General Marshall about a meeting he attended at the White House on November 25, 1941, where the main issue was how to maneuver, goad and incite Japan into firing the first shot. General Marshall admitted being present at the White House meeting and that Secretary of War Stimson's recollections as stated in his diary were correct.

At the Atlantic Conference, August 1941, President Roosevelt conferred with Prime Minister Churchill regarding an agreement to protect the British interests in the Far East. The proceedings have never been released to the American public, but Churchill's speech in the Parliament on January 27, 1942, confirmed such an agreement. He said, "The probability since the Atlantic Conference, at which I discussed these matters with President Roosevelt, that the United States even if not herself attacked would come into the war in the Far East and then make victory sure, seems to allay some of the anxiety."

There are some people who for their own reasons do not want the truth of history known, particularly when it directly changes the meaning of history or treads on the toes of outspoken advocates of the war. But no one has the right to obscure the truth of history. It must be discovered so that it may serve as a guidepost for the preservation of peace throughout the world.

In case some ardent interventionists and prowar friends or supporters of former President Franklin D. Roosevelt question the ethics of criticizing the public actions of a former president, they should read and digest the advice of former President Theodore Roosevelt, one of our greatest American presidents, who had this to say *in the midst of World War I*: "To announce that there must be no criticism of the president, right or wrong, is not only unpatriotic and servile, but it is morally treasonable to the American people. Nothing but the truth should be spoken about him or anyone else, but it is even more important to tell the truth . . . but the flood of memoirs, diaries, reminiscences else."

Napoleon Bonaparte once said, "When events occur in the heat of contrary passions, it is difficult to obtain the truth . . . but the flood of memoirs, diaries, reminiscences (and now present releases from government sources), that, my friend, is history."

For personal, political and obvious reasons, I purposely refrained from publishing this book during the lifetimes of former President Franklin Roosevelt, former Prime Minister Winston Churchill, former Secretary of the Treasury Henry Morgenthau and former General of the Army Douglas MacArthur; all of whom were prominent and controversial public officials during World War II.

I am not an iconoclast seeking to tear down or destroy the reputation of any public official, but a devotee of history endeavoring to present the truth and to show the other side of the coin. This was impossible during or shortly after World War II. The wartime propaganda continued for a number of years and the truth was not then always palatable. It is only now that these long-buried, hidden facts are beginning to seep through the governmental archives and are available to the American people, previously kept in the dark.

Even Democratic members of Congress admitted that the president had already asked Congress to do everything but declare war. Senator George, a leading Democrat from Georgia, said in September 1940: "Do not deceive yourselves, gentlemen: do not try to deceive the American people. They will know you are not preparing for peace, or for national defense, but you are preparing for war." This was probably the reason that President Roosevelt tried to purge this distinguished Democrat. But there were ten other Democratic senators on FDR's purge list, including Huey Long.

In this Bicentennial year it is well to remember the advice of President George Washington to the American people: "Real patriots who may resist the intrigues of the favorite (FDR) are liable to become suspected and odious; while its tools and dupes usurp the applause and confidence of the people to surrender their interests. Against the insidious whiles of foreign influence I conjur you to believe me, fellow citizens, the jealousy of a free people ought to be constantly awake."

The above quotation, from President Washington's Farewell Address, applied to such patriots as former Democratic Governors Charles Edison, Alfred E. Smith and Harry Woodring, to former President Herbert Hoover, to well-known editors William R. Hearst, Joseph Patterson and Col. Robert McCormick, to Col. Charles Lindbergh and to such distinguished Senators as Bill Borah, Weyland Brooks, Arthur Capper, Champ Clark, Hiram Johnson, Edwin C. Johnson, Robert Lafollette, Jr., Pat McCarran, Gerald Nye, Bob Reynolds, Bob Taft, Arthur Vandenberg, David Walsh and Burton Wheeler. And in the House of Representatives to Carl Bachmann, Martin Dies, Everett Dirksen, Claire Hoffman, Royal Johnston, Harold Knutson, Louis Ludlow, John O'Connor, Alvin Olkonski, Caroll

Reese, James Richards, Joe Starnes, Dewey Short, Francis Walters, Martin, Barton and Fish.

In celebrating the 200th anniversary, we must reaffirm our faith in our government by the consent of the governed, in our own freedoms and independence, and in the United States as the greatest, freest and best nation in the world. Napoleon in his last instructions to his son, the King of Rome, wrote: "Let my son read and reflect on history: this is the only philosophy."

FDR
THE OTHER SIDE
OF THE COIN

Whatsoever will remain of mortal man in generations to come is that which appeared in black and white upon the printed pages of books. A century hence, even the greatest of this generation will have been forgotten, unless historical pages contain some reference to him and to his deeds. All Americans should be interested in the truths of their history. The author hopes that this unpretentious historical book will be read by oncoming generations until our Tricentennial, if not beyond.

1

THE INDISPENSABLE PRESIDENT AND HIS PERSONALITY CULT

*From a Jeffersonian Democrat
to a Fabian Socialist*

I have often stated that FDR was personally attractive, good looking and replete with charm. He had an appealing honeyed voice and excelled in delivering his fireside chats over the radio. Most of his radio speeches were ghostwritten by the best professionals in the nation, starting with Louis Howe, Ray Moley, Tommy Cochran, Stanley High, Sam Rosenman, and ending with Robert Sherwood, the ablest of all his ghost-writers.

When he was not reading his ghostwritten radio talks to the public, he was a very ordinary speaker, but his golden voice, often interspersed with sarcasm and humor, was extremely effective over the radio. His delivery was excellent, he was somewhat of an actor when he addressed large crowds but the words and ideas were not his own.

He apparently did not read widely and knew little about economic or fiscal matters. One does not absorb history, government or economics except through serious reading and patient study, over a long period, of the best sources available. Miss Frances Perkins, a member of his cabinet, knew FDR from early manhood until his death. She said he was not a student, knew nothing of economics, and that he admitted he had never read a book on that subject. Edward J. Flynn, his campaign manager in the 1940 election and closely associated with him as a friend and as secretary of state of New York while Roosevelt was governor, said he never saw FDR read a book. Others closely associated with him in the White House said they never saw him interested in a book, save an exceptional detective story. The only books that he really seemed to care for were about the navy. I submit that the history of the navy and its battles is not the history of the United States or Europe, or their tremendously complex political and social movements.

His education before he entered Groton School was mostly by governesses and tutors, and he attended a German school for one month while his parents visited a German spa. At Groton and at Harvard his academic standing was merely average. He did, however, become an editor of the *Harvard Crimson*.

At Groton he came under the influence of its distinguished headmaster, Dr. Peabody. Peabody was not only a fine educator, but a strong and religious character and a leading Episcopalian. Young Roosevelt was influenced by this association and remained throughout his life a churchgoing Episcopalian.

However, his intellectual qualifications were limited. He read little, and was not interested in writing books, unlike presidents Theodore Roosevelt, Woodrow Wilson, Herbert Hoover, John F. Kennedy and Dwight D. Eisenhower. However, FDR outclassed the rest in one category—he was a master politician, thanks to Louis Howe and James A. Farley at first, although he soon outshone them as well. After his election as governor of New York, he lived and breathed politics to the end of his days. But he bitterly resented opposition and developed an unfortunate tendency toward intense vindictiveness, surprising in a person with his background. At times it almost verged on sadism, according to Jesse Jones, a member of his cabinet. In no sense," said Jones, "did I feel his superiority over other men except that he was the greatest politician our country has ever known and ruthless when it suited his purpose." FDR indulged his vengeful spirit in numerous political purges, even against a dozen Democratic United States senators.*

It is not for me, a dyed-in-the-wool Republican, to depict President Roosevelt's political characteristics at length. It is inappropriate for any well-known Republican whose views might be regarded as partisan or prejudiced. That should be left to well-known Democrats.

I admired FDR for the fine courage he showed in the long fight to recover from his paralysis. For twenty years, 1913–1933, we were very good friends. I have a score or more of intimate and personal letters from him. In one, he wanted me to succeed him as state senator as a Theodore Roosevelt progressive and said he would not only get me the Democratic endorsement but would break his rule by campaigning for me. In another letter he recommended to President Woodrow Wilson the appointment of my father, who was then head of the Sub-Treasury in New York, to the Federal Reserve Board. I supported most of Roosevelt's crisis legislation, but after six months I split politically with him over unconstitutional legislation creating the NRA and the AAA, which I felt were socialistic measures, and the recognition of Soviet Russia. The split was not on personal or partisan grounds: There were numerous Democrats who did not mince words either. Alfred E. Smith called FDR a demagogue, a repudiator of the 1932 Democratic national platform and denounced him for turning the Democratic Party to socialism.

It is extremely difficult to portray President Roosevelt's chameleon individuality. As Al Smith used to say, "Let's

*For a detailed report on the purge attempt, see Turner Catledge, *My Life and the Times*, op. cit., chapter 9.

look at the record and see what the record discloses."

Franklin D. Roosevelt, in accepting the nomination of the Democratic Party for president in 1932, made crystal clear his approval of the party platform. In his own words, "that admirable document, the platform, I accept it 100 percent." Throughout the presidential campaign, FDR openly supported the Democratic platform, promising "a saving of not less than 25 percent of the cost of the federal government" (p. 661).* This extraordinary promise was deliberately thrown into the wastebasket soon after the inauguration, ignored and forgotten, as were so many of his promises made in later campaigns.

He said "I accuse the present administration (Hoover) of being the greatest spending administration in peacetime in all our history. And I ask you to assign to me the task of reducing the annual cost of the operating expenses of the national government" (p. 761). He said further, "High-sounding newly invented phrases cannot sugarcoat the bill. Let us have the courage to stop borrowing, to meet continuous deficits and stop the deficits" (p. 662). This is the same man who later on was referred to as "Franklin Deficit Roosevelt."

Of course there are not many people alive today who remember FDR's promises to the American people in the 1932 campaign. It is almost beyond the comprehension of any fair-minded person to reconcile the enormous avalanche of spending deficits and regimentation of the American people with FDR's commitments in the 1932 campaign. He even told the American people, "I dislike regimentation when it is done by the government of the United States" (p. 680). These are just some of the definite promises made by FDR in support of the Democratic national platform in 1932, all of which were repudiated, to put it mildly, soon

---

*The page numbers in parentheses used in this and succeeding paragraphs refer to the pages in Vol. I of *The Public Papers and Addresses of Franklin D. Roosevelt, 1928–1932*, issued by the president and edited by Judge Samuel I. Rosenman.

after his inauguration. This should have provided a clue as to the sincerity of his subsequent pledges in the 1940 campaign to maintain peace. In fact, he was doing everything in his power to involve us in the war *sub rosa*.

The Congress turned over 4 billion dollars emergency and relief funds to FDR without restrictions or accountability forty years ago, which would be equivalent to 10 billion dollars today. The control of the purse strings is a principal responsibility of the Congress. Whenever a weak, partisan rubber-stamp Congress surrenders that power to a president, Democrat or Republican, it virtually changes our form of government.

Fiscally the most significant product of Roosevelt's administration was that it borrowed money by issuing tax-exempt bonds and treasury notes. Here, it surpassed all previous world records. It was the only consistent policy of an administration elected on a platform to balance the budget.

A few quotations from FDR and from the Democratic national platform during the 1932 presidential campaign.

Relief: "I am opposed to any form of dole. I do not believe the state has any right merely to hand out money" (p. 42).

"Under no circumstances," he said again, "shall any money be paid in the form of a dole or any other form by the local welfare offices, to any unemployed or family" (p. 463).

FDR said, "Revenues must cover expenditures by one means or another. Any government, like any family, can for a year spend more than it earns, but you and I know that a continuation of this habit means the poor house" (p. 663).

FDR opposed the government's borrowing at the banks (p. 806). He repeated condemned Hoover in the strongest language for permitting deficits. "I regard it as a constant duty of the Government to raise by taxes whatever sums may be necessary" (p. 798).

At a campaign speech in Pittsburgh on "The Budget," FDR said, "Now I am going to give you good people a real shock—. The true deficit of June 30, next year will be over one billion six hundred million dollars . . . a deficit so great that it makes you catch your breath" (p. 805). Later on, the FDR deficits were enough to make the angels weep.

He adopted the traditional Democratic position against "the tendency to concentrate power at the top of the Government structure, alien to our system" (p. 96). But later on, he built the greatest centralized alphabetical bureaucracy in history.

The political secret of FDR's popularity was his almost complete control of approximately $3 billion annually for seven years for recovery and relief up to our entrance into the war. Much of it was distributed by the big bosses and his alter ego, Harry Hopkins.

Instead of reducing the running expenses of the government by 25 percent and stopping borrowing and deficits, he started a long-range, reckless, cowardly policy of squandermania which gave birth to our present-day ruinous inflation.

When elected to the State Senate in 1910, FDR was a Jeffersonian Democrat and continued to be until after his inauguration as president in 1932. Then he brought to Washington a host of young extreme liberals and Marxists who proceeded with FDR's cooperation to build a socialistic welfare state. He was surrounded with leftists, radicals and Fabian Socialists like Rexford Guy Tugwell, Henry Wallace, Sidney Hillman, Harry Hopkins, Alger Hiss, Harry Dexter White, and Lauchlin Currie, his executive secretary. FDR downgraded the Constitution and spurned the free enterprise system which he had pledged to support via his party platform. He compared the Constitution with the horse-and-buggy days and undermined free enterprise with a bureaucratic socialistic welfare state.

I have no personal animosity or ax to grind against

FDR, although I knew he disliked me very much and with good reason. I continuously opposed his socialistic New Deal measures and his prowar foreign policy in Congress, and remained undefeated in Dutchess County, New York, in his own congressional district, which included Orange and Putnam counties.

I remember his reaction when I introduced an amendment providing for volunteers for thirty days to fill the military quota before the draft went into effect. It was adopted by the House of Representatives by seven votes in spite of a 100-man Democratic majority. Whereupon Roosevelt went into a tantrum. He called the Democratic leaders of the House to the White House and upbraided them for permitting the Republicans to amend his allegedly vital prowar measure. When one of the Democratic leaders told the president that it was *his* congressman who offered the amendment and led the fight, the conferees told me on their return that Roosevelt almost had apoplexy. They grinned and said, "Ham, you almost killed the President." I defeated him on a number of other occasions, and in general did not elicit much of the Rooseveltian bonhomie.

I was not only the leader in the House against Roosevelt's prowar foreign policies, but as chairman of the first Congressional committee to investigate Communism, I was very much against appeasement of the Communists at home and abroad. I was convinced then and still am that the Communists are the greatest enemies of freedom and democracy in the world. It was doubly menacing under FDR's regime because there were then so many fashionable apologists for communism and its bloody master, Stalin. They included President Roosevelt and his wife, Henry Wallace, Harry Hopkins, Sidney Hillman, Harry Dexter White, and Alger Hiss. Friendly towards the Chinese Communists then were Gen. George Marshall and Assistant Secretary of State Dean Acheson, who later changed his views.

The New Deal leftists, radicals and Fabian Socialists

piled commission upon commission, bureau upon bureau, and taxes upon taxes, and set up the greatest concentration of alphabetical organizations in Washington ever conceived. Shades of Thomas Jefferson, who became the first forgotten man!

What now of the "great white father," invincible in peace but invisible in World War I? What about the ex-Jeffersonian Democrat? Why, he would say he had progressed with the times. What a progression!

From a Jeffersonian Democrat, which signifies a liberal, he progressed rapidly to be an extreme liberal, then a radical, and finally to a Fabian Socialist and an apologist for Communists.

Franklin D. Roosevelt admitted that he had Communist friends and was the friend of the red dictator, Joseph Stalin, the world's greatest mass murderer. FDR himself was not a Communist. His religious faith lasted to the day of his death. The charge that he was a Fabian Socialist may arouse some New Dealers to rush to his defense, but the record cannot be ignored or washed away.

The New Deal, with its huge spending program, was certainly socialistic; it paved the road for collectivism and state socialism. When a president of the United States out-socializes Norman Thomas and recommends a limit of $25,000 on individual salaries, that in itself is a hallmark of Fabian socialism. But believe it or not, he approved the original Roosevelt-Morgenthau tax bill which the Democratic Ways and Means Committee threw into the wastebasket. This bill called for a limit of $12,000 on individual salaries and a 99 percent tax on large incomes. That bill out-socialized socialism and was as confiscatory as any Communist measure. I still have in my possession my speech in Congress exposing this most outrageous, un-American, socialistic and demagogic of all of FDR's New Deal policies.

His double-crossing and tricking of the American people in sending a secret war ultimatum to the Japanese government (as set forth in detail in Chapter 15) and in making Admiral Kimmel and General Short scapegoats for the disaster at Pearl Harbor, to cover up his own direct responsibility, is a black mark in American history. Admiral Halsey was right when he said "scapegoats and naval martyrs" were made to protect the higher-ups.

James D. Warburg, referring to Roosevelt, said, "He is undeniably and shockingly indifferent and ignorant about anything that relates to finances. This is not, I think, because he is incapable of grasping these subjects, but because he does not like them and therefore refuses to make any great effort to understand them. FDR was largely governed by his *personal emotional desires, predelictions and prejudices.*" (Italics mine.)

This would explain his vindictiveness against all those who opposed the New Deal or his prowar objectives. His personality cult came into being after his election to a third term as president. He became the first president to attain a third term and he felt now that he was all-powerful. Lord Acton's famous dictum that "power tends to corrupt; absolute power corrupts absolutely," is confirmed by history. After breaking the traditional American third-term barrier, FDR fell into the tangled web Lord Acton described. His personality cult grew steadily in proportion to the vast increase of his war powers. His unprecedented war ultimatum to Japan is a typical example of power's corrupting influence, and his actions at the fatal and disastrous Yalta Conference is another ghastly demonstration that absolute power corrupts absolutely.

FDR in his third term had accumulated so much power from Congress that he deluded himself that he was indispensable, that he alone was greater than the Congress, the Supreme Court and the American people. The next step was to ignore and bypass the Congress, the Supreme Court and the American people.

Senator Hiram Johnson, former governor of California, turned down the vice presidency under Harding, which, had he accepted it, would have brought him the presidency at Harding's death. He was prophetic when he said, "I want to do everything within my power to keep this country out of war, but I believe there are people in high places in government who will trick the American people into war."

This is exactly what Roosevelt did by provoking and forcing Japan into war in defiance of the Congress, the Constitution and the people. Then this masterful politician joined in a consortium of silence to cover up the very existence of this drastic war ultimatum so that today very few Americans have ever heard of it. It was done by ruse, trickery, and deception—by hiding and veiling the truth as expertly as Lenin ever did.

It was an immoral and infamous act. This shrewd and astute politician covered his tracks by shouting from the housetops and denouncing the attack on Pearl Harbor as a day of infamy, blaming it entirely upon the Japanese.

This propaganda travesty was believed by all Americans, including myself (see Chapter 16). Can anyone, Republican or Democrat, imagine any other American president since the days of George Washington, leading this country into war by subterfuge and trickery? Does anyone believe that George Washington, Thomas Jefferson, Abraham Lincoln, Grover Cleveland, or Theodore Roosevelt would have taken any part in such an infamous betrayal of the American people?

Despite the bitter criticism of him, FDR should be credited with having secured the adoption of a number of much-needed legislative reforms, most of which I supported, which helped to restore confidence and stability during the financial crisis at the beginning of his first term. Later he forced a rubber-stamp Congress to adopt many of his socialistic measures and started the New Deal alphabetical merry-go-round on its dance of destruction.

At the end of his second term, he lost faith in his own creations and began to lose interest in the New Deal's failures. At the beginning of the third term, he shoved the astute Jim Farley aside and took Harry Hopkins into the White House as his close friend and adviser. Hopkins was an able former relief worker who had no knowledge or experience in economics or international affairs.

Walter Lippman, a well-known commentator and author, said of the president that "his mind is not very clear, his purposes are not simple, and his methods are not direct."

The sanctity of promises cannot morally be ignored or thrown out of the window. Turner Catledge, who represented the *New York Times* for many years in Washington, expressed a low opinion of FDR in his excellent book, *My Life and The Times*. He stated that he felt the Congressional code of conduct was higher than the White House's under Roosevelt. "It seemed to me," he wrote, "that FDR brought to Washington politics a cynicism, a degree of double-dealing that had not existed before." In another connection he stated that "Over the years I had many experiences which caused me to question his sincerity and his honesty where political matters were concerned. Roosevelt was a consummate manipulator, a man who misled, deceived, lied outright when it was necessary to gain his ends."

John Flynn, in his book *The Roosevelt Myth*, criticized President Roosevelt seriously: "The White House goes into business and asks what sort of a man was this who permitted his family to make the White House into a headquarters for their commercial operations."

I prefer to bypass in silence charges which make less pleasant reading in two chapters of Flynn's book. I want to confine my remarks to telling the truth about the vital and important issues affecting the interests of our country and our people in order to help prevent similar mistakes, tragic blunders and ruinous policies that could jeopardize the destiny of our republic in the future.

Although Roosevelt, like Hitler and Stalin, sought to

accumulate power for himself, he was not a real dictator. He did not have the makeup to be an American dictator. He lacked determination, courage and vigorous faith in the operation of his own New Deal. He liked to be known as the commander in chief of our armed forces, but he made no attempt to control his generals as Hitler, Stalin, and, at times, Churchill did. Yet he was proud, vain, egotistical and enjoyed the use of his political powers. He was highly vengeful against everyone who opposed him, even to the extent of using the income tax process to frighten and punish his pet enemies. He tried to purge the Supreme Court, ten Democratic senators, and particularly Huey Long. He issued a crucial war ultimatum to Japan in secret. He sought the political persecution of the more active noninterventionists; it resulted in a trial of a score of Americans that finally collapsed because it violated the Constitutional rights of freedom of speech. He surrendered half the world to Stalin, including China, secretly. He had my telephone tapped and those of numerous senators and representatives who opposed his policies. These were all acts of political dictatorship. Perhaps he would have interpreted them as acts in the interest of the country or in defense of himself and his policies.

John L. Lewis, on October 24, 1940, charged over the Mutual Broadcasting System that President Roosevelt was "overweening, abnormal and selfish, craving for increased power while protesting that he hates war and will work for peace. The president has shown by his acts that war was his motivation and his objective from the time of his quarantine speech in Chicago. Above all, war perpetuates in imperishable letters on the scroll of fame and history the names of its political creators and managers."

General Hugh S. Johnson, former head of the NRA, was outspokenly against American involvement in war. He is reported as having said, "Regardless of an 8-to-1 popular majority against our getting into a foreign war, we are headed straight towards it by the shortest path." He placed the blame squarely on FDR.

Among the most devoted disciples of FDR were Elmer Davis and Archibald MacLeish. They would denounce anyone who disagreed with FDR's personality cult or prowar views as subversive and destructive of national unity. The high priest of the Library of Congress and the head of the OWI, like the ancient priests of Baal, cried out against the iconoclasts who would destroy the image of the king (FDR) and overthrow New Deal idols and war gods.

Arthur Krock of the *New York Times*, who had known Franklin D. Roosevelt for many years, gave a multifaceted portrait of the president's virtues and political assets as well as his defects.* His virtues included "A very special charm in private and public behavior—or, as it is now called, charisma. . . . A quality of leadership rare in history."

Inasmuch as the title of this book is *FDR: The Other Side of the Coin*, Arthur Krock's views of the president's defects are given in full:

Lack of intellectual depth. Too great a reliance, when thinking problems through got too tough, on what is clever and slick. A cynical approach to the trade of politics by which he ascended, notably by alliance with even more cynical city bosses. Fundamental weaknesses as an administrator. A callous or negligent reaction to the commercialization of his fame and office, that some members of his family openly engage in. Too ready to persuade himself that the national interest justified glossing over or withholding the facts due the people. A disposition to view honest critics with personal prejudice, and often to punish them by questionable use of the great powers of the Presidency. Conceit and arrogance particularly illustrated by his third-term ambition, in his estimate of his own talents as protean and absolutely indispensable to mankind. A shallow grounding in history, including that of the United States.

*Flynn, *Country Squire in the White House*.

Mr. Krock goes on to say, "But though my tally of 1945 attributed to him 'conceit and arrogance,' these traits did not manifest themselves until his election as President, and until he became aware of the great powers of the office . . ."*

Frances Perkins, secretary of labor in FDR's cabinet and a personal friend, described him as "the most complicated man I ever knew." This is a fair and accurate description. He was complicated because he had a habit of playing Russian roulette with important issues and was seldom sure of his final decisions. He was often influenced by the last man or advice. This created a credibility gap among his advisers and newspaper reporters and gave an impression of insincerity and untruthfulness.

FDR enjoyed usurping its legislative powers from Congress, particularly monetary and war powers, leaving the New Deal rubber-stamp Congress with no more clothing than Gandhi. In addition, he planned unsuccessfully to take over the powers of the Supreme Court; those plans blew up in his face.

---

*Arthur Krock, *Memoirs* (New York: Funk & Wagnalls, 1968), pp. 145–6.

2

THE MARCH TO WAR

FDR's prowar obsessions;
noninterventionists versus interventionists

The internationalists' and interventionists' cauldron began to seethe and bubble in the United States two years before the outbreak of World War II. The ingredients which Macbeth's witches used for their hell's broth were not more terrible or infernal than those thrown into the prewar brew by President Roosevelt and his belligerent prowar cabinet. What were those ingredients? Quarantining the aggressor nations with the lives of American boys, policing the world with blood and treasure, proclaiming war embargoes, undermining our traditional neutrality and peace for so-called collective security around the world—one-worldism and demands by the president for unlimited power and money from Congress to involve us in war without a declaration of war.

This was the power and war brew that enabled FDR to meddle and interfere with the foreign policies of European and Asian nations and to involve us in their age-old conflicts. Roosevelt was a determined internationalist and interventionist. He had been a candidate for vice-president on the Democratic ticket in 1920 on a rigid internationalist pro-League platform. He rarely departed from his internationalist views except for a third term. FDR had a secret obsession about using the high office of the presidency to influence, cajole, threaten, and directly or indirectly interfere with the foreign policies of England, France and Poland. He sought to persuade Poland to refuse to negotiate for the restoration of Danzig, 90 percent German, to the Third Reich, the main cause of the war, until it was too late. Not satisfied with direct meddling, he indulged in provocative name-calling against the heads of totalitarian nations such as Italy, Germany and later Japan, but never about Soviet Russia or Joseph Stalin. His language and epithets, and those of Secretary Ickes, were so inflammatory that he automatically ruled himself out as a potential peacemaker. That did not bother him because war was his objective and to act as a peacemaker, except early in 1940, was not what he had in mind. His constant thought, from September 1, 1939, to December 7, 1941, was to maneuver the United States into war.

Once World War II had begun, FDR was determined to involve us in it. Why? 1) To keep promises and implied promises. 2) To relieve a tragic unemployment situation, ten million unemployed after six years of New Deal policies and failures. 3) Desire as an internationalist to intervene actually in the conduct of the war. 4) Lust for power and a place in history as a war president. 5) The creation of the United Nations with FDR as the de facto ruler or coleader with Stalin.

Jesse H. Jones was a member of Roosevelt's cabinet as secretary of commerce, and a Democrat who also headed the Reconstruction Finance Corporation. In his book, *Fifty Billion Dollars*, he refers to Roosevelt as the "total politician." He helps to clarify FDR's desire and determination to get into war: "Regardless of his oft-repeated statement, 'I hate war,' he was eager to get into the fighting, since that would insure a third term. A third term would have gratified his two highest ambitions—to get into the war,

For Hamilton Fish Jr from Franklin D Roosevelt — Jan. 29 - 1934.

and his vanity to be re-elected as the first third-term President." He accomplished both by assuming the character of Doctor Jekyll and Mr. Hyde, posing as the peace candidate while he and his cabinet were doing everything in their power to maneuver the American people into war against their will.

There is an inexorable law greater than man-made laws. It is that truth will prevail. The minions of truth are stirring in the womb of history. History must uphold the realities of truth so that it may light the darkness.

FDR's prowar policy was like the bird who feigns to have a broken wing in order to decoy the enemy from destroying its nest and fledglings. He publicly pursued a policy of guile and subterfuge. He proclaimed his love of peace and hatred of war, but war was in his mind.

"War was in his heart: his words were softer than oil, yet were they drawn swords" (Psalms 55:4).

If Roosevelt had refrained from meddling in the European situation by encouraging England and France to believe that we would fight their battles, they would have reached an agreement by peaceful means to settle the Danzig issue, avoid the disastrous war, and protect their own colonial interests. The American people, regardless of their antipathy to Nazism, were opposed to sending their sons to fight over the possession of Memel or Danzig, or other territories seized under the Versailles Treaty, or to be slaughtered in defense of communism and Soviet Russia, or to defend French and British colonial empires. With Soviet Russia the most despotic and dictatorial nation in existence allied to Great Britain and France, a European war could not be fought for freedom and democracy, but for world power and the support of vast colonial empires.

As far back as April 21, 1939, four months before the outbreak of the war, the American people began to realize that the Roosevelt administration was openly prowar. It stood for internationalism, intervention, collective security, secret diplomacy, military alliances, and against our traditional American foreign policy of neutrality, nonintervention and peace. FDR and New Deal spokesmen, including members of the cabinet, stirred up war hysteria into a veritable frenzy. The New Deal propaganda machine worked overtime to prepare and condition the minds of our people for war, and once again to send our youth to foreign battlefields.

What was behind his far-reaching and continued campaign of hate emanating from the White House and discovering daily a new crisis? One word from the president would have stopped the hysteria and talk of war. But no such word came. Instead there was a steady flow of alarming and provocative statements that added fuel to the flames of war.

On April 11, 1939, President Roosevelt endorsed an editorial in the *Washington Post* that stated, "If war broke out in Europe, our participation in it would be a virtual necessity." The facilities of the president and the New Deal administration to disseminate war propaganda and hysteria, to prepare the youth of America for another bloodbath in Europe, was so enormous that a national organization to counteract these provocative and dangerous policies, the America First Committee, was formed to keep America out of foreign wars.

"Would that mine enemy write a book," is an old saying, but it is even worse to have a friend write a book like *Roosevelt and Hopkins: An Intimate History*. The author, Robert E. Sherwood, proves beyond a shadow of a doubt that what the noninterventionists (whom Sherwood always called "isolationists") were claiming was correct—that FDR was a militant, prowar interventionist. From the time of his quarantine speech of October 5, 1937, up to and after the beginning of World War II on September 3, 1939, his foreign policy was to meddle in the bloody game of European power politics.

The great rank and file of the American people had been appalled by the casualties and huge costs of World

War I. After the victory, largely won by United States troops, we asked for nothing and got exactly what we asked for. No thanks, no war booty, no reparations, nothing at all except to be called Uncle Shylock. Britain and France did not repay their war debts to us, or even the interest. An indignant President Calvin Coolidge remarked, "They hired the money, didn't they?" Is there any wonder that most Americans were in favor of keeping out of European wars? They were rightly noninterventionists in war, not the isolationists depicted by Mr. Sherwood, one of FDR's ablest ghost-writers.

Mr. Sherwood states in his book that FDR realized the strong antiwar sentiment in the country and did not dare to meet it head-on. Consequently, he was careful from the beginning to avoid getting too far out on a prowar limb where there could be no reconsideration. Instead FDR tried in every way to alarm the nation by propaganda that German planes would bomb Denver and that German panzer divisions would cross over from Africa to Brazil on their way to attack New York. The hysteria unleashed by the vast government propaganda sources alarmed the people without any justification. It was an abominable attempt to excite peace-loving Americans by ghost stories of bombing by Nazi airplanes and attacks by panzer divisions. (In Brazil they would be much farther away from the United States than from Germany and could not have gotten through the impassable swamps and forests of northern Brazil.) We do learn from Mr. Sherwood that FDR was a cloak-and-dagger internationalist who used extraofficial channels. There was Lord Beaverbrook, and once the war had broken out, there was a still partially unpublished historic correspondence of 1,700 messages with Winston Churchill; some of the most critical may never see the light of day.

Why aren't Americans now entitled to know their contents? All—not some exceptions. We were then living in the midst of an inspired and gigantic campaign of hysteria and fear that sought to break down the attitude of the American people against involvement in foreign wars by depicting us as being defenseless, like Norway and Holland, and that in self-defense we needed to go to war at once, or become a victim of Hitler later on. This was like jumping off a cliff or committing suicide from fear of having cancer in the future.

We were told that we might be attacked from Dakar in darkest Africa and that Hitler would fly himself with his panzer divisions to Brazil in order to invade us. In other words, he would attack us by going backwards: Dakar is twice as far as Germany is from the United States, and Brazil is again twice as far from Germany.

This was cowardly and craven talk to inspire fear of Hitler's invading the American continent. What in the name of heaven would our navy, the greatest in the world, and our army and air force be doing when Hitler discovered America? If the armed might of the German army could not cross the 20-mile English Channel, crossing 3,000 miles of Atlantic Ocean to the United States would be utterly impossible.

This was typical of the administration's prowar propaganda of hysteria, fear and emotionalism that sought to drive the American people into a global war despite their open opposition in every opinion poll.

My ancestors came to America from England 337 years ago to get away from the ceaseless religious and civil wars of Europe, and so did the ancestors of most other Americans. However, Field Marshall Harry Hopkins, Secretary Ickes, Morgenthau, Harriman, Henry Wallace and President Roosevelt, most of whom were invincible in peace, but invisible in war, were determined to send our sons back into the ceaseless wars of Europe and Asia. I have much more respect for Secretaries Stimson and Knox, two leading red-hot interventionists and warmakers, because they had served in the armed forces of the United States in the previous war.

In speaking about FDR's prowar propaganda, no one

knows more about it than his secretary of the navy, Frank Knox, who, referring to the effectiveness of New Deal propaganda, said, "This is a political propaganda machine the like of which this country has never seen." It went into high gear when Knox and Stimson joined the cabinet—not to support the New Deal, which both disapproved of, but to aid a massive, gigantic continuous prowar propaganda machine not even limited to the United States.

When the people of the U.S. began to take sides over going in or keeping out of World War II, the administration started a totally false and fictitious creation of word images. The image makers coined the word "isolationist," purposely designed as a disparaging word, to the delight of the warmakers, interventionists and one-worlders. Ninety percent of the forefathers of the American people migrated from foreign lands in order to avoid the hardships, privations and wars of the Old World. But actually, there was no such animal as an isolationist—that is, a person who is opposed to dealing with, trading, and maintaining diplomatic relations with other countries. Instead, the overwhelming majority of Americans were noninterventionists. Remembering the disillusionments of World War I they were openly opposed to our entrance into World War II unless we were attacked.

The new epithets—"obstructionists," "Nazis," "Fascists," "ostriches," "copperheads" and "isolationists"—were of no avail, because the American people could not be moved from their honest convictions that we should keep out of the bloody feuds and power politics of Europe.

The late President John F. Kennedy said at Yale University, June 11, 1962: "The greatest enemy of the truth is very often not the lie—deliberate, contrived and dishonest—but the myth—persistent, persuasive and unrealistic."

Most historical interpretations contain polemics and controversy. The main objective of the historian is to dispel with truth the innuendos, half-truths and misrepresentations that have been perpetuated over the years on an unsuspecting and uninformed public.

On the walls of Hunter College, New York City, engraved in large letters is the following quotation from Ralph Waldo Emerson: "We are of different opinions at different hours, but we always may be said to be at heart on the side of truth."

The following is part of a speech I made over the National Broadcasting Company's radio network. It was about the only way to reach the American people.

The interventionists and prowar press of the east and south would not carry a line, if they could help it, giving the views of an overwhelming majority of our people who want to stay out of war unless attacked. The American people have long since seen through the interventionism of the eastern press, columnists and prowar commentators, and the moving picture industry, to drive them into the war against their will. This inspired propaganda left the American people cold, even in the summertime.

Every American has a right to his or her views on the vital issue of war or peace, and to express them openly and freely. The 15 percent who are for participation in war, represented by the Fight for Freedom Committee, a misnomer after Yalta, had an absolute right to urge an immediate declaration of war without being called names or being denounced as placing the interest of the British Empire before that of America.

I agreed with Senator Pepper that if we entered the war it might last five years and cost 100 billion dollars a year. I do not believe that many American mothers wanted their sons to die in darkest Africa, in the vastness of China, fight for Soviet Russia, or to make Europe safe for communism. On the other hand, every American mother would have been willing to give the life of her son in the defense of the United States and the American continent.

President Roosevelt in a letter to the Young Democratic Clubs of America urged all isolationists to leave the Democratic party. Thomas Jefferson, the founder of the party, would turn in his grave. Jefferson was the leading noninterventionist of American history. He repeatedly urged that we keep out of the eternal wars of Europe. Jefferson founded the Democratic party and Franklin D. Roosevelt unfounded, or dumbfounded, Jefferson. President Roosevelt wanted to purge and read out of the Democratic party such able and courageous senators as Wheeler of Montana, Clark of Missouri, Clark of Idaho, Walsh of Massachusetts, McCarran of Nevada, Reynolds of North Carolina, and even Senator LaFollette, a progressive from Wisconsin, for seeking to keep America out of war unless attacked.

If FDR had succeeded in reading the noninterventionists out of the Democratic party north of the Mason-Dixon line, he would have had nothing left but the office holders of the party and the Fight for Freedom Committee, somewhat misnamed after the U.S.S.R. entered the war and more so after the Yalta betrayal.

Roosevelt's statement injected reckless partisanship into the greatest single issue before the American people, that of our involvement in foreign wars. Noninterventionists in both the Democratic and Republican parties representing most of the American people were strongly for national defense. The difference is that the noninterventionists wanted to protect and safeguard the United States and the American continent, and not go out looking for war all over the world.

· The American people should decide their own destiny within the confines of the Constitution. If FDR had sent a war declaration to the Congress it would have been defeated by a vote of four to one. Every American is in favor of making the United States invincible on land, sea, and in the air, so that we can meet and defeat any attack by any group of aggressor nations upon us or South America. Our navy, the largest and finest in the world, and many times greater than the German navy, guaranteed that there could be no successful attack made upon us. Within a few years our two-ocean navy will be completed. And within a year, our army will be equipped with artillery, tanks, airplanes, and antitank and antiaircraft guns sufficient to repel any possible invasion of this continent.

This sums up in a nutshell the vast antiwar sentiment that prevailed in the U.S. from the outset of the war in Europe. Now, what about the 15 percent of the population who were prowar advocates? Where did they come from?

They were a small, but very well and heavily financed

group, representing the international bankers, newspapers in the big northeastern cities, such as the *New York Times*, the *New York Herald Tribune* (Republican), the *Washington Post*, the *Baltimore Sun*, the *Boston Globe*, and most of the Philadelphia papers. They were a tremendous source of constant interventionist propaganda. In addition, in the Northeast, well-to-do socialite families through European marriages or business associations were belligerently pro-British or pro-French. They were few in number but vociferous, rich, and powerful. Then there was a so-called intellectual element which was distinctly prowar, such as presidents Conant of Harvard, Seymour of Yale, Nicholas Murray Butler of Columbia and Dodd of Princeton.

These prowar groups were small but powerful in financial circles, in the press, and on the radio. But by far the most important and effective prowar sentiment came from the Southern states. There was still in the South a considerable latent sympathy and goodwill for the British because of its moral support of the Confederate States during the Civil War. But there were other ties to Britain among the prowar Southerners. Many were of British origin and, even more important, were dyed-in-the-wool Democrats.

If it had not been for the hard-core Democrats from the South in the House and in the Senate, most of FDR's step-by-step unneutral and prowar measures would have been scrapped in Congress. The South was by far the most warlike section of the nation and naturally inclined to follow a Democratic president. Only one senator from the South, Robert Reynolds from North Carolina, was an active noninterventionist. However, he was fearless, outspoken, and held an important position as chairman of the Military Affairs Committee in the Senate. He also had the courage of his convictions, and FDR could not intimidate him.

The Southern members of Congress can justly claim major responsibility for the passage of Roosevelt's prowar measures and for the steps toward American involvement in war. But in fairness to them, probably not more than 20 percent would have voted for a *declaration* of war unless there was a definite attack on the United States or its armed forces.

Speaker Sam Rayburn, a likable and able Democrat from Texas, was as internationalist and interventionist as FDR but never served a day in our armed forces, and neither did Harry L. Hopkins, the alter ego of FDR, Sidney Hillman, the left-wing labor leader, Vice-President Henry A. Wallace, Clifton Woodrum and others in the House. But the Republican party had such men, too: Thomas E. Dewey and Nelson A. Rockefeller, both of whose presidential ambitions were ruined by the votes of the American war veterans, and their families.

The Northern and Western Democrats were fairly solid for my volunteer amendment to the draft bill, which passed the house by a vote of 207 to 200. Later on in the final extension of the draft bill, it was adopted by a vote of 211 to 210, with the Southerners voting for it.

There is a definite reason for describing the antiwar sentiment in the nation and the different situation in the Congress which was two-thirds Democratic in both the House and the Senate. Above and beyond the Congress stood the "great white father" and Harry Hopkins, with his spend-tax-and-elect program that had been so helpful in electing Democrats to Congress. It is not surprising that those Democratic members of the House who stood for election every two years were willing to follow the president on all measures allegedly short of war.

One of the most courageous and outspoken Democrats, who opposed every step towards war in the House, was Louis Ludlow of Indiana. He introduced a referendum war measure which came very near to winning a majority of the votes in the House. It took all the power of the administration to prevent its passage.

Who were the main opponents in the United States to war? The American Federation of Labor headed by William Greene; John L. Lewis head of the United Mine Workers;

farm organizations; the church elements, Catholic, Methodist, Baptist, Lutheran and many others; a majority of our women; the America First Committee and other peace organizations; Norman Thomas; many liberals; most of the large German and Italian population; and many disillusioned veterans who served with distinction in World War I, such as General Robert Wood, Theodore Roosevelt, Jr., and Hanford McNeider, later national commander of the American Legion.

All of these groups combined with the rank and file of the American people who preferred peace to war.

On June 29, 1941, former President Herbert Hoover exposed the entrance of Soviet Russia into the war as undermining the interventionists' pleas that the United States "should join the conflict to preserve Democratic principles and ideals," as Stalinist Russia was "one of the bloodiest tyrannies and terrors ever created in human history."

Hoover then predicted what has since become true—if we did join the war and won, "then we have won for Stalin the grip of Communism on Russia and more opportunity for it to expand over the world."

Senator Bennett Clark (Dem.) of Missouri pointed out that Stalin was "as bloody handed" as Hitler, and the United States should let these bloody dictators destroy themselves.

Senator Harry Truman, later president, denounced both dictators and said: "If Russia were winning help should be given to Germany and if Germany were winning, help should be given to Russia."

Looking back on history, Truman showed great foresight. Senator Robert M. La Follette of Wisconsin, with whom I debated in numerous cities across the nation, also had the same views as expressed by Senator Truman. "The American people will be told to forget the purges in Russia by the OGPU, the confiscation of property, persecution of religion, the invasion of Finland and the vulture role Stalin played by seizing half of prostrate Poland, all of Latvia, Estonia and Lithuania." La Follette as quoted above also foresaw the menace to freedom from Soviet communism.

Roosevelt's consistent war propaganda failed to achieve his objective as regards Germany. He did, however, succeed in getting us into war with his war-provoking ultimatum to Japan, still almost unknown to the American public.

3

"I HAVE SAID THIS BEFORE AND I SHALL SAY IT AGAIN, AND AGAIN, AND AGAIN:

Your boys are not going to be sent into any foreign wars"

Noninterventionists who had naturally suspected President Roosevelt ever since his quarantine speech of October 7, 1937, were confirmed in their opposition to him by his selection of Henry Stimson as secretary of war and Frank Knox as secretary of the navy. Both of them were leaders in the Republican war camp. Stimson was a war maker par excellence. He made no attempt to conceal his views.

On June 18, 1940, Stimson delivered a radio speech that was virtually in favor of an undeclared war. He urged opening our ports to British and French war vessels and sending our own ships into the war zones as convoys. Exactly at this time, Stimson was invited to serve as secretary of war. Before accepting, he asked President Roosevelt over the telephone whether he had read the text of his speech. The president replied that he had read the speech and approved of it. Of course the public did not know this, but they did know of Stimson's strong wish for war.

The insincerity and barefaced dishonesty of FDR's subsequent peace promises constituted an all-time high of misrepresentation, hypocrisy and deception of the American people. At the end of the 1940 presidential campaign, the Democratic leaders, fearing the strong peace vote, urged Roosevelt to counteract it by making a powerful peace plea. This was the origin of the most shocking, contemptible and untruthful public utterance of any president in our history.

It was in Boston on October 30, 1940, a week before the election that he said, "While I am talking to you mothers and fathers, I give you one more assurance. I have said this before, but I shall say it again and again and again: Your boys are not going to be sent into any foreign wars."

On November 3, a few days before his third-term election over Wendell Willkie, he added, "The first purpose of our foreign policy is to keep our country out of war."

These outright peace promises and pledges coming from the president of the United States were believed and acclaimed by voters in every village, hamlet, town and city in the country. Wendell Willkie, the Republican candidate, was pursuing a zig-zag course between peace and war and ended up running the wrong way with the peace ball. He was nominated by the internationalist Republican warmakers and did not dare to denounce the Democratic war party or President Roosevelt. He conducted a shadow-boxing campaign regarding the peace issue, the issue closest to the hearts and minds of the great majority of the electorate.

Roosevelt's deliberate deception on a matter involving the life or death of hundreds of thousands of young Americans was unforgivable, unforgettable and unconscionable. Before making such total peace promises, and actually *while* making them, he was using his vast powers to involve the United States in another European war. Certainly the American people should take another look at his Boston promise—"Your boys are not going to be sent into any foreign wars." He omitted the words, "except in case of attack," which were always used by antiwar and noninterventionist speakers.

Robert Sherwood, who suggested the all-out peace pledge for Roosevelt's Boston speech, wrote years later, "I burn inwardly whenever I think of those words, again—and again—and again."

President Roosevelt and those associated with him never sought to apologize to the American people. But by his secret ultimatum to Japan he did send ten million American soldiers, sailors and marines to fight in foreign lands, of whom almost 300,000 were killed and 700,000 wounded or missing.

FDR's peace assurance outpromised, outpledged and outdeceived any other public statement ever made by a president. Why did he make it? Because he was determined to get elected by hook or crook, so that he could carry out his obsession, to take the American people into World War II. Remember he said just days before his election, "The first purpose of our foreign policy is to keep our country out of war." This is the same president who issued a drastic war ultimatum a year later to the Japanese government for the sole purpose of forcing Japan, like a cornered rat, to fight and fire the first shot.

Two months after his pre-election promise of October 30, 1940, in Boston to the American fathers and mothers that their sons would not be sent into any foreign wars, FDR sent Harry Hopkins, his alter ego, to London to tell Churchill a different story. "The President is determined that we shall win the war together. Make no mistake about it. He has sent me here to tell you that at all costs and by all means he will carry you through . . . There is nothing that he will not do, so far as he has human power."

Harry Hopkins pledged American support to Britain at an official dinner. He quoted from the Book of Ruth: "Wither thou goest, I will go, and where thou lodgest, I will lodge . . . Where thou diest, I will die."

Robert E. Sherwood, Roosevelt's main ghost-writer, condoned Roosevelt's repeated deception of the American people by saying: "The inescapable fact is that this was what Roosevelt was compelled to say in order to maintain any influence over public opinion and over Congressional action." Deception is another word for cover-up.

A number of distinguished and loyal Americans honestly believed that we should have entered the European war at the outset when Poland was invaded by Hitler, or at least when France was invaded and conquered. But most public opinion in the United States opposed our involvement in another world war at those times.

I have no quarrel with any American who honestly believed it was in our interest to enter the war in Europe when Hitler's armies invaded Poland on September 1, 1939. That is the right of all Americans under the free speech guarantee in the Constitution, but it works both ways—for 'war interventionists and noninterventionists alike.

The question is sincerely raised, why didn't we enter the war in the beginning when Poland was attacked? The answer is that most Americans did not know the cause of the war or even where Danzig was. The Congress, under the Constitution, has the sole power to declare war. At that time over 96 percent of the American people, and the Congress, were opposed to joining another European war. Seven months later when Hitler's armed forces invaded Norway, a Gallup poll showed 3 percent of the American people in favor of entering the war and 97 percent in favor of keeping out. It is very evident from this that there was almost maximum sentiment in the U.S. against entering the European conflict, either at the beginning when Poland was invaded, or later when Norway and France were likewise invaded. Over the years the percentage was reduced from 97 to approximately 85 percent and remained the same right up to the attack on Pearl Harbor.

FDR was then surrounded by a group of appointees who were interventionists; many were Communist apologists. Among them was Averell Harriman, who like Assistant Secretary of State Acheson realized after the barn door was open that Stalin and communism were bitter enemies of freedom and the United States.

Roosevelt boasted that "Harry Hopkins and Uncle Joe Stalin got along like a house on fire. They have become buddies." Hopkins never tired of plugging for his friend Stalin. He said it was ridiculous to think of Stalin as a Communist. He was a Russian nationalist.

Sidney Hillman took the same distorted view of Stalin and so did Harold Ickes. Hopkins and Hillman, and in addition former Ambassador Joseph Davies, were deceived by Stalin and passed on their illusions to Roosevelt, who assured visitors that Stalin was not a Communist at all, just a Russian patriot.

Henry Wallace, when vice-president, was an outspoken Communist-appeaser and even talked about encouraging a people's revolution in Europe to advance the cause of the common man. When Truman became president, Wallace wrote him a letter which was released to the press, stating his views on what the American policy on Russia should be. He was so pro-Russian that he urged yielding on every issue. President Truman, who had little use for communism, requested his resignation soon afterwards.

Thirty-five years ago the vital issue was to stop FDR's march to war. As ranking Republican member of the Committee on Foreign Affairs and as the ranking member on the Rules Committee, I led the noninterventionists in the House of Representatives. It was always an uphill fight, as the Democrats had a 100-man majority. In addition, Roosevelt and his prowar cabinet, and Harry Hopkins and his relief organization, continuously exercised a tremendous influence to help the passage of most war measures. Allegedly they stopped short of war, but actually they enhanced the president's powers in the march to war.

If President Roosevelt had been able by the sheer power of patronage and propaganda to involve the United States in war six months or a year before the Japanese attack on Pearl Harbor, then Hitler would never have attacked Stalin and Soviet Russia on June 22, 1941. It must be clear to most people that if FDR had involved us in war before that time, Hitler would have avoided war with Russia, where he lost a large portion of his army, most of his artillery, tanks, air force, and oil—all of which would have been available to defend the coast of France and Africa. With such a German army equipped and intact, we could not have landed troops in France or Africa.

The war might have lasted for years and ended in a stalemate through exhaustion with the loss of over one million American boys killed and more millions wounded and disabled. Every American family would have had a father, a brother, or a son killed, wounded or mutilated.

The American people owe a lasting debt of gratitude to all the noninterventionists in Congress for keeping the United States out of war until Pearl Harbor.

I was amazed reading in a recent biography entitled *Roosevelt, the Soldier of Freedom*, by Professor James MacGregor Burns, in which I was mentioned fifteen times, that I was Roosevelt's worst enemy. This was news to me as I always thought that Huey Long, General Charles de Gaulle or Alfred E. Smith held that honor. I thought I was further down the list, behind Senators Burton Wheeler, Tydings, Robert Reynolds, Pat McCarran, Bennett Clark, David Walsh, and Congressman Martin Dies. These were all Democrats but I am willing to accept the laurel wreath as the top Republican, followed by Robert Moses of the Triborough Bridge Authority, Robert Taft, Thomas E. Dewey, Senator Nye, Colonel McCormick, Colonel Lindbergh, Joseph Martin and Bruce Barton, of the political firm of Martin, Barton and Fish.

I do not blame FDR for hating me; not only did I come from his own congressional district, where I remained undefeated, but as ranking member on the Foreign Affairs and the Rules committees I was constantly criticizing both his socialistic domestic and war-provoking foreign policies in the House and over the major radio networks. I did not mince words, but they were based on the pending issues, not on personalities or sentiment. I can truthfully say that I never hated FDR, but did feel very strongly about some of his socialistic and prowar measures. I believe that he really feared and hated Huey Long, who denounced him in bitter language and who had a big political following. I believe he feared that I might become chairman of the Rules Committee, where I would have been in a position to have blocked his path to socialism and his road to war and, if warranted on Constitutional grounds, to have introduced impeachment proceedings. Certainly, looking back, the infamous ultimatum to Japan was in violation and open defiance of the Congress and the Constitution. The truth is that the entire foreign policy of the president—from the time of the transfer of fifty destroyers to Britain, the stationing of troops in Iceland, and his shoot-at-sight order—proceded without the consent of the Congress. FDR's foreign policy was a policy of deceit; it double-crossed the American people. As a candidate for reelection to a third term, he repeatedly assured the voters of his devotion to the preservation of peace. His peace pledge in Boston was a vivid example of his hypocrisy and trickery towards the American people while soliciting their votes.

It is time that the searchlight of truth should be turned on FDR's foreign policies, exposing to the American people that he sought through subterfuge and false propaganda to trick the United States into war in brazen repudiation of his peace pledges. It makes no difference what his close admirers or firm supporters may think or say; there is no substitute for truth.

Nine months after his Boston speech, Roosevelt sent U.S. marines to Iceland in July, 1941, prepared for battle and ready to resist any German attack. Five months after that we were involved in World War II, in which one million Americans were killed or wounded in battle.

It is difficult now to reconcile Roosevelt's policies with his message on the State of the Union to the Congress on

January 6, 1941. He said we were "committed . . . for our own security which will never permit us to acquiesce in a peace dictated by aggressors and sponsored by appeasers. *We know that enduring peace cannot be bought at the cost of other people's freedom."* (Author's italics.)

Looking back on the destruction of the freedom of Poland, Czechoslovakia, Hungary, the Balkans, and the Baltic states, the peace was a travesty on freedom everywhere. It is also difficult to understand FDR's statement to Congress about not acquiescing in a peace with which we were not involved. We were not then even committed to go to war. Congress had never voted for it.

The following is part of my testimony on February 15, 1938, before the Naval Affairs Committee of the House of Representatives, headed by the Honorable Carl Vincent, an able and respected Democrat. This was eighteen months before the outbreak of World War II.

Mr. Fish: I am convinced that the American people are absolutely opposed, except for the 10 percent internationalists, to President Roosevelt's request for power to establish blockades, sanctions, embargoes, concerted actions, or to determine the aggressor nation. They all amount to justifiable causes for war, in policing and quarantining other nations by coercion and force.

These acts of aggression have been going on for several hundred years. Great Britain seized half the world, France seized large colonies, and Italy and other nations have, including Russia and Germany, and we have not interfered.

I am putting in the record the recent speech of former President Herbert Hoover who stated it a little more strongly, and my reply in support of his speech: Hon. Herbert Hoover, Palo Alto, Calif., Telegram, January 17, 1938: As ranking Republican member, House Foreign Affairs Committee, commend your peace program. Am inserting it in the Congressional Record. Glad to know you do not endorse the internationalism of Henry L. Stimson who agrees with FDR in concerted action through embargoes and armed force in quarantining other nations. The American people are for peace, not war. Hamilton Fish.

4

FDR SURROUNDED BY RADICAL APPEASERS

How we helped to spread communism at Yalta

I have been asked many times whether I thought FDR was a Communist. The answer is no. I am sure he always registered as a Democrat in his home town of Hyde Park. There is no question but that he was a left-wing liberal Democrat and closely affiliated with socialist ideology. Most Socialists, however, feared and hated totalitarian Communist police governments, but for some strange reason, FDR not only admitted that he had Communist friends, but it is well known that he appointed numerous pro-Communists to important positions in the federal government.

Martin Dies, Democrat from Texas and chairman of the House Committee on Un-American Activities for many years, submitted the names of 2,000 subversives, Communists and pro-Communists in the federal government and the jobs they held. This infuriated FDR who did everything in his power to purge Martin Dies, who was merely carrying out his sworn constitutional duty by reporting the results of the investigations of his committee to President Roosevelt. He should have welcomed this report and aided in purging the federal payrolls of all Communists, pro-

Communists and enemies of our country. However the president of the United States, sworn to uphold and defend the Constitution and the security of the nation, ignored the fact that there were a host of subversives and pro-Communists in the various departments of the government.

There is no question that FDR did a great deal, wittingly or unwittingly, to strengthen the Communists in the United States. Later on at Yalta, the record shows he helped his friend Stalin in promoting the spread of world communism, particularly in China and in eastern Europe, more than anyone outside of Russia.

The fundamental and most realistic question is why did he associate with Communists, pro-Communists and Communist-appeasers, call them his friends, appoint them into the federal service, place them in key positions and invite them to visit the White House? Why did he almost singlehandedly, against the overwhelming sentiment of the country and of former presidents and secretaries of state, recognize Soviet Russia in 1933? He did this despite the opposition of the American Federation of Labor, the American Legion, the Veterans of Foreign Wars, the Chamber of Commerce and almost all members of the Congress. Why did he do all this and more, if he was not a Communist-appeaser?

The answer is very simple. He was obsessed with an overwhelming love of power and the retention of his unprecedented powers by reelection to a third term and later to a fourth term. He was by far the shrewdest and most cynical politician ever to occupy the White House. No president ever acquired or controlled such vast powers for good or evil. He would have preferred death rather than to relinquish any of them. He knew better than anyone that he was sick and deteriorating, both physically and mentally, when he sought a fourth term. He grew to consider himself an indispensable ruler, both in peace and war. His passion for power may have been the result of his disease and disability, but whatever it was, it was overwhelming and, at times, ruthless.

As a consummate politician with eyes fixed on re-election to the presidency, FDR always cherished and sought popularity. He knew he had the solid Democratic South, through big governmental handouts. As president he catered to the Liberal Party in New York, to radicals, Communist-appeasers and even to Communists like Earl Browder. It paid off politically in the big cities—New York, Philadelphia, Chicago, Detroit, San Francisco and Los Angeles.

Franklin Roosevelt's personal charm was often marred by what Robert Sherwood in *Roosevelt and Hopkins* referred to as a capacity for vindictiveness. He also had a capacity at times for sadism and demagogery. Frank Knox, writing two years before he accepted the appointment as secretary of the navy under Roosevelt, said: "Sadistic anti-capitalism is illustrative of the methods used in the working out of Roosevelt's programs."

Governor Alfred E. Smith did not mince words even before FDR's inauguration as president. At the Jefferson Day Democratic dinner held in Washington in 1932, where he was the main speaker, he said: "In a recent speech which has been criticized widely, Governor Roosevelt based his first campaign appeal for president on his plan for relief of forgotten men and women at the bottom of the pyramid." Mr. Smith went on to say,

This is no time for demagogues. At a time like this when millions of men and women and children are starving throughout the land, there is always the temptation of some men to stir up class prejudices, to stir up the bitterness of the rich against the poor, of the poor against the rich. Against that effort I set myself uncompromisingly. I protest against the endeavor to delude the poor people of this country to their ruin by trying to make them believe that they can get employment before the people who would ordinarily employ them are also again restored to the conditions of normal prosperity. A factory worker cannot get his job back unless business conditions enable the factory owner to open up again. And to promise the great masses of the working people that they can secure renewed employment by class legislation is treachery to those working people, to the principles of the Democratic party and to the United States itself. I will take off my coat and vest and fight to the end against any candidates who persist in demagogic appeals to the masses of the working people of this country to destroy themselves by setting class against class and rich against poor.

These were the words not of a Republican, but of Alfred E. Smith, who had been a presidential candidate on the Democratic ticket and was one of the ablest and most popular Democrats in the nation.

In case some of the ardent and devoted followers of FDR should feel that my comments about him are too harsh, I would remind them that I have acknowledged his attractive and charming personality, good looks, and winning friendliness when it suited his purposes, and his melodious honeyed voice which was his greatest asset as a radio speaker. He was a most accomplished radio orator; his delivery and acting were of the highest order. He was not a natural orator when speaking without notes, as Churchill was, but on the radio he had great appeal.

I have never questioned his loyalty or his patriotism, but I seriously question why and how he became a dupe of the Communists or pro-Communists, and particularly of Joseph Stalin, the bloody tyrant and the greatest mass murderer in the history of the world.

If Franklin D. Roosevelt had retired after the end of his second term, following the footsteps of Washington, Jefferson, Jackson and many other presidents, he would have gone down in history as one of our great presidents. But his record in his third term and particularly his fourth term is one of the darkest spots in American history. His infamous secret ultimatum to Japan was sent deliberately to provoke, incite and force Japan into war. At Yalta, without any representation from the Republican party, and surrounded by Harry Hopkins and Alger Hiss, this sick and dying man betrayed half the world to communism. This included the

Polish people and government which had, at his request, stood up to Hitler and refused to make any concessions at Danzig or elsewhere. It is one of the most shocking betrayals in all history. As a result of the Yalta legacies more than 700 million people, formerly free and independent, were turned over to the bloody hands of Stalin.

The tragic legacies from Roosevelt's concessions to Stalin caused the war in Korea, the war in Vietnam, and has cost the American people since the end of World War II in defense against Russian communism, in excess of one trillion dollars of the taxpayers' money. This was the cost, according to a letter to me from Melvin Laird, secretary of defense.

A president can only be judged on his record—not by his intentions—and on that record in his third and fourth terms, Franklin D. Roosevelt, "the great white father" who could do no wrong in his first and second terms, should stand near the bottom of the ladder on the list of presidents of the United States.

This I believe, that he deceived the Democratic Party about the state of his health when he was nominated to a fourth term, so that the Democrats had no responsibility for the tragic concessions made to Stalin and the Communists at Yalta, or for the betrayal of the freedom and democracy for which 300,000 Americans gave their lives and 700,000 more were wounded, mutilated and blinded.

Only one man was responsible for the infamous war ultimatum against Japan and for the betrayal of the principles of freedom and democracy at Yalta, and that was FDR, the president of the United States.

I remember taking the floor of the House of Representatives, representing FDR's congressional district, to deny the unfounded charges of his being a Communist that were spread by many of his bitter opponents.

The reason he was denounced as a Communist was that he had a number of Communist friends and appointed pro-Communists to important key positions in his own administration. That he was friendly with Communists and with Stalin and his Communist regime in Soviet Russia is a matter of historical record.

The following is a letter written to me by former Congressman Dies, a Democrat from Texas, who was head of the House Committee on Un-American Activities for a number of years and a man of integrity and ability. His father had served in Congress with distinction before him.

February 12, 1962

Col. Hamilton Fish
12 W. 44th St.
New York, N.Y.

Dear Col. Fish:

I wish to acknowledge receipt of your letter of February 1. As I have reported many times, the President told me that he had several good friends who were Communists and that he did not regard communism as a danger to the United States. He said that he thought that Russia would be our greatest ally and that while he did not believe in communism, the Soviet government was an improvement over the Czarist government.

With kindest regards I am,

Sincerely yours,
Martin Dies

President Roosevelt's statement that the Soviet government was an improvement over the Czarist government is open to very serious challenge. During the 30 years of Stalin's bloody dictatorship, 30 million or more of his own people were killed either by the secret police or in slave labor camps.* In the 23 years of the reign of the last czar,

---

*For the horrifying details, consult *Encyclopaedia Britannica* (Macropaedia). Chicago: Encyclopaedia Britannica, Inc., 1974, Vol. 17, pp. 576ff.

Nicholas II, less than 2,000 Russians were killed by his secret police or in Siberian prison camps. The people living under the czar, by and large, had the right to travel, a very broad right of free speech, and a free press, and the absolute right of freedom of religion, the right to own property and to enjoy the use of their savings, and to live in a political atmosphere that was free from terrorism on the part of the government, except against bomb throwers, anarchists and militant revolutionists, approximately the same atmosphere that now exists in the United States and in most free nations.

However, I do not want to go on record extolling the Czar's autocratic regime, or in condoning the persecution of the Jews which existed then as it does now by a more lethal tyranny over their minds and souls and by drastic control of their conscience, education and religion. FDR had the right to appease communism if he wanted to, but as for me, I am convinced that communism is the most deadly enemy of freedom and peace in the world, and that its own people are enslaved under the worst type of tyranny that has existed in a thousand years. It is also the black-out of religion both for Christians and Jews.

I supported President Nixon's efforts to lessen the nuclear war tensions by his visits to Soviet Russia and Red China. There is one thing I want to make crystal clear—that I have no quarrel with the Russian people, the Chinese people, or any people living in Communist-dominated police states—only with their despotic, totalitarian dictatorships, the negation of all freedoms.

In 1961 the U.S. Department of State published a volume containing the long overdue secret papers documenting the Teheran Conference held in Iran, November 28—December 1, 1943. They reveal FDR's exaggerated sense of personal power. In one of the meetings between Roosevelt and Stalin they agreed that France should be punished for her attitude during the war and that Indochina should not be returned to France. Roosevelt said, "No Frenchman over forty . . . should be allowed to return to positions in the future." Roosevelt told Stalin that "Mr. Churchill was of the opinion that France would be very quickly reconstructed as a strong nation," but that he did not personally share this view.

Mr. Eden (Lord Avon) in his book, *The Reckoning*, acidly referred to a conversation with FDR at the White House in 1942 when he was told by the president that he thought "the Americans, the British and the Russians should police Europe after the war, allowing the smaller powers nothing but rifles."

This statement evidently shocked Mr. Eden. Naturally it would not have great appeal to the freedom-loving people of France, Belgium, Holland and Norway. If they had known this during or immediately after the war, they would probably have burned Roosevelt in effigy as the betrayer of the Atlantic Charter and the freedom and democracy for which the war was fought. Even more remarkable was the fantastic suggestion by FDR at the Casablanca Conference in 1943 to Mr. Eden "to create a new state to be called 'Wallona' to be 'composed from the Wallon parts of Belgium, Luxemburg, Alsace-Lorraine, and parts of northern France'." Eden wrote critically that he suspected that Roosevelt's knowledge of world geography largely rested on his experience as a stamp collector. He did not try to hide his contempt for FDR's personal hostility against de Gaulle, and called it both "absurd and petty."

5

HOW ROOSEVELT PRODDED AND GOADED THE BRITISH GOVERNMENT INTO WAR

The full extent of the American diplomatic intervention and international prodding of England, France and Poland, prior to the outbreak of World War II, is still little known, particularly the aggressive activities of our ambassador to Paris, William Bullitt, who was FDR's spokesman in Europe.

The following is an extract from an interesting article by Drew Pearson and Robert S. Allen, dated April 14, 1939, that might well be entitled, "How Roosevelt and the State Department Served an Ultimatum on Prime Minister Chamberlain."

The authors were interventionists and friendly to the Roosevelt administration. It is historically important to relate what they said at that time to show how far President Roosevelt went to influence British diplomacy in 1938 and 1939, to turn Britain from peaceful negotiation with Germany into war.

The State Department has just heaved big sighs of relief after terminating one of the most crucial episodes of international prodding. The objective of the State Department, or perhaps it is more accurate to say of the president himself, has been to push, goad, or cajole the British Empire into the realization that democracy is at stake in Europe. (*Author's note*: What happened to the democracies and free nations of Europe—Poland, Czechoslovakia, Hungary, the Baltic and Balkan nations?) All this took place during the period of diplomatic double-crossing in which British banks actually were lending money to Germany for rearmament and the Federation of British Industries were negotiating a secret pact with German industries in violation of the Anglo-American agreement.

These double-crossings finally became so flagrant that when Roosevelt, Hull and Welles got the full drift of it, they sent a virtual ultimatum to Chamberlain declaring that as far as the U.S. was concerned, Great Britain was either a Nazi nation or a democracy, and that the United States would watch Chamberlain's future policy for the answer. To get the full picture of British double-crossing and to understand what led up to this crisis in Anglo-American relations, it is necessary to trace the events after the Munich crisis last October (1938).

After Munich, the Roosevelt administration instructed Ambassador Joe Kennedy to suggest to Chamberlain that the only thing Hitler understood was the straight arm and that it would be an excellent idea to call an abrupt halt on appeasement. Supposedly Chamberlain agreed, whereupon Roosevelt and his State Department mapped out a program carefully calculated to show Hitler that he could give the democracies no more lip. (*Author's note*: The Communists made mincemeat of the democracies of eastern and southeastern Europe.) To this end the United States deliberately recalled the ambassador from Berlin, (*Author's note*: A bad blunder as we were unable to exert any influence in Germany for peace just before the outbreak of World War II) and deliberately planned that Secretary Ickes should scold the German chargé d'affaires for his effrontery in protesting. It was no accident that Roosevelt's address to Congress on the State of the Union vigorously slapped down the dictators.

Later it was discovered that whenever the State Department would take a stern stand against Hitler, Sir John Simon or other Tory members of the British Cabinet would trot around to the Nazis and tell them that Britain was not in sympathy with the United States pronouncements. Finally, just before the last Czech crisis, the State Department learned that the powerful Federation of British Industries in which several cabinet members were represented, had worked out a secret trade agreement with the Nazis, undercutting the United States and the Anglo-American trade agreement so laboriously negotiated by Cordell Hull.

By this time the sentiment of Roosevelt, Hull, et al., towards the British would have burnt up the printed pages. Their almost inescapable conclusion was that the oligarchy, which actually rules Britain at heart, was anxious to preserve the dictators and secretly feared the strengthening of democratic governments similar to the popular front in France or the Negrin Regime in Spain.

The Pearson-Allen article was published four and a half months before the start of the European war, and inserted in the Congressional Record. It proves to what an extent President Roosevelt prodded, pushed and goaded Prime Minister Chamberlain and his cabinet. It shows how far we interfered with and influenced the British foreign policy, from negotiation with Germany into the most bloody, costly and disastrous war in the history of the world that left half of Europe bled white, ruined and devastated, and the democracies of eastern Europe overwhelmed by Communist dictatorships.

England itself was a major victim, both in blood and treasure, was virtually bankrupt after six years of war, and lost a large part of its Empire.

This statement by two American columnists, both ardent supporters of the Roosevelt administration, clearly sets forth the brazen attempts of FDR for more than a year before the outbreak of World War II, not only to influence, but to dictate the policies of the British government regarding Germany.

If President Roosevelt could dictate to the prime minister of Britain, he could, and did, do the same to the prime ministers and foreign ministers of both France and Poland through his main spokesman William Bullitt, who although our ambassador to France, was also FDR's roving ambassador extraordinary for all of Europe.

6

THE GREAT BRITISH FIRSTER, WINSTON CHURCHILL, WHO HATED AND FEARED COMMUNISM

Churchill was a far greater man in every respect than FDR, but he was never permitted to forget that Roosevelt held the purse strings and the military might, the two controlling cards in the game of war or peace. When Churchill sat down with FDR and Stalin at the Teheran and Yalta conferences, he was, in poker parlance, squeezed out of the game. Roosevelt with the money, Stalin with a powerful army, and Churchill with a navy that had a glorious war record but was no longer needed towards the end of the war, at the time of Yalta. The weakest spots in Churchill's historical armor are Teheran and Yalta. Despite Churchill's great ability, personal grandeur, courageous and brilliant leadership in the conduct of the war, Great Britain suffered huge casualties, virtual bankruptcy and disintegration of the empire. No one can deny these facts, which had their origin in the ancient and outmoded balance-of-power policy in Europe that Churchill inherited and supported. That policy was one of the fundamental causes of the war.

It is true, however, that Churchill was stymied by both Roosevelt and Stalin when he tried to open up a western

"I HAVE NOTHING TO OFFER BUT BLOOD, TOIL, TEARS, AND SWEAT."

front by a tremendous attack from Italy into Yugoslavia and Bulgaria, in order to drive the Nazis out of Austria, Hungary, and Poland before the arrival of the Russian army. Churchill envisioned what would happen to these countries if Stalin's armies arrived there first. His plan, if successful, would have saved their independence and the freedom of the people of eastern Europe.

The determined opposition of Stalin and Roosevelt prevented Churchill from stopping the march of communism on the eastern boundaries of Europe.

In 1938 Churchill predicted, "I have watched this famous island descending incontinently, fecklessly, the stairway which leads to a dark gulf. It is a fine, broad stairway at the beginning, but after a bit the carpet ends. A little farther on there are only flagstones, and a little farther on these break beneath your feet." *This was before the war.*

Is the destiny of England and the relic of the British Empire as secure today, confronting world communism and its arsenal of nuclear weapons? Might not these words of Winston Churchill describe the present and future, rather than the past?

In all fairness to England's greatest prime minister of the twentieth century, he went along with Roosevelt because of the force of circumstances. Actually, unlike FDR, he had an obsession to destroy bolshevism, which we in America call communism. He feared international communism as a world force that would strangle the lifeline and lifeblood of the British Empire and stir up rebellion and civil war. He was quite right. That is exactly what happened, and the end of his tragic vision is not yet in sight. The tragedy is that he appeased Stalin when the chips were down.

Churchill and Roosevelt loomed large as wartime leaders, but not as protectors of democracy, defenders of Christianity, or preservers of the independence of small nations against Communist aggression. The Atlantic Charter and the four freedoms were merely used as slogans to arouse the people against Hitler, Mussolini and Tojo. They were soon discarded.

The four freedoms—freedom of speech, freedom of religion, freedom from want, and freedom from fear—were beautiful, sublime and idealistic. Actually, they were used as a propaganda hoax and as political chicanery, and forgotten at both the Teheran and Yalta conferences which betrayed Poland, Czechoslovakia, Hungary and other eastern European nations into Communist slavery.

How could Winston Churchill play ball with Stalin and the Communist conspiracy unless forced to by FDR, since he understood its duplicity and bad faith? Churchill seldom minced words in unmasking and exposing communism. He once said, "It is not only a creed, it is a plan of campaign. A Communist is not only the holder of certain opinions, he is the pledged adept of a well-thought-out means of enforcing them. The anatomy of discontent and revolution has been studied in every phase and aspect, and a veritable drill book prepared in a scientific spirit of sabotaging all existing institutions. No faith need be kept with non-Communists. Every act of good will, or tolerance or conciliation or mercy or magnanimity on the part of governments or statesmen is to be utilized for their ruin. Then, when the time is ripe and the moment opportune, every form of lethal violence, from revolt to private assassination, must be used without stint or compunction. The citadel will be stormed under the banners of liberty and democracy, and once the apparatus of power is in the hands of the Brotherhood, all opposition, all contrary opinions must be extinguished by death. Democracy is but a tool to be used and afterwards broken."

This statement of Winston Churchill is a veritable masterpiece of eloquence and truth—no description of communism approaches it as a brief, concise and apodictic summary of this evil nightmare.

I am one of Churchill's admirers because he always put the interests of England and the British Empire first. He realized the menace of world communism. But he reluctantly, once Soviet Russia became an ally against Hitler, permitted Roosevelt to lead him down the ruinous path of appeasement, a tangled web from which he was never to emerge during Roosevelt's life. That he failed to maintain British power and security, which were closest to his heart, was because he was frozen into a financial and military situation that compelled him against his wishes and better judgment to support FDR in his abject appeasement of Stalin. He was reluctantly forced to follow Roosevelt's footsteps; helped in downgrading de Gaulle, supported FDR's insistence on the unconditional surrender of Germany, the monstrous Morgenthau Plan, and even worse, participated in the ghastly betrayal at Yalta of the freedom and democracy for which a million American, British and French soldiers paid the supreme sacrifice.

Churchill joined in the betrayal of Poland, Hungary, Czechoslovakia, Yugoslavia, and other free nations because he believed he could thereby gain the goodwill and support of Stalin for British imperial interests at Hong Kong, Singapore, Malaya, Ceylon, Burma, India and spheres of influence in Greece, Palestine, Iraq, Iran and Africa, and for delay in establishing a second front. It was a shameful and unholy bargain.

There can be no denying the genius of Churchill both in war and peace. The biography of his father, his memoirs, the power, mastery, dignity and scope of his speeches and, above all, the extraordinary resilience and activity of his mind, were clear attributes of genius.

He also excelled not only as a masterful statesman, but as a war correspondent, polo player, amateur painter, biographer, historian, orator and brandy drinker. It would, however, be a mistake to believe that Churchill was a paragon of virtue, and depository of sweetness, light and righteousness.

E. T. Raymond, writing about Winston Churchill many years ago, said, "Perhaps the chief reproach lies with his ancestors. At this distance, there is visible in him more than a trace of the termagant humour, the restless levity and the inordinate vanity of Sarah Jennings. He has the blood also of that Spencer whose name was a byword for unprincipled intrigue in the most unprincipled period in our political history. From the great Duke he inherits, perhaps, his courage, his warlike tastes, much of his intellect, and no little of his facility for espousing new causes and deserting old ones. With John Churchill's steady baseness, cool treachery and single eye to the main chance, he might easily have rivalled the glory and shame of the founder of his house."

The fact is that Churchill did emulate the glory of the great Duke of Marlborough but not his alleged shame. Churchill may well have inherited his persistent towering ambition and love of intrigue from his ancestors. He was a past master in English and international intrigues and power politics. He and FDR, another past master in intrigue, wove such tangled webs separately and together that Neville Chamberlain was tripped up at every turn in his efforts to maintain the peace of Europe for several years prior to the outbreak of war on September 3, 1939.

Churchill's forensic powers, magnificent personality, and fighting spirit combined to make him the greatest statesman of World War II, far excelling Adolph Hitler, Benito Mussolini, Joseph Stalin and Franklin Roosevelt. All these were wartime leaders and dictatorial or near-dictatorial heads of state. All had a lust for power and renown, but none had the wide experience, remarkable ability, compelling eloquence, mental brilliance and forceful leadership of Winston Churchill.

Churchill succeeded in winning the war and losing the peace. The only victors were Stalin and communism. As a result, the British Empire was smashed instead of Germany. What a tragedy!

The stability of the British Empire had been the most powerful factor in preserving law and order, parliamentary government, international law, and protection of world trade for 150 years. Gone is the glory, the grandeur, the might and the stability of the most powerful empire in the world since the conquering legions of Rome. What a paradox! The brilliant and dynamic Churchill, one of England's greatest prime ministers, was largely responsible for the decline and liquidation of the British Empire. This was furthest from his thoughts and policies.

Now thirty years later, Britain waits with head unbowed before the Russian colossus, the Red bear who walks like a man, that Churchill reluctantly helped to strengthen at Teheran and Yalta. Her courage remains, but her policies are and will continue to appease Moscow as Britain knows she would be wiped out and destroyed in a nuclear war.

The mighty Communist claws took over China four years after the end of the war and reached out into South Korea, South Vietnam, Indonesia, Malaya, Zanzibar, Tibet, the Congo, Africa, Cuba, the Arab nations in the Near East, Chile, Italy and France, the last line of British defense.

If Soviet Russia ever overran France by infiltration or by armed force, it would mean the beginning of the end of England and the British Isles. Heaven forbid. But only her wartime enemy, West Germany, and a lukewarm France stand between her and 20,000 Russian bombers and fighters that could be based in France, to say nothing of the Soviet nuclear threat. How long could valiant England withstand such an onslaught? Even the British bulldog, whose courage and tenacity is known throughout the world, would not be able to save England.

The only effective protection would be from the American stockpiles of nuclear weapons. If it were not for them, all of western Europe and Britain would fall like ripe plums under the blood-red flag of communism.

Roosevelt alienated both de Gaulle and France, and so did Churchill at the instigation of FDR, but to a lesser degree. Actually, behind the scenes, Churchill admired de Gaulle.

FDR's personality cult clashed with de Gaulle's—the justly popular leader of the Free French. The enmity began at the Casablanca Conference in January, 1943, and continued to FDR's death. The bitterness of that era, the result of his personal quarrel, vindictive criticisms, and humiliating actions against General Charles de Gaulle, still exerts a negative influence on the traditional friendly relations between France and the United States. The withdrawal of French troops from NATO and its ousting from France by de Gaulle in 1966 was probably one legacy of that bitterness.

At numerous meetings of the big three at Yalta, Stalin strongly implied that Churchill had a secret affection for Germany and favored a soft peace. Among the conditions Stalin said must be met were that "at least fifty thousand and perhaps one hundred thousand of the German officers and all the staff must be physically liquidated." Stalin was a political general who distrusted and feared top staff and general officers. He probably had in mind his own liquidation of thirty-eight thousand Russian officers only five years before.

Churchill had fought as an officer in the British army as a young man and later in World War I, which FDR sidestepped, claiming important public duties as assistant secretary of the navy. His cousin, the great Theodore Roosevelt, risked his life in defense of his country in the Spanish-American War, and was also the assistant secretary of the navy when that war broke out.

The prime minister took a strong stand against what he termed "the cold-blooded execution of soldiers who fought for their country." He said that "war criminals must pay for their crimes as individuals who had committed barbarous acts." He objected vigorously to "executions for political reasons." Churchill's remonstrance was a tribute to his courage and statesmanship.

Churchill and Eden vigorously argued and supported by logic the recognition of de Gaulle and the Free French and particularly the right of France to maintain troops in German territory after the anticipated victory. Both Roosevelt and Stalin were bitterly opposed to de Gaulle and against any concessions to him or France. But the masterful and persuasive reasoning of Churchill prevailed over FDR's personal vindictiveness and Stalin's objections.

Stalin really wanted a free hand to deal with, or rather to control, Europe after the war and Roosevelt approved, as outlined in his statement to Bishop Francis Spellman. Naturally Stalin objected to French participation in the control of Germany, as he did not want to strengthen French prestige or influence. That is why both Roosevelt and Stalin refused to invite de Gaulle to attend the Yalta Conference.

The tragic fact is that Churchill, who publicly proclaimed he had not been made prime minister to liquidate the British Empire, ended by doing the very thing he dreaded most. Great as Churchill was as a wartime leader, fate and the world communist conspiracy combined in undermining the British colonial interests against his well-known devotion to imperial Britain. But to his credit, he was able to obtain more than 35 billion dollars from the United States, in Lend-Lease aid, munitions, and outright grants.

The decline of the British Empire began as a result of World War II and has continued ever since. But as long as Canada, Australia and New Zealand remain in the British Commonwealth, Britain will survive as a strong, free and independent nation unless there is an atomic war. As Britain relinquished its colonies, Soviet Russia became, through seizure of the captive countries, the greatest colonial and imperialistic nation in the world. Britain and the United States, through Churchill's and Roosevelt's fatal appeasement at Yalta, sacrificed the free nations of eastern Europe and China to the bloody hands of Joseph Stalin and the Communists.

These captive nations may seek to restore their own

freedom and the right of self-determination in case of war between Soviet Russia and Red China. This may break out in five years or earlier. The Peking Communists have their hungry eyes on sparsely settled eastern Siberia. If Red China builds a large arsenal of nuclear weapons in the next five years and succeeds in its plans to industrialize the nation, Soviet Russia may suddenly have a fighting tiger at its throat, no longer an old-fashioned paper tiger.

These Chinese Communists could afford to lose 100 million or more of their people, and perhaps be better off—but not Soviet Russia.

The great British-firster, Winston Churchill, who hated and feared communism, had one trait in common with Roosevelt and Stalin: an overweening ambition to achieve and maintain absolute power. This was the relentless driving power of all three—power and more power. This is what created the personality cult of all three. It was the power that corrupts, and the greater the power, the greater the corruption. It certainly applied to Stalin and Roosevelt, who both delighted in purging their enemies, one by the bullet and the other by the ballot. But Churchill had other qualifications and interests. He was an accomplished author, historian, painter and orator. He enjoyed his unprecedented influence and power, but he was not a power-mad autocrat.

Churchill, with his "blood, sweat and tears" program, was one of the greatest and most famous wartime leaders in the history of Britain. But at the peace table at Yalta he remained complacent when he should have protested. He permitted Roosevelt and Stalin to jointly destroy the principles of freedom and democracy for which the western European nations and the U.S. had fought, and in so doing, made half the world safe for communism. This was the crucifixion of Churchill's brilliant and successful efforts of more than five years to turn the tide of defeat into a glorious victory. The outmoded balance-of-power policy that had caused Britain's entrance into the European war brought disaster to the free world, as world communism was the only winner.

Stalin and communism buried Churchill's ancient balance-of-power policy in a mound of postwar ashes, unmourned and beyond resurrection.

7

FDR'S IMPLIED PROMISES IN 1939 OF MILITARY SUPPORT TO FRANCE

General de Gaulle was a brigadier general when the German army occupied France in May, 1940. He probably was not informed of the efforts of FDR to cajole, push and goad France into war against Germany with implied promises of military support. Only Premier Reynaud, former Premier Daladier, Foreign Minister Bonnet and our Ambassador Bullitt, would have had factual knowledge then; all are now dead. Bidding farewell to his neighbors at Warm Springs *in 1939*, Roosevelt said, "I will be back around Thanksgiving if we don't have war." The *Washington Post* explained Roosevelt's statement in an editorial which was later upheld by the president as expressing his views at his April 13 press conference. The *New York Times* the next morning carried a front page story which began as follows:

ROOSEVELT SEES AMERICA INVOLVED

President Roosevelt strongly implied that he believed the involvement of the United States in any general European war was inevitable and that this nation should stand shoulder to shoulder with Great Britain and France against Nazi-Fascist machinations.

Here is a crystal clear public statement by FDR, five months before the outbreak of World War II, implying that the U.S. would join Great Britain and France if war broke out against Germany and Italy. Naturally, the war hawks in Great Britain and in France were given a helpful shot in the arm by FDR's implied war commitment.

There were powerful peace sentiments in both the British and French governments against war, as well as among the people who would do the fighting and dying.

There could be only one interpretation in the minds of British and French government officials—that the United States would join them right away against the Nazi-Fascist nations. FDR made no secret of his prowar views in 1939 among his intimate friends and cabinet members. This was recorded by both Secretary of War Harry Woodring and his wife.

On June 9, 1940, Paul Reynaud, premier of France, sent a telegram to President Roosevelt in which he said, "It is my duty to ask for new and even larger assistance." He followed it up with a radio broadcast appeal on June 13th in which he said, "France, wounded, has the right to turn to other democracies and to say, 'We have claims on you'. None of those with a sense of justice can deny this. Will they hesitate still to declare themselves against Nazi Germany? I have asked this of President Roosevelt as you know. I am sending him tonight a new and last appeal."

On the night of June 22, 1939, I spoke as the ranking Republican on the House Foreign Affairs Committee over a nationwide NBC broadcast in which I said, "France lies prostrate and bleeding from the velvet glove and secret diplomacy pledges of President Roosevelt, which left her defenseless to her enemy because she relied on his implied and false promises of support."

Stanley Clark in his story of General de Gaulle, *The Man Who Is France*, stated that Churchill resisted every effort to have the Royal Air Force used in France against the German invaders as urged by Premier Reynaud and the

French high command. Churchill said, "It is essential to conserve intact the Royal Air Force, which I regard as the instrument on which depends perhaps the *intervention of the United States in the conflict.*" (Author's italics.) Premier Reynaud declared, "History will say without a doubt that the battle of France was lost through want of aircraft." De Gaulle, who had been taken in the government as undersecretary of state to the French minister of national defense, wanted the French army to establish a defensive position in Brittany. Churchill argued, "If we can do this and find a method of stopping the tanks and maintain a bridgehead on the Atlantic, we may gain a month necessary to obtain the *intervention of America.*" (Author's italics.)

It is obvious from Churchill's statement and Premier Reynaud's actions that they believed they had assurance of American intervention at the very outset of the war from FDR, who was the only one who could have given such promises.

General de Gaulle is also quoted in *The Man Who Is France* as saying to Mr. Boris in London (a noncommissioned French officer, one of his earliest French recruits), "*If Britain can hold out, America will come into the fight within several months, or at most a year and all will be well.*" (Italics mine.)

History will show that Roosevelt, through Ambassador Bullitt, was largely responsible for plotting, prodding and pushing France into war before she was adequately prepared, by secret promises of armed support. I predicted years ago that some day a disillusioned French statesman would tell the truth about the diplomatic duplicity and implied intervention that will shock both the French and the American people. Now Georges Bonnet, French foreign minister in 1939, has let the cat out of the diplomatic bag.

I received a letter from Monsieur Bonnet from Paris, dated March 26, 1971; I knew him personally and had written asking if he would state briefly his views regarding the efforts made by William Bullitt to influence the French government to stand firm against Hitler just prior to the beginning of the war. He sent me an extract from a book that he had just written entitled *Dans la Tourmente* in which he referred to Bullitt and added:

This is what I can tell you on this subject. As much as Bullitt counseled Daladier, the French premier, and myself (to have) prudence about the Czechoslovakia affair in 1938, he however in 1939 urged France to take a strong stand against Hitler. I am convinced also that he gave Daladier the conviction that Roosevelt would intervene (in the war) if he saw that France and England were in danger. I add that Bullitt held in a large measure the illusion of many other people at that time, that Hitler was bluffing and that his army and his aviation did not have the strength which he pretended, and that he thought it would be enough to speak firmly to make him concede. I have no doubt whatever that this was his belief . . . I will be however at your disposition to discuss these matters. One thing is certain is that Bullitt in 1939 did everything he could to make France enter the war. Accept, my dear Hamilton Fish, expression of my sentiments and devoted friendship.

Georges Bonnet

Georges Bonnet was virtually the only living French statesman of that period. His statement confirms my views that Bullitt did everything he could in 1939 not only to make France stand firm but to urge France to go into the war against Hitler. Ambassador Kennedy in London and Colonel Charles Lindbergh both believed that Germany was far stronger in airpower at that time and was superior in armament to France. Unfortunately FDR listened to Bullitt and downgraded the views of Ambassador Kennedy and Colonel Lindbergh.

When the attack actually came, the German Luftwaffe was vastly superior and literally destroyed the French resistance because of their lack of airplanes. This is the view of former Premier Reynaud, who was very explicit about blaming the defeat of the French army on the lack of air support. It was for this reason that he appealed to Churchill to send over a large number of British airplanes.

Georges Bonnet's statement is one more piece of evidence that Bullitt did everything in his power to urge France to go to war against Germany—and he could not have done so unless he were carrying out the orders of President Roosevelt.

8

FDR'S PROPOSED BETRAYAL OF FRANCE AND FREEDOM
Communism triumphant

Stalin and communism triumphed with the help of FDR aided by Churchill at Teheran and Yalta. Actually the sellout, or more accurately, betrayal, was prearranged by FDR.

Churchill is alleged by FDR to have acquiesced three months before Teheran in a conference between them, held in Washington, D.C., on the first two days of September, 1943. Churchill's part is still vague and questionable as are whatever commitments were made to him by Roosevelt.

FDR outlined his odious plan to his close friend Bishop Francis Spellman, later Cardinal, on September 3, 1943, at the White House. Bishop Spellman took copious notes and wrote out a precise account of the statements made to him by President Roosevelt. This memorandum of two typewritten pages is contained in *The Cardinal Spellman Story* by Reverend Robert Gannon.

I knew Cardinal Spellman well. He was of the highest character and integrity. The statement is bloodcurdling in its appeasement or rather abject surrender. The memorandum is headed, "Here Are a Few Outstanding Points of the

Conversation." Bishop Spellman merely reported the facts and made no comments of his own. The following are extracts in quotes, under the title "Russia." (It is important to understand that this was three months before the Teheran Conference.)

Stalin would certainly receive Finland, the Baltic states, the eastern half of Poland and Bessarabia. Furthermore, the population of eastern Poland want to become Russian.

It is interesting to know that FDR, out of the great generosity of his heart, even agreed to give Finland to Russia without the consent of the Finns, who remained free through their own indomitable courage.

According to FDR's carefully devised plan, the world would be divided into spheres of influence:

China gets the Far East; U.S. the Pacific; Britain and Russia get Europe and Africa. But as Britain has predominating colonial interests, it might be assumed that Russia will predominate in Europe.

In other words, more than a year and a half before the war had been won, and before any peace conferences had been held, FDR planned to give Russia not only Europe as a sphere of influence, but allow her to act as a predominating force there. That is enough to make the angels weep and the French, Belgians, Dutch, Danes and Norwegians who suffered the horrors of Nazi invasion and conquest for four years to have hanged FDR in effigy rather than submit to Russian Communist domination. But the kind-hearted American president hoped

although it might be wishful thinking, that Russian intervention might not be too harsh, it is probable that the Communist regime will expand—France might eventually escape if it had a government à la Leon Blum. The Front Populaire would be so advanced that eventually the Communists might accept it.

The freedom-loving French will be shocked by FDR's postwar plans for France. They do not even once refer to de Gaulle!

President Roosevelt proceeded to say,

> We should not overlook the magnificent economic achievement of Russia . . . Their finances are sound. It is natural that the European countries will have to undergo tremendous changes in order to adapt to Russia. The European people (which includes France, Belgium, Holland, Denmark and Norway and of course our wartime enemies Germany and Italy) will simply have to endure the Russian domination in the hope that in ten or twenty years they will be able to live well with the Russians.

This statement of FDR's is shameful; it proposes betrayal of the freedom of France and other western European nations. It is interesting to note that Roosevelt almost always referred to the Russians, not the Communists. His statement was a travesty on Allied war aims, a mockery of the Atlantic Charter, and a repudiation of the sacrifices made by our own soldiers in Europe. It would have meant that those heroic veteran dead had died in vain.

If France had been dominated by the Communists from Moscow, British influence in Europe would have disappeared into thin air, and instead a Communist Sword of Damocles held by a wire from the Kremlin would have been held over the heart of London and all of Britain.

It is puzzling and difficult to believe that FDR thought up this scheme for the control of western Europe all by himself. And as one who had often disagreed with him on his foreign policies, I would be inclined to believe that this abominable plan was not conceived by him alone. Roosevelt had advisers who were known to be friendly to Stalin and his regime. Among them were Lauchlin Currie, Roosevelt's executive secretary and adviser on foreign affairs, who was publicly denounced as a pro-Communist and later fled to Columbia; Harry Dexter White, the top representative of the Treasury Department on foreign affairs, and who was also alleged to be a pro-Communist; Alger Hiss, who held a high position in the State Department and whose Communist activities did not become public until much later; and possibly, Harry Hopkins, FDR's right arm, who Roosevelt had said got along with Stalin "like a house on fire," whatever that means. Hopkins had more influence with Stalin and also with Roosevelt than anyone else. Any one of these might well have helped in writing a plan that virtually turned over all of western Europe to Russian domination.

Some future historian I hope will make a thorough investigation of the story of Bishop Spellman's written memorandum on September 3, 1943, three months before the Teheran Conference. The searchlight of truth should expose its origin, protagonists and motives. It is one of the most shocking documents of the entire war, and of great historical importance. The fact that it was a written verbatim report of a statement made by FDR to Bishop Spellman, a political friend and supporter of the president, confirms the authenticity and truth of Roosevelt's shameful postwar plans. The public may draw its own conclusions.

The real question is, who sowed the seeds in Roosevelt's mind for this odious domination of Europe by the Communists? It may never be known definitely. One thing is certain—it did not originate from Churchill, Eden, Hull, Byrnes or Sumner Welles, none of whom had any use for communism. Hull did not like General de Gaulle because of the seizure by his Free French of the islands of Saint Pierre and Miquelon, close to the southwestern coast of Newfoundland, without the knowledge or consent of our State Department.

But Cordell Hull was not vindictive. I am sure he would not have been a party in attempting to punish France to spite de Gaulle by supporting FDR's plan, and there is no evidence that Hull had any knowledge of or approved of it.

On February 15, 1971, the State Department released a

number of long-withheld documents to the public. They revealed an almost incredible and vindictive hatred of de Gaulle expressed by President Franklin D. Roosevelt in 1943, at the time of the meeting of de Gaulle and Roosevelt at the Casablanca conference.

It is just as well that these bitter comments were pigeonholed for all these years, and perhaps it would have been better if they had never been released. Much of FDR's personal dislike of de Gaulle was published many years ago in his son Elliott Roosevelt's book, *As He Saw It*. Now it is the inescapable duty of an historian to add insult to injury and make the new diatribes against de Gaulle public property, although they will not make many friends for the United States among the numerous Gaullists in France.

But historically, these documents disclose the main weakness in the composition of Roosevelt's character. His personal denunciation of de Gaulle was vindictive, bad manners, and bad politics. De Gaulle was then the great hero of the Free French and of most of the French people, an acknowledged savior of France, and the almost unanimous choice of the people as the head of the provisional government. Roosevelt's attitude did not represent that of the American people, who generally admired de Gaulle for the courage of his convictions in France's darkest hours.

These tirades are typical of FDR's personality cult in their arrogance, vindictiveness and personal animosity. There was no reason for him to be hostile to de Gaulle, who was not a political opponent but merely a courageous and honorable Frenchman whose chief objective was the freedom and restoration of the French Republic.

In a letter to Churchill on May 8, 1943, FDR accused de Gaulle of stirring up trouble in Algiers and said, "I do not know what to do with de Gaulle; possibly you would like to make him Governor of Madagascar." Roosevelt went on to recommend the reorganizing of the French National Committee, the resistance movement de Gaulle headed. "I am sorry but it seems to me the conduct of the bride (de

Gaulle) continues to be more and more aggravating." The bridegroom, according to the president, was General Henri Giraud. Roosevelt tried to bring them together. Actually he favored General Giraud over de Gaulle as chairman of the French Committee of National Liberation in exile. Roosevelt wrote, "I am inclined to think when we get into France itself we will have to regard it as a *military occupation run by British and American generals* . . . I think that this may be necessary for six months or even a year after we get into France." About 90 percent of the mayors and subordinate officials of French cities and departments could be used, Roosevelt suggested, *"but the top line of national administration must be kept in the hands of the British or American commanders-in-chief*. The old former government simply will not do." (My italics.)

This would mean nothing more than a foreign military autocracy or dictatorship. What a travesty on American fundamental principles and ideals of government based on freedom and self-determination of the people. This State Department release differs from Roosevelt's conversation with Bishop Spellman, four months later. Perhaps the president found that Churchill and the British were not in favor of assuming control of the government of France with the United States, so substituted Stalin and the Communists to dominate France and the other western European nations.

Roosevelt sent the draft memorandum on de Gaulle to Secretary of State Hull with a note saying he thought of taking up its contents with Churchill, according to a State Department footnote to the document. Hull answered, "It is very evident that the French National Committee is basing its whole policy on the idea that when France is liberated from the Germans, organized elements under de Gaulle will be in control."

These documents released by the State Department have been hidden away for the last 32 years. The recent documents confirm Roosevelt's intense antagonism for de Gaulle and account to some extent for his odious plan to have the Russians dominate France after the war.

It is time that the French and British people knew the truth and have an agonizing reappraisal of FDR's attitude towards them.

Again quoting from Bishop Spellman's carefully prepared written report of what FDR told him on September 3: "The Russian production is so high that American help, except for trucks, is negligible." What a misleading and incredible statement. The truth is that the bulk of the Russian factories had been destroyed by the invading German armies. The U.S. loaned Soviet Russia eleven billion dollars. Under the terms of the Lend-Lease agreement, Stalin received from the West twenty thousand aircraft, close to 400,000 trucks, twice as many tanks as the Communists had at the time of the invasion of Russia, vast quantities of leather for shoes, cloth for uniforms, hundreds of miles of barbed wire and telephone lines, railroad locomotives, automobiles, much-needed food supplies on a huge scale, and equipment for setting up new industrial plants.

These statements by FDR are so incredible and outrageous that I could not have believed them except from such an exceptional source as Francis Spellman, a trusted ally of FDR at that time. He had just returned from a six-month mission, as Roosevelt's personal representative, to Europe, Africa and South America, when he had this appalling interview with the president of the United States. The night before, he had dined at the White House with the president and Winston Churchill. I have dealt only with the facts as stated specifically by Bishop Spellman, but I ask the reader's forebearance while I digress to conjure up a picture of FDR and Churchill, carving up the postwar world at the White House three months before the Teheran Conference. How else could FDR have spoken to Bishop Spellman as he did, outlining such a terrible postwar program?

It is a mystery to me why Churchill ever consented to such ruinous terms. It is more than likely that Churchill gave only limited or lukewarm support, even though Britain was to participate in control with Russia over western Europe and Africa. In his fear and dislike of communism, Churchill was as constant as the north star. Besides, he was a realist and must have understood that FDR's postwar plans for western Europe and Africa would be disastrous to Britain and to freedom everywhere. He probably quietly and effectively undermined the whole project. Certainly the English did not want Stalin to control France, Belgium and Holland any more than they wanted Hitler to.

As for the French, they were never consulted and knew nothing about Roosevelt's shameful plan. His proposal of Russian domination for twenty years was, of course, meaningless. The Communists would have seized complete power in a few years and communized France and western Europe by force and violence. Freedom would then have been sorely stricken throughout the world. I must repeat to my French friends that FDR's anti–de Gaulle and anti-French views were not that of the American people who disliked and distrusted Soviet Russia's tyrannical Communist dictatorship.

On the contrary, the American people have had a long, traditional friendship for France, and will continue to maintain it as long as France is free. If the French people are shocked at Roosevelt's attempt to make Stalin the master of France, no one would be surprised if they reacted by changing the names of avenues and streets in his memory, to Lafayette, the champion of freedom, or to Franklin, the great American friend of France, or to Pershing or Eisenhower, who commanded the American troops in World Wars I and II.

However, in time, despite agonizing reappraisals and changes, even past mistakes are forgiven. The traditional friendship between our two great republics must continue for generations to come in upholding and preserving our mutual dedication to the cause of freedom, democracy, and peace.

9

AMBASSADOR
JOSEPH PATRICK KENNEDY

*Our controversial ambassador to the
Court of St. James*

Young Joe Kennedy, son of an Irish immigrant saloon-keeper, and successful politician, graduated from Harvard in 1912. Almost immediately, his attractive personality, dynamic energy and determination launched him on the road to financial success. He became the youngest bank president in New England. However, the most fortunate thing he did was to marry the lovely Rose Fitzgerald, the daughter of Mayor John J. Fitzgerald of Boston, often known as Honey Fitz. At that time, the Fitzgerald family stood at the top echelon of Boston Irish society and the mayor was not too pleased about the marriage.

When he graduated from Harvard, young Kennedy did not waste time in his zest to accumulate a large fortune and family. He and his wife gave birth to nine children, three of whom became U.S. senators, and one of them, president of the United States. Joseph Kennedy was the founder of an almost unparalleled political dynasty. Like most beginners, he had his ups and downs in business, but more ups than downs. He campaigned as vigorously to make a fortune as his sons did later in political life. Most everything Joe Kennedy touched turned to gold: real estate, movies, stock market manipulations in the 1920s bull market and the 1929 panic, and a monopoly on imported scotch whisky after the repeal of prohibition. The millions, once started, kept flowing until his wealth was finally estimated at 200 million dollars.

As a born and bred Irish Democrat whose father was in politics and with a distinguished Democratic father-in-law, Kennedy, too, was naturally interested in the political game. He met and liked Franklin D. Roosevelt as a candidate for president in 1932. Joe Kennedy was a realist. He felt that it would be a Democratic year so he decided not only to support Roosevelt, but to contribute generously to the campaign. This he did with a $25,000 gift, and a $50,000 loan, and persuaded his wealthy friends to get on the financial bandwagon for Roosevelt. Evidently young Kennedy enjoyed the campaigning, the political intrigues and conferences. He made quite an impression on FDR and on a number of his associates.

After an initial appointment to the Maritime Commission, FDR decided to name Kennedy as head of the Securities and Exchange Commission where he sat in judgment on the same stock exchange manipulations at which he had been so adept. He had already demonstrated his executive ability and he went to work with the same untiring energy to reform and control the security markets. There is no question but that he was a remarkable financial wizard; he took the chairmanship of the important Securities and Exchange Commission in his stride and proceeded to manage it with ability, integrity and success. However, the ambitious Kennedy, with all his money, was not satisfied. He tired of this position and apparently had his mind set on being appointed secretary of the treasury. The President, however, had other ideas. He had no intention of dismissing his loyal and faithful friend, Henry Morgenthau, Jr., who knew no more about economics than he did, but could be relied on to carry out all presidential wishes. Nevertheless, no matter what anyone may think about President Roosevelt, he was a masterful politician. He realized that Joe Kennedy was one of his biggest campaign contributors and influential not only in Irish circles, but with many prominent and wealthy businessmen. He therefore proceeded to find an important position for him to fill. There was a vacancy in the ambassadorship to Great Britain, a highly important office of influence and dignity. Although young Kennedy would have preferred the Treasury, he did not waste much time in accepting the appointment as American ambassador to the Court of St. James.

At the American embassy in London our red-headed ambassador was known to have a flaming temper, a rough tongue and a friendly, cautious personality; he soon became a popular ambassador. He openly supported Prime Minister Neville Chamberlain's efforts to maintain peace with Germany. Kennedy, the appointee of FDR, who was the leading American interventionist and internationalist, stood firmly for his own convictions. He told reporters in December, 1939, during the European crisis, "I am pro-peace. I pray, hope and work for peace." He told Lord Halifax the foreign minister that he himself was "entirely in sympathy and a warm admirer of everything that Prime Minister Chamberlain has done."

However, Kennedy was a cautious and faithful ambassador. After the Munich settlement, Roosevelt cabled him a congratulatory message for Chamberlain. "I went over to 10 Downing Street the day I received the cable," Kennedy said, "but instead of handing the cable to Chamberlain as customary, I read it to him, as I had a feeling that the cable might haunt Roosevelt some day, so I kept it."

Morgenthau wrote in his diary, "He (FDR) became increasingly irritated at Kennedy. Who would have thought that the English (the Clivenden Set) could take into camp a red-headed Irishman?"

As for Chamberlain, the president called him "slippery" and added with some bitterness that "he was interested in peace at any price, if he could get away with it and save his face."

Roosevelt referred to Joseph Kennedy as "my ambassador." It was typical of FDR's colossal egotism.

On March 31, 1939, Britain reversed the course of her foreign policies of the previous five years and announced a guarantee of the independence of Poland which included Danzig. This infuriated Hitler and turned friendship into hate overnight. Chamberlain had given this blank-check guarantee of Poland with the utmost reluctance. He had to do so because he was on the defensive both in England and vis-à-vis the White House. Due to pressure from the British prowar elements and Roosevelt, he was forced to take a firm stand against Hitler.

Unfortunately, the timing of this turned out to be a strategic blunder of the worst kind and led directly into war. Both Chamberlain and Ambassador Kennedy, his close friend, were anti-Communist and hoped and anticipated that Hitler would attack Soviet Russia, thereby making any Anglo-Russian alliance unnecessary. However, the shrewd former prime minister, Lloyd George, thought that Chamberlain's guarantee of Poland was a futile blank check and a step towards war. He said, "If we go into war without the help of Russia, we will be walking into a trap."

Neville Chamberlain, the avowed man of peace, was directly responsible for making the war inevitable. He tied his own hands over the final Danzig controversy. No one wanted peace more than Chamberlain. Ambassador Kennedy received from Sir Horace Wilson, acting on Chamberlain's behalf, a highly secret peace proposal which the ambassador promptly relayed to Washington. Kennedy said that "the British wanted one thing of us and only one thing. Mainly that we should put pressure on the Poles. They felt that they could not, in view of their obligation under their recent treaty, do anything, but we could."

FDR and Secretary Hull scorned the proposal, according to J. Pierpont Moffat of the State Department. This reaction by the State Department was natural in view of the fact that Ambassador William Bullitt for almost a year had been urging the Poles not to negotiate with Hitler for any concessions of territory at any time, including Danzig, the cause of the war. This action turned out to be a tragedy and resulted in World War II. It could have been settled by mediation and arbitration of the Danzig issue. Once that was out of the way, Hitler would have returned to his first love and dominating obsession—the march towards the east, and not the west.

As a result, we mourn not just the terrible casualties of World War II, but the destruction of freedom and the communization of half the world. Roosevelt had the opportunity to have been a great peacemaker. Instead he chose to be a disastrous warmaker. He could have prevented the outbreak of World War II and turned Hitler and the German army against Stalin and his communist hordes. If there had only been a crystal ball there might have been a different decision to use American influence with Poland to arbitrate the Danzig issue instead of pushing, shoving, cajoling, and influencing almost-defenseless Poland to refuse to negotiate. This was not only the direct cause of the war, but the end of the American-created Polish Republic.

In December 1945, Kennedy had a conversation with James V. Forrestal. Later Forrestal wrote in his diary,

Played golf today with Joe Kennedy. I asked him about his conversations with Roosevelt and Neville Chamberlain from 1938 on. He said, Chamberlain's position in 1938 was that England had nothing with which to fight and that she could not risk going to war with Hitler. Kennedy's view, that Hitler would have fought Russia without any later conflict with England if it had not been for William C. Bullitt who urged Roosevelt in the summer of 1939 that Poland must make no concessions to Germany. Neither the French nor the British would have made Poland a cause of war if it had not been for the constant needling from Washington. Bullitt, he said, kept telling Roosevelt that the Germans wouldn't fight, Kennedy, that they would, and that they would overrun Europe. Kennedy stated Chamberlain said that "America (President Roosevelt) . . . had forced England into war."

In his telephone conversations with FDR in the summer of 1939 the president kept telling him to "put some iron up Chamberlain's backside." Kennedy's response always was that putting iron up his backside did no good unless the British had some iron with which to fight, and they did not.

I was president of the congressional group to the Interparliamentary Union at the Oslo Conference on August 16, 1939, two weeks before the outbreak of the war. Ambassador Kennedy of course knew this. I arrived in London on September 1 to meet my wife and children who were coming in from Paris. I telephoned the American embassy and asked for seats for my wife and myself in the distinguished guests gallery in Parliament. This was not difficult to arrange; I had previously on several occasions sat in the distinguished guests gallery. I admit of some annoyance when I found the two tickets for the famous meeting of Parliament on September 3, to declare war, were not in the distinguished guests gallery. I said to myself, I suppose Ambassador Kennedy thinks, he is an awful Republican and it doesn't make much difference what we do with him. I am glad to apologize publicly even at this late date, because the ticket he sent for my wife was in the box with the duke and duchess of Kent, and mine was for one of the six reserved seats on the floor of Parliament. This shows that Joseph Kennedy was a fair-minded ambassador who rose above partisanship in matters of this sort. Of course it was a highly historic occasion for anyone to witness.

Neville Chamberlain, prime minister of Britain, who for five years had sought honestly through his leadership and activities to preserve the peace of Europe, stood up before the Parliament and confessed, "Everything that I have worked for, everything I have hoped for, everything I have believed in during my public life, has crashed into ruins."

Talking soon after this with Sir John Simon, chancellor of the Exchequer, Ambassador Kennedy asked him what the British were fighting for. How could they restore Poland even if Hitler were defeated? Germany would be thrown into chaos and might go Communist (half did). The war would exhaust England and France, leaving them vulnerable to radicalism. What, Kennedy demanded, was the sense of fighting? Simon glumly shook his head and said that he did not know, but once in the war, it was difficult to get out. That was partially true. But Churchill could have made an advantageous peace half a dozen times that would have freed France, Belgium, Holland, and Norway, and would have saved millions of lives in western Europe by giving a green light to the Nazi dictator Hitler to fight the Communist dictator Stalin.

10

MY INTERVIEW WITH THE GERMAN FOREIGN MINISTER JOACHIM VON RIBBENTROP ON AUGUST 14, 1939

This is an account never before published of my exclusive and unique interview with Joachim von Ribbentrop, the German Nazi foreign minister at his mountain villa near Salzburg, Austria, two weeks before the outbreak of World War II. It was prepared and written from copious notes taken at the time, and is now presented to the American people and to all others interested in truth and history.

The interview took place 36 years ago. Certainly the facts can now be told without arousing political animosity between nations. It might even serve to scotch misleading rumors and absurd implications that may have existed at the time. Herr von Ribbentrop was sentenced many years ago by the Nuremberg Court and hanged. I went to Salzburg at the invitation of the German foreign minister in my official capacity as president of the American delegation to the Interparliamentary Union. I was on my way to the annual convention to be held at Oslo, Norway, August 15–19, 1939.

The American delegation was composed of twenty-four

members of the House of Representatives, equally divided between the two parties, and four U.S. senators. Two of these, Senator Theodore Francis Greene and Senator Alexander Wiley, later served with distinction as chairmen of the Senate Foreign Relations Committee.

For a number of years, Senator Alben W. Barkley, later vice-president of the United States, had been elected as president of the American delegation to the Interparliamentary Union by the members of the House and Senate. In the early part of 1939, there was a good deal of war talk and fear that President Roosevelt would involve us directly or indirectly in another European war. A majority of the Congress, both Republicans and Democrats, were in favor of keeping out of foreign wars unless attacked. My views as ranking Republican member of the House Foreign Affairs Committee were well known in Congress and throughout the nation.

I was openly opposed to having the U.S. dragged into the ancient European blood-feuds and balance-of-power politics, and so were approximately 90 percent of the American people at that time. A number of my friends in the Congress asked me if I would serve as president of the Interparliamentary Union if there were enough votes to defeat Senator Barkley. I agreed, and to my surprise I was elected by a two-to-one margin.

The result was even a greater surprise to Senator Barkley, who had for years been the supreme autocrat of the Interparliamentary Union and considered politically unbeatable. Hitherto, Barkley had distributed the $10,000 appropriated by Congress each year to seven or eight senators, mostly Democrats, and to two or three representatives. In view of the fact that my election over Senator Barkley was almost revolutionary, I decided to fill the entire American quota of twenty-eight members, which I proceeded to do by appointing twelve Republicans and an equal number of Democrats from the House, and two Democrats and two Republicans from the Senate. The

$10,000 appropriation, at $500 per member, took care of twenty members and the others agreed to pay their own expenses. Then I received a contribution of $3,000 from Bernard Baruch which provided $500 for most of the others. This was the first time that the full American quota had been appointed and the first time that the membership had represented both parties equally.

For several years I had realized the crucial and delicate balance of the scales in Europe between war and peace, and had determined both in Congress and as president of the American delegation, to exert my utmost influence towards the preservation of peace, as opposed to an utterly ruinous European world war. I remember telling or warning von Ribbentrop that no matter which nation won, if the war broke out, every European nation engaged in it would lose in lives, and endure destruction and bankruptcy. It did not take much of a prophet to foresee that eventuality. At no time did I receive any cooperation from President Roosevelt; he was, I am reliably informed, very much annoyed at my election as head of the delegation, and likewise by my efforts at Oslo to settle the Danzig issue by peaceful means instead of by another European bloodbath.

After Congress adjourned at the end of July, 1939, I went by boat to Ireland where I met President De Valera at his office in Dublin. He was a tall, intelligent, kindly and outspoken public official. He stated without reservations that if the European war broke out and England were involved, Ireland would remain neutral but would sell food and other products to England.

From Dublin I flew to London to keep a Saturday afternoon appointment with Lord Halifax, the British foreign minister at his office. He later became the British ambassador to Washington. He was very tall, charming and able—a cultured gentleman and statesman. He looked something like Abraham Lincoln. He was outspokenly against war with Germany and told me that the Nazi government had proposed to limit its army to 300,000, provided France would also, and he deplored France's refusal to agree. He felt, as I did, that another European war would be ruinous and that every possible constructive effort should be made to avoid it.

I then flew to Paris to meet my wife and children who had preceded me there by boat from the United States. I met the French foreign minister Georges Bonnet by appointment. I thought him a talented and experienced diplomat but inclined to the defeatist attitude that war was inevitable and would break out within a few weeks. Obviously he did not want France to become involved in a war with Germany, but from reports I received he was being pressured into it by certain powerful public figures both in the United States and Great Britain. He realized that France was not sufficiently prepared in air power and lacked enough armored tanks.

Also while in Paris, I met at a small dinner party given by our amiable and astute Ambassador William C. Bullitt, at his exquisite chateau at Chantilly near Paris, the good-looking young French air minister, Guy LaChambre. He was only thirty-seven but had served in the French army in World War I and had been decorated for gallantry. He was then in somewhat the same position in France as Goering was in Germany. He had revived and reorganized the French air force and was in the process of building it up into a powerful weapon for the defense of France. Had he had another year, he could have succeeded. I talked with him for an hour after dinner, and he told me in a calm and deliberate manner that France was preparing for any eventuality and that war would probably break out by August 24. I argued as best I could, pointing out that in modern wars all nations lost, including the victor, and that it was not too late to reach a peaceful agreement with Germany. I told him I expected to see von Ribbentrop in a few days and asked him if what he had told me was confidential and he answered most emphatically, "No." The French air minister evidently greatly underestimated the size and power of the German air force as events later proved.

During the first week of August while I was staying at the Roblin Hotel in Paris with my family, I received a telephone call from a German friend of mine, Mr. Sallett in Berlin, asking me if I would like to meet the German foreign minister, von Ribbentrop. I told him I would be glad to stop off on my way to Norway for the interparliamentary convention. I knew of no reason then (nor know of any now) why I shouldn't have met the German foreign minister. In fact, I felt it my duty as head of the American congressional group to meet von Ribbentrop and obtain all available information about the intention or plans of the German government as it affected the peace of Europe and the world. I had already seen Lord Halifax, the British foreign minister, in London, Monsieur Georges Bonnet, the French foreign minister, and Guy LaChambre, the French air minister, in Paris. I suggested Monday, August 14th at Salzburg, the day before the Oslo Conference.

Herr Richard Sallett, an official of the German foreign office and a graduate of Harvard University, whom I had known in America, entertained me in Berlin. I went with him to the foreign office where I met Baron Weizbaecker, who ranked next to von Ribbentrop. He was, I believe, formerly in the naval service, and spoke English well. His only son was killed three weeks later while serving as an officer in the Polish campaign. He apparently was not a Nazi, nor in favor of the invasion of Poland. I arrived with Mr. Sallett at Salzburg by train from Berlin on Monday morning, August 14, and was taken straight to the same hotel at which Count Ciano was staying. At breakfast I met von Ribbentrop's personal liaison officer, Colonel Huwell, later an ambassador. He was killed escaping from Hitler's bunker at the end of the war. He informed me that my appointment had been postponed until four o'clock that afternoon as the result of Ciano's visit. This delay aroused my Holland Dutch blood and I informed him that I had come by special invitation and would have to catch the noon train for Berlin in order to be in Oslo the next morning to attend the opening session of the Interparliamentary Congress. In a short time a message came back from von Ribbentrop that if I would wait until four o'clock that afternoon to see him he would provide one of his airplanes to fly me to Oslo and promised definitely that the plane would arrive there by nine o'clock the next morning. As head of the American delegation I had to attend a meeting of the Executive Committee of the Interparliamentary Conference at ten the next morning and be received by the king of Norway at ten-thirty with the entire American delegation. In fairness to von Ribbentrop, the plane did arrive at the Oslo airport on time.

It must be remembered that the United States had no ambassador to Germany. I believed then, and still believe, that this was a serious blunder on the part of the Roosevelt administration. Our chargé d'affairs in Berlin, Mr. Alexander Kirk, although an able and trained diplomat, was unable to see Hitler or von Ribbentrop and might as well have been in Timbuktu. We should have maintained an American ambassador in Berlin to be in a position to exert our influence in behalf of peace before Europe committed suicide and communism devoured a large part of central and eastern Europe. The fact that our ambassador had been recalled from Berlin a year before left the United States without influence or leadership in the prewar crisis.

I spent four delightful hours wandering around Salzburg, one of the most picturesque cities in Europe with its ancient castle perched up above the town. The inhabitants, men and women, still wore the old peasant costumes, the women in bright red and blue and the men in leather shorts with green or black Alpine hats.

At 3:30 P.M. an automobile arrived at the hotel for me. It took me over some country roads and hills for about seven miles to von Ribbentrop's villa overlooking an exquisite mountain lake called Fuschel. His villa was formerly a hunting lodge of the archbishop of Salzburg. I relate unemotionally my interview with von Ribbentrop as accurately as my notes and my memory serve me.

He met me as I entered his country residence in a most cordial manner. I was impressed by his youthful appearance. He was then forty-five years old, good-looking, and while I suppose many people believed that he was some kind of a demon and would have liked me to describe him as such, I was able to observe only that he was a gracious and charming host and spoke English fluently.

He told me he had worked for six years in the United States and Canada. I believe he said on the railroads and in the contracting business in the Middle West. At any rate, his English was excellent and he was never at a loss for the right word or expression. I had been in politics for over twenty years but I had never spoken with anyone in a more informal and open manner. We sat at a tea table on the porch of his villa overlooking the lake, the huge mountains, surrounded by clouds, in the distance.

My purpose in seeing the foreign ministers of England, France, and Germany before attending the Interparliamentary Union Conference was to obtain firsthand information about the European situation, particularly concerning the preservation of peace. I was also interested in a possible solution of the refugee problem by establishing a homeland for them in a suitable part of the underdeveloped highlands in the vast territories of England or France in North Africa, backed by funds from American philanthropists and men of vision. I had already discussed the refugee problem with Mr. McDonald, the British minister of colonies, who was interested and cooperative. Mr. Mandel, the French colonial minister, was a highly intelligent and dedicated French patriot. He became so interested in the project that he said he would invite the three top French governor generals in north and west Africa to meet me at his office in Paris on September 1 to determine what land was the most suitable and available for a refugee colony. Mr. Bernard Baruch, an American philanthropist endowed with humanitarian vision, was the real sponsor of this project. He agreed to raise sufficient funds to start it on a moderate scale. Unfortunately Hitler invaded Poland on September 1 and after France was overrun by the German army, George Mandel was killed by the Nazis.

I was primarily interested in the preservation of peace and wanted to find out if there was anything that I could do to promote peace at the conference or to influence von Ribbentrop. This I found extremely difficult. Herr von Ribbentrop told me at length and in detail that the English encirclement of Germany by guaranteeing Danzig and the boundaries of Poland was regarded by Hitler as not only provocative, but a hostile act. He said that he and Mr. Beck, the Polish foreign minister, had practically agreed to the return of Danzig to Germany and to a Polish Corridor. He claimed that after the British encirclement policy was proclaimed in April, 1939, Poland refused to negotiate and that even her foreign minister, Mr. Beck, was powerless in the hands of what von Ribbentrop called "the Polish military clique" who were preparing for war with the backing of France and England. He further stated that Germany had come to the end of her patience and unless Danzig were restored and German minorities' rights guaranteed in Poland, war would break out within two weeks. I mentioned that the French thought that war would begin any time after August 24, and he replied that it would come very soon unless agreement were reached on Danzig. Von Ribbentrop made it very clear that Germany was ready to fight to restore Danzig to the German Reich regardless of the English encirclement.

The question of a thirty-day armistice or moratorium was never discussed between us, nor was the settlement of the Polish issue by arbitration and peaceful methods. He presented me with considerable data about the maltreatment and attacks on Germans in Poland, much of which I thought was sheer propaganda. He spoke of half a dozen German boys who had been castrated in Poland and said he feared to publish the facts, as they would arouse the German people to immediate revenge. He did say, however, that war with Poland would be popular with the German people as they believed that they had freed Poland from Soviet Russia only to be deprived of their own territory by the Versailles Treaty. He told me that the German army was prepared, and that if disorders continued in Poland, war was inevitable. I remember he said that "the mechanized German army can crush and overwhelm Poland in two weeks." I laughed at that and said, "You mean two months don't you?" To which he replied, "No, in two weeks," and continued, "We are familiar with every road in Poland from the last war and know Poland as well as the Poles, and the muddy roads of Poland do not frighten us."

Herr von Ribbentrop reiterated that for years Hitler, whom he called the Fuehrer, was animated by racial consideration and belief in the stability of the British Empire. He said he had flown twenty times or more to London with friendly proposals and goodwill messages to the British government from Hitler. For a number of years von Ribbentrop was the German ambassador to London. He referred to Hitler's offer to limit the German army to 300,000 which France had rejected; and to the offer, which was accepted, to limit the German navy to one-third the size of the British navy. He went even further and said that Hitler believed that cooperation between England and Germany was essential for the maintenance of peace, and that Hitler had "offered to place fifteen German army divisions and the entire fleet at the disposal of the British government to support her empire in case of war anywhere in the world."

This I did not believe at the time, but it was substantiated years later. He said it was not until the British inaugurated their program of encirclement and guarantee of the status quo of Danzig that Hitler turned from friendship to bitter enmity. Although von Ribbentrop did not use the words, "like a woman scorned," that was the impression I received. He did say that now the Fuehrer "would stop at nothing to destroy the British Empire even to the last German soldier."

I asked von Ribbentrop who wrote the remarkable reply of April 1939 to President Roosevelt's proposal to guarantee the neutrality of certain nations. I thought that he, as the foreign minister, had done so. However, he claimed that he had shown a translation of the proposal to Hitler, who exclaimed on reading it, "This is an act of Providence," and that Hitler had stayed up the entire night working on the answer himself.

Herr von Ribbentrop told me that he had, himself, written to Monsieur Bonnet, the French foreign minister, that the German Westwall (the Siegfried Line) was completed and was invincible and that the Germans had no quarrel with the French but if the French insisted on attacking, they would lose a million men and bleed to death. That, he said, was France's responsibility, not his. It should be easy for any historian to check up and find out whether any such letter was ever received.

It was not my mission to quarrel with the foreign minister; the only dispute I got into was when he tried to make out that the German army did not lose the last war. I reminded him that I too was an officer in that war and that the German soldiers and replacements were either young boys of sixteen or men over forty-five and that Germany was exhausted in manpower and resources and could not have lasted another six months regardless of the revolution at home. He did not press the issue any further.

During the conversation, which lasted over an hour and a half, we drank tea and ate cookies and preserves. My reception throughout was most cordial and courteous. He invited me to go to the opera with Hitler that evening and assured me that if I did, he would arrange for his plane to get me to Oslo by nine the next morning. I declined for several reasons; one of which was that I did not believe it worth the risk of being late in reaching Oslo, and the other political. Looking back I am intrigued in not having met the megalomaniac Hitler at the apex of his power.

It did not take me very long to come to the conclusion that von Ribbentrop was very antagonistic to the British, despite Hitler's friendly attitude.

History has often shown that small things have caused enmity and war between nations. The British aristocracy, despite the fact that von Ribbentrop was ambassador of the German Reich, one of the most powerful nations in Europe, apparently could not overlook the fact that he had been a former champagne salesman. This form of snobbishness was carried to the extent that von Ribbentrop's son was blackballed and turned down for Harrow and Eton. This is something that no father, whether ambassador or not, can forget or forgive, and from then on he used his influence against the British wherever possible. It is a sad commentary on diplomacy, but human nature has not changed for thousands of years, and this little family episode was a contributing factor towards World War II. This I believe as the father of an only son.

When the motor car arrived to take me to the airfield, von Ribbentrop politely escorted me to the car and that was the last time I ever saw or heard from him. Ten days later he signed the pact with Stalin for a German-Russian alliance, one week after the Interparliamentary Union failed to adopt my resolution for a moratorium of thirty days in order to settle the Danzig issue by arbitration.

Years later von Ribbentrop was hanged. Just why I do not know; it may have been because he succeeded in making a war alliance with Stalin and Molotov in August, 1939, when England and France failed to secure the same type of treaty. In any case many lawyers have raised the issue of *ex post facto* law at the trials. I do know that von Ribbentrop, condemned for alleged crimes at the Nuremberg Trials, knew as most other people did of the terrible Communist atrocities that included the murder of 12,000 Polish officers (prisoners), 38,000 of their own officers, and the brutal liquidation of millions of Russian people.

Certainly those Germans responsible for direct atrocities, such as the killing of innocent people in concentration camps or otherwise, should have been held guilty for their barbaric actions. But I have always, along with Senator Taft, doubted the legality of holding a foreign minister and top officers of the army and navy responsible for atrocities with which they had no connection nor knowledge, any more than General Marshall, General Eisenhower or Secretary of State Cordell Hull should be held responsible for the killing of over 150,000 Germans in the bombing and burning of Dresden or that President Truman and his advisers should be held responsible for the death of 120,000 Japanese by atomic bombs at Nagasaki and Hiroshima.

Of course individuals should be held responsible for war crimes. But to have Soviet Russia, which invaded Poland two weeks after the Nazi invasion in 1939, participate in the Nuremberg Trials, made them largely a farce and a travesty of justice if their purpose were to establish a definite standard for wars of aggression, war crimes, or atrocities.

11

THE FAMOUS INTERPARLIAMENTARY UNION CONFERENCE

The plane which Foreign Minister von Ribbentrop had placed at my disposal was a sixteen-passenger commercial type with two pilots and an assistant, not the famous smaller plane that had been provided for Prime Minister Chamberlain when he visited Hitler. Herr Sallett, a representative of the German foreign office, accompanied me to Berlin. We were the only passengers. The airplane took off just before seven o'clock from the Salzburg airport as the sun began to disappear. The first hour's flight over the Austrian and Bavarian Alps was very beautiful, but after that all was darkness as we crossed Czechoslovakia. We landed at Berlin at ten o'clock, where Mr. Sallett left me, and I continued on to Copenhagen, Denmark, where we arrived at midnight. The plane took off again at six in the morning, flying over numerous small islands and arriving at the Oslo airport precisely at nine, as promised. One hour later when I arrived at the Interparliamentary Union Conference I was surrounded by reporters who wanted to know all about my interview with von Ribbentrop. I refused to make any statements except to say that I had flown over in one of his airplanes and that I believed that war would break out between August 24 and September 1, and that my information came from both high French and German sources.

This was obviously cabled to America where I was attacked viciously in press editorials as being an alarmist and not knowing anything about the foreign situation, although for over twenty years I had been a member of the Committee on Foreign Affairs in the House of Representatives. The war did break out two weeks later, but I do not remember receiving any apologies from the editorial writers or columnists who denounced me as an alarmist. However, public officials are accustomed to that kind of treatment.

King Haakon of Norway gave an official reception to the 300 delegates of the Interparliamentary Conference and diplomatic corps at the palace in Oslo. The crown prince and the royal family were also there to meet the guests. Only seven months later they were forced to flee from Norway to escape from the Nazi invasion.

The reception was held in the spacious and beautiful ballroom of the royal palace. I was standing talking with a group of delegates when an equerry of the king invited me to meet His Majesty, King Haakon, who was standing alone in front of a large mantlepiece in the middle of the ballroom. He was a very tall, handsome, intelligent individual, past middle age. He greeted me cordially and immediately began asking me in perfect English about my interview with von Ribbentrop. He, like all the heads of the western European delegations, was anxious to know if von Ribbentrop had said anything about German intentions to invade France, Belgium, and Norway. I could only tell him what von Ribbentrop had said—that if Germany recovered Danzig, it would be the final liquidation of the Versailles Treaty and that Germany had no desire for any additional territory in the west. I repeated his statement about the invincibility of the Westwall, which seemed to me a clear indication that in case of war, Germany did not originally intend to invade France or Belgium. The fact is that Germany did not invade either nation for seven or eight months. Then the king cross-examined me on what the German and French foreign ministers had said regarding the timetable for a shooting war and also my proposed moratorium of thirty days to settle the Danzig issue. After the first fifteen minutes, I reminded him that I was in an embarrassing position as all the delegates were waiting to meet him. He insisted on continuing the conversation, which he did with marked intelligence and knowledge of the vital issues of war and peace. I told him what I have written in this chapter. I finally received permission of the king to leave, but I am sure not without making numerous enemies among the waiting diplomats, delegates and their wives.

At the opening of the Interparliamentary Congress, I introduced a thirty-day moratorium resolution for the peaceful settlement of the war-provoking Danzig issue. The Free City of Danzig was 90 percent German, and I believed then and am convinced now, that it could and should have been settled by peaceful means instead of war. My resolution read as follows:

RESOLVED, that the Interparliamentary Union, in its session at Oslo, urges upon the governments of Great Britain, France, Germany and Italy, the immediate consideration of a moratorium on war (Danzig) for thirty days or more with a view to the settlement of international disputes by arbitration, mediation and peaceful methods, consistent with the principles for which the Interparliamentary Union was founded.

I urged the adoption of the resolution in the most important and dramatic speech I ever made, asking the conference to rise above the deadlock in which Europe was engulfed, into the daylight of peace and humanity. Hatred and revenge had to be subordinated to the nobler principles of arbitration and peace. There had to be a peaceful way out of the existing deadlock to prevent another bloody and disastrous European war from breaking out within the next two weeks.

I am taking the liberty of quoting parts of my Oslo

speech, in view of the subsequent events, from an article in *World Affairs* magazine, December 1939.

The following selections from my remarks indicate more fully the spirit in which they were made. Announcing that I proposed to speak on the peaceful settlement of international disputes, and paying a respectful tribute to the Scandinavian countries and their contributions in America, I said:

We are all members of representative and parliamentary governments from throughout the world which believe in the fundamental rights of the people to govern themselves under free institutions and in the preservation of peace as a paramount and continuous policy. I never had more faith in the final triumph and extension of democracy and the right of the people to rule than I have today, in spite of its temporary challenge by dictatorships of the left and of the right. The answer to all dictatorships is to make democracy work in our own countries and to put our own houses in order. Parliamentary and representative forms of government are still the hope and aspiration of the struggling masses of mankind throughout the world.

Free institutions, including free speech, free press and radio, and free assembly, together with personal liberty and economic justice, are the natural aspirations of free men and women throughout the civilized world.

I regret deeply to state that I believe that a European war is more imminent today than at any time since last September. If the Danzig and the Polish agitation continues, the slightest spark may start a world conflagration. This conference has listened to numerous interesting and able speeches from the point of view generally of the nation involved. As one who served in the World War I and for most of the time in the French Fourth Army under General Gouraud, I hate and loathe war, and do not offer any apologies for raising my voice in behalf of peace. I refuse to admit that the door to peace is closed or to yield to the defeatist war talk that apparently covers Europe. I refuse to believe that if there is a will and sufficient determination, a way cannot be found to open the door of peace and the road to a peaceful settlement of international controversies.

Pointing then to the horrors of war, I went on to say:

> We have no power as delegates to enforce peace, but we have a solemn and sacred duty to exert our moral and political influence in our own countries to preserve peace through arbitration, mediation and conciliation. We cannot dodge or evade the peace issue. We would be shirking our obligation to humanity and our duty as representatives of millions of free people throughout the world if we join in any defeatist attitude towards peace and wash our hands, like Pontius Pilate, over the crucifixion of Europe, and maybe of civilization and Christianity. I urge this conference to make a strong, united plea to the governments of the world, including the Vatican, in support of a thirty-day moratorium on political and international disputes and, in the meantime, to explore anew every avenue and possibility for a fair and peaceful settlement of the issues that are leading European nations into war, and to provide for a program of world recovery.
>
> If we refuse to act and no armistice on war is arranged, the whole peace issue may go by default. Peacemaking machinery has broken down. The tension has been so continuous and so acute that it is not surprising if the statesmen of Europe are worn out and find themselves in an impasse or a deadlock that leads directly to war. If this conference can contribute the leadership in a democratic manner, to world peace, it will deserve the grateful thanks and prayers of millions of peace-loving people throughout all of Europe and the world.

I also quote, from the official records, my concluding words in French, "Je dis aux membres de cette Conférence Interparlementaire: À bas la guerre. Vivent la démocratie et la paix." (Loud and prolonged applause.)

The applause showed that my proposal was very well received by most of the delegates of the twenty-five nations represented at the conference. The head of the French delegation told me that he favored it, but unfortunately, for reasons best known to themselves, the British and Norwegian delegations later opposed it. To this day I believe that FDR had quietly slipped a dagger into the back of the proposed moratorium. I was reliably informed that Mussolini and the Italian government strongly and urgently favored the adoption of the moratorium resolution. I stated I would not press for its adoption if any of the nations mentioned in my resolution were opposed to it. Mr. Hambro of Norway, aligned with British interests, was the only speaker against it but he took occasion to say in his remarks that the United States had never done anything to help any of the European nations. (After the war started no nation suffered more than Norway.)

The next day at the Executive Committee meeting, composed of two members from each nation, I rose and withdrew my resolution because I believed that, to be effective, it should have British support and be unanimous. But in doing so, I asked the chairman of the Executive Committee who was a former Belgian foreign minister if it were not true that the United States, through Herbert Hoover, had given great quantities of food relief during World War I to the Belgian people. He jumped to his feet and said that no nation had ever done more, unselfishly and on such a large humanitarian scale, as the United States. I then turned to the Polish representative and asked him if he did not remember the food supplies and relief that were sent to Poland by the United States during and after World War I, and he too took occasion to praise the humanitarian efforts of our country. By that time, Mr. Hambro sneaked out of the committee room. However, the net result was the adoption of an innocuous and futile resolution, nothing but a scrap of paper, praising peace but utterly ineffective and worthless as a deterrent in preventing the onrushing tidal wave of war that broke over Europe two weeks later and wiped out millions of people including the youth of Europe.

If my proposed moratorium had been adopted it would have put the moral stigma upon Hitler and Mussolini to turn down a proposal emanating from the representatives of twenty-five democratic nations seeking to avert war through peaceful settlement of the Danzig issue. On my return to

America after the war began, I received numerous pathetic cablegrams from the Finnish, Hungarian, Lithuanian, Estonian and Latvian foreign ministers, saying what a tragedy it was that my resolution had not been adopted. It might only have delayed war for a month or a year, but it might have averted it entirely and prevented the wreck and ruin of Europe and the advent of communism throughout eastern and central Europe.

It might well have headed off the holocaust in western Europe in 1940 and resulted instead in a war between the Nazis and the Communists, with the people of Europe and America sitting peacefully at home listening in on their radios and saying, "A plague on both Nazism and Communism. Let the bloody dictators destroy each other."

On September 1, the German army invaded Poland, and France declared war two days later. That ended the proposed refugee project. I never got back to Paris but went straight to London to join my family on September 2. They had left Paris the day before. The next day I heard Prime Minister Chamberlain make his declaration of war speech in Parliament. The die was cast and it was to be an arbitration of blood, tears and death instead of peaceful methods.

The telling of these critical events that occurred just prior to the beginning of World War II may arouse the American people from their lethargy and apathy to use their influence to remain strong militarily, but against our involvement in a nuclear war except in self-defense. The United States must try to prevent any igniting of the spark that will start World War III and the destruction of most of the civilized world. A nuclear war would be mutual suicide. The preservation of peace should be our permanent policy.

The American people should remember the words of Abraham Lincoln: "To sin by silence when you should protest makes cowards of men." This is particularly true in our nuclear age. The American people have the constitutional right to protest to their members of Congress who alone have the sole power under our Constitution to prevent our involvement in unnecessary and undeclared wars. Let Soviet Russia and Communist China, as much as we would deplore it, fight it out in the next decade. It would be their war—not ours.

It is my definite conviction that if my thirty-day Danzig moratorium proposal had been adopted at the Oslo conference on August 17, 1939, and submitted for implementation to England, France, Germany and Italy, that the Danzig issue could have been settled on a friendly basis and could have stopped Hitler from signing a nonaggression pact with Soviet Russia to partition Poland. But far more important, it could have avoided the war in the west by Germany against England and France. No fair-minded person, in view of history, can deny that my moratorium might have prevented the beginning of World War II in 1939. When my proposal was turned down by the British, probably at the instigation of Roosevelt, it was followed within a week by Hitler's entering into a nonaggression pact with Soviet Russia, which contradicted all of his principles and policies of many years of anti-Communism.

The proof that my moratorium proposal was justifiable and historically right is crystal clear. As soon as Hitler made his pact with Stalin on August 23, 1939, he ordered the mobilization of the German army. This immediately electrified and aroused the British, French and Belgian governments, the Vatican, and even Mussolini to try to prevent World War II from breaking out over Danzig by the invasion of Poland by Hitler's army. The protest from Mussolini and all others was so determined that Hitler canceled the mobilization orders subject to direct negotiations with Poland for the return of Danzig.

The British, led by Prime Minister Chamberlain, Lord Halifax, and Ambassador Nevile Henderson completely reversed the position taken by the British delegates at the Oslo conference the week before and now urged the settlement of the Danzig issue by negotiation. They were urgently supported by the French prime minister, Daladier, and Foreign Minister Georges Bonnet, by the pope, the king of Belgium, and even, at the last minute, by FDR.

Unfortunately time was running out on the Polish government. Armed with its totally useless agreement with Britain, it evaded open negotiations in spite of the united pressure of the western European powers. It must be obvious now that if the British had gone along with my moratorium proposal that a settlement could have been reached and Hitler, having achieved the final termination of the Versailles Treaty, would have been free to go towards the east, which was his constant plan, instead of going to war with France and England.

As I look back, it was a stark, naked tragedy that the lives of millions of Europeans and Americans were sacrificed in an unwanted and unnecessary war over Danzig.

12

PEACEFUL ARBITRATION OF DANZIG OR WAR?

The subject of this chapter is of such tremendous importance—involving as it does the direct cause of the greatest war in the history of the world, based on casualties, destruction and the loss of freedom—that the full story must be told, without omissions. The magnitude of the issue involved, and the great efforts made by most of the prewar statesmen to prevent the outbreak of World War II, have an important place in history.

In *The Rise and Fall of the Third Reich* by William L. Shirer, there are at least fifty pages of material outlining the efforts of England, France, Germany, and numerous others, including the pope, Mussolini, the king of the Belgians and even, at the last minute, President Roosevelt, to prevent such a catastrophe.

Nearly everyone of prominence was anxious to avoid war by having Poland agree to enter into direct negotiations with Germany. There was one stumbling block: Polish Foreign Minister József Beck had previously recognized the German viewpoint, but after he obtained the utterly useless guarantee of British armed protection made an about-face and took a very strong position against negotiation. Danzig had a German population of ninety percent who voted overwhelmingly in a referendum to be restored to the German Reich in accordance with the principles of self-determination. The German aggressions against Czechoslovakia were ruthless and impossible to defend, but the desire of Nazi Germany to negotiate for the return of Danzig and a Corridor, is understandable, and should never have been permitted by England and France to become the cause of World War II.

What were the real reasons that delayed, obstructed and prevented direct negotiations between Germany and Poland for the restoration of Danzig? By this time England and France, through their top officials, urged Poland to send emmisaries with full powers to determine the Danzig issue on a peaceful basis. England and France had both made it very clear that if Germany invaded Poland, they would declare war on Germany. However, Prime Minister Chamberlain was exceedingly anxious to head off a catastrophic war and had even appealed to President Roosevelt through Ambassador Kennedy to have the president use his influence.

Hitler was also very anxious to settle the Danzig issue peacefully to avoid bringing England and France into the war. He was greatly annoyed by the Polish refusal to even consider any concessions about Danzig or to appoint plenipotentiaries to discuss them. He finally ordered an invasion of Poland on August 24, but at the last minute canceled it because of pleas from various quarters.

The frantic pleadings of both France and England and messages from the pope, the king of the Belgians, and the president of the United States, finally at the eleventh hour, induced the Poles to authorize their ambassador in Berlin, Lipski, to see von Ribbentrop and state that Poland was interested in the German proposed terms of negotiations. Von Ribbentrop asked Ambassador Lipski, "Do you come here with powers to negotiate?" and when he admitted he did not, that was the end of the tragic efforts to preserve the peace.

The ultimate blame rests on Hitler for forcing the issue and not having the patience to wait another few days, as it was evident that the pressure from all sources would have compelled Poland to enter negotiations. Poland was also to blame for its refusal to even consider concessions regarding Danzig, the final liquidation of the Versailles Treaty. It was especially heartrending in view of the fact that Hitler had made a nonaggression pact with Russia only six days before, and obviously Russia would now be on the side of Germany.

It is almost unbelievable that Foreign Minister Beck and the other high officials of Poland could have been so completely deceived about the actual military situation, when confronted by Germany with the finest army in Europe on the west and the vast Russian army on the eastern border. Words almost fail to describe such an awesome and pathetic military situation.

England had only two or three divisions available at that time and could not even provide a pop gun or a fire cracker to help Poland militarily. In fairness to England and France, they did not force the war on Poland. They did everything within their diplomatic power to persuade Poland to enter into negotiations for the restoration of Danzig. This would in no way have reflected on the honor of Poland, as Danzig was a German city and Germany agreed, if it were restored, to sign a treaty to guarantee the independence and integrity of Poland.

The negative reaction of Poland in view of the military situation is almost beyond comprehension. It was a futile, tragic policy on the part of her top political and military leaders, especially as the Polish people were far more hostile to the Communist regime at Moscow than they were to the Nazi regime in Berlin.

Marshall Pilsudski was one of the greatest heroes and statesmen in the history of Poland. Had he been alive, he would have arranged to submit the Danzig issue to arbitration with Germany and would have secured a guarantee from Germany for the independence and integrity of Poland. It is not that Marshall Pilsudski was partial to Nazi Germany, but he knew Soviet Russia and feared and hated communism. Unfortunately for Poland, he died five years before the outbreak of World War II. He was such a forceful character and great military leader that he would have been respected even by Hitler. I have spoken to numerous Polish exiles and they invariably agree that if Marshall Pilsudski had been alive, the Danzig issue could have been arbitrated peacefully and there would have been no invasion of Poland, no World War II, no murder by the Communists of 12,000 Polish officers and no communization of free Poland.

The most vital, controversial prewar problem in August, 1939, was the status of the free city of Danzig. Recovery of that German city was a *sine qua non* to Hitler and to German prestige. Everyone, even the Polish Foreign Minister Beck, recognized, however reluctantly, that Germany had justifiable claims to Danzig. Perhaps that is why Beck sidestepped negotiations until too late.

A few months later, the freedom-loving Baltic nations, all except Finland, were seized by Soviet Russia, and soon after, communized. That was what I had warned against for several years—that the Communist vulture, once war broke out, would swoop down and pick up the bloody remains in eastern Europe.

Now that the hysterics and emotions of World War II have cooled, let us consider what might have happened if Poland had agreed to restore Danzig and a Corridor. Foreign Minister Beck was willing to do so, but pressure from Roosevelt and top Polish generals prevented it until too late.

The return of Danzig to Germany would have deprived the Nazis of an excuse to invade Poland, headed off the Stalin-Hitler nonaggression pact, saved Poland from being a Communist state, and would have aborted Hitler's extermination policy of the Jews in Poland.

Hitler would not have made an alliance with Stalin and communism, not if he could have avoided it. The net result was that Chamberlain's ill-considered plan played into the hands of the advocates of war and actually checkmated his own aspirations for peace. Lloyd George, as well as many conservatives of vision, foresaw the trap, that this commitment to Poland would inevitably involve England in war, regardless of the consequences to British vital interests, which it finally did. But why could not World War II have been avoided and millions of the finest youth of Europe saved from death and mutilation, by civilized methods of mediation over Danzig, which I did my utmost to achieve at the Oslo Conference? With the Danzig issue settled, that reason for World War II would have been eliminated.

Hitler and Stalin, Nazis and Communists, would certainly sooner or later have fought a ruinous and exhausting war. The people of Europe, preserved from the ever-present threat of war, would have watched while Hitler and Stalin, the two brutal dictators, destroyed each other. If that had happened Britain and France would not have been participants in the war, and peace, freedom and democracy would have prevailed throughout western Europe.

I am convinced, now more than ever, that World War II in Europe could have been avoided by restoring Danzig and a Corridor to the German Reich. No one, of course, could guarantee Hitler's future actions, but in all probability western Europe would have been saved from a ruinous war, and Hitler and Stalin would have fought to mutual destruction; Poland would have been neutral or possibly allied with Germany against Soviet Russia; and the bestial butchery of six million European Jews by Hitler's orders might thus have been averted.

These are events that might have happened, and if they had, they would have saved Europe from the scourge of war, and America from participation in it. It would probably have prevented the communization of eastern Europe and the growth of the powerful Communist world conspiracy that now threatens the peace and freedom of the world. If Hitler had won, he would have had his hands full in eastern Europe and Russia during his lifetime. Because of his numerous enemies, this bigoted and cruel dictator's chances for a long life would have been very slim.

The German contention was that if there had been no British blank check, Hitler could have contrived to solve peacefully the Polish Danzig problem, provided England had not interfered. On March 21, 1939, von Ribbentrop told the Polish ambassador, Lipski, in Berlin that he hoped Danzig would be restored to the Reich, with a Polish Corridor to give access to it.

But on May 5, 1939, after the British guarantee in a memorandum, the Polish government refused von Ribbentrop's suggestion and the fat was in the fire. Almost immediately Hitler declared that the Polish-German declaration of nonaggression agreed to in 1934 was ended and he also abrogated the Anglo-German nonaggression pact and the agreement to limit the size of the German navy with Great Britain.

Most people now admit that it was a legitimate goal of German policy to try to get Danzig returned to the Reich. Unfortunately the worthless blank-check guarantee stood in the way of the peaceful settlement I tried to accomplish and almost did at the Interparliamentary Conference on August 16, 1939, two weeks before war broke out.

The dilatory action of Poland turned out to be the spark that set off World War II. Roosevelt had the opportunity to have been the great peacemaker, but by turning down Chamberlain's request and delaying too long, he failed to do anything to prevent the outbreak of World War II.

The doom of the freedom of the young Polish republic created by Woodrow Wilson, and the communization of eastern Europe was a tragedy of tragedies.

Illustrating Roosevelt's prewar dealings with Poland is a report by Jerzy Potocki, the Polish ambassador in Washington in the 1930s. This was found among the Polish diplomatic files seized by the Germans at Warsaw and confirmed later by Mr. Potocki, who was then living in South America.

The statement was made after an extensive interview on January 16, 1939, with Ambassador William C. Bullitt, President Roosevelt's key representative in Europe, who was about to return to his post in Paris. It read as follows:

> It is the decided opinion of the president (Roosevelt) that France and Britain must put an end to any sort of compromises with the totalitarian countries. They must not let themselves in for any discussions aiming at any kind of territorial changes. *They have the moral assurance that the United States will leave the policy of isolation and be prepared to intervene actively on the side of Britain and France in case of war.* (Author's italics.)

This is damning evidence of FDR's prewar interference, promises of intervention and positive opposition to any peace compromises regarding Danzig.

The above statement made by Ambassador Bullitt to the Polish ambassador in 1939 is also discussed in Chapter 13; it is cited here because of its relevance to the Danzig issue. It is proof positive that Roosevelt, from the beginning of 1939, was using his influence with Britain and France "to put an end to any sort of compromises with the totalitarian countries." And further, Bullitt gives definite assurances that the United States was *"prepared to intervene actively on the side of Britain and France in case of war."*

Bullitt's statement confirms precisely what the American noninterventionists were saying before the outbreak of the European war. It also goes a long way to substantiate the charge that if FDR had not meddled and pressured Britain and France into the war, there would have been no war in Europe and the Danzig problem would have been solved by peaceful arbitration. Both Prime Minister Chamberlain and Foreign Minister Georges Bonnet of France have publicly admitted the pressure and influence of Roosevelt to get them into war against Germany.

Ambassador Potocki's statement after his interview with Ambassador Bullitt is just another link in the chain of positive proof that President Roosevelt was exerting through Bullitt, and directly with Chamberlain, his powerful prowar influence. It is the first time in American history that a president of the United States intervened directly in European politics, let alone to promote war, not peace.

I graduated from college with a *cum laude* degree in history and government at the age of twenty and was, upon graduation, offered an appointment to be an instructor in history at Harvard, which to this day I am sorry I did not accept for one year. However, I did serve on the Committee on Foreign Affairs in Congress for twenty-five years and have generally kept up with the diplomatic history of our country. I know of no instance in which a president of the United States sought to provoke a war in Europe through ambassadorial and other channels. All of our presidents have stood for peace as a permanent policy, and none has ever used his influence to incite or promote war before. FDR's efforts to encourage a war against the Axis powers in Europe are made clear by Bullitt's activities and statements, the letter from Georges Bonnet, the French foreign minister in 1939 previously cited, and a similar statement by Prime Minister Chamberlain to Ambassador Kennedy, as repeated to Secretary of the Navy James Forrestal and quoted in his diary. The article by Pearson and Allen quoted in Chapter 5 also shows how President Roosevelt helped push Chamberlain into war with Germany. All these statements prove FDR exerted his influence to urge England, France and Poland to go to war with Hitler throughout 1939.

When Foreign Minister Beck, a very fine Polish official, went to England and persuaded Chamberlain to give him the utterly worthless guarantee of English support in case of war with Germany, it was the height of reckless diplomacy on both sides. England was in no position to fire a shot, even from a shotgun or pistol, in defense of Poland.

But Mr. Beck must have known that, and also that it would infuriate Hitler and the entire German nation, and incense Stalin and the Russians, neither of whom relished any implied control or domination by Britain in eastern Europe. It caused the rapprochement of Germany and Soviet Russia and the signing of the nonaggression pact on August 23, 1939. Once that pact was signed, Foreign Minister Beck should have seen the writing on the wall and immediately taken steps to arbitrate the solution of Danzig by peaceful means regardless of the views of some of the Polish generals and marshalls.

There was no valid reason for Poland not to realize that Germany had a justifiable claim to get back a German city that was lost by the Versailles Treaty. To risk the freedom and independence of Poland on such an issue was unfair to the 30 million Poles whose freedom was sacrificed to both the Nazis and the Communists.

If Danzig and a Corridor had been ceded to Germany it would have been the final liquidation of the Versailles Treaty. Thus the major designs of Hitler would have been fulfilled. The long-delayed march east for the wheatfields and oil production of Soviet Russia, with the consent and approval, if not the active cooperation, of Poland was next on Hitler's schedule. The people of Poland were bitterly opposed to the Communists and probably would have been rewarded by additional territory.

Looking back, it is a stark tragedy that the fate of Poland and of all eastern Europe had to be sacrificed over the small city of Danzig. Most Americans had never heard of it. It was an unnecessary and unwanted war, the most destructive and ruinous in all history—the tomb of freedom for over 100 million Europeans, not only in Poland, Czechoslovakia and Hungary but in the Baltic and Balkan nations and even in eastern Germany.

Lord Lothian, later British ambassador to Washington during the war, said in a speech at Chatham House on June 29, 1937: "Now if the principle of self-determination were applied on behalf of Germany in the way in which it was applied against them, it would mean the reentry of Austria into Germany, the Union of the Sudeten Deutsch, Danzig, and probably Memel with Germany, and certain adjustments with Poland in Silesia and the Corridor." Lord Lothian, a highly intelligent, well-informed, patriotic Englishman, made this statement more than two years before the Danzig crisis.

Wars are made by overt acts, acts of omission or by dilatory tactics. The catastrophe of World War II resulted partially from the dilatory tactics of Col. Józef Beck, foreign minister of Poland, who delayed until it was too late. He refused to comply with the request of the British foreign minister, Lord Halifax, and the British ambassador in Berlin, Sir Nevile Henderson, supported by the French ambassador at Berlin and French Foreign Minister Bonnet, urging that the Polish government negotiate directly with Germany over the restoration of Danzig. Ambassador Henderson stated openly that the German proposals were fair and reasonable. Presumably Mr. Beck did not realize the seriousness of the situation and took upon himself the responsibility of delaying direct negotiations until it was too late to stop the war.

The New York *Daily News*, which has the largest circulation of any newspaper in the United States, said editorially in June, 1940:

The French catastrophe is a part of one of the great tragic ironies of history, as we see it. Hitler said in *Mein Kampf* that he wanted to go east into Russia. The Ukraine looked to him like the ideal place for Germans to colonize and build up a farming and industrial civilization.

Hitler devoted pages in the same book to kind words about the British, how he considered them the same kind of people as the Germans, what fierce fighters the British were in an emergency, and how Germany's best single bet would always be an alliance with England.

Mein Kampf contains some harsh words about France, but by

building the Westwall, Hitler indicated that he didn't want a war with France—but what he still wanted last August was to go east. The allies wouldn't let him go east. They insisted that he come west. He has come west, with a vengeance.

How true! The *News* editorial was a breath of truth and prophecy in the midst of the hysteria of the war era. Who changed Hitler's mind? Who stopped him from going east? Who compelled him to come west, with disastrous results?

Roosevelt, Bullitt, Churchill, Eden, Vansittart, Amory, Duff Cooper, Daladier, Col. Józef Beck, Marshall Smigly Rydz, and strangely, Neville Chamberlain, prime minister of Britain, who desperately sought and wanted peace with Germany but was forced by FDR and the British prowar element to guarantee Poland support against German aggression. This was the catastrophic green light to World War II.

I was in Danzig the day before the German invasion of Poland, on my way back from a trip after the Oslo conference to Finland, Estonia, Latvia and Lithuania. I telephoned our American ambassador to Poland, Anthony Biddle, a longtime personal friend. He immediately invited me to come and spend a week with him in Warsaw. Nothing could have been more appealing; he was attractive, gay and charming, and would have been a delightful host. I told him there was nothing I would rather do, but that the war would probably break out within forty-eight hours and there would be no way for me to join my family in Paris except by a long detour through Constantinople and then by ship. He was most emphatic that there would be no war, but I knew otherwise. He evidently knew nothing of Ambassador Bullitt's prowar activities with the Polish government behind his back. Tony Biddle was a popular ambassador and was obviously in no way responsible for urging the Poles to become involved in the war with Germany.

The war broke out within two days. It was an abomination of desolation for free Poland—torn apart by a Nazi wolf pack on the west and a Communist wolf pack on the east.

Among my files, I recently found an interesting letter from former President Hebert Hoover to me:

THE DRAKE
Chicago

February 11, 1940

My dear Congressman:

Please find enclosed a copy of a section of an address which I delivered here last evening.

It bears upon the problems with which you are so earnestly engaged.

With kind regards,
Herbert Hoover

My part tonight is to discuss an immediate task. We are faced today with a gigantic task of alleviating the sufferings of the people of Poland. There are destruction and suffering in Poland that I could not adequately portray even if I wished to do so. Millions of people must have food; they must have clothing; they must have shelter. Whatever can be done by public charity must be done. But before the next harvest, imports of food from abroad on a large scale must be found. It may cost as much as $20,000,000. Charity can be of great aid, but starvation can be prevented only by the cooperation of governments.

With views to securing this cooperation I joined last fall in organizing the Commission for Relief in Poland. Its primary purpose was to serve the people of German-occupied Poland. It has the presidency of Mr. McCormick and the direction of Maurice Pate, both of whom so ably administered the relief of Poland in 1919.

This problem must be understood by you to whom it is so vital. In order for it to succeed the following conditions must be met:

First: Supplies to German-occupied Poland must pass the British blockade. The British must be guaranteed that these supplies are going to the Polish people and not to their enemy.

Second: Any supplies must be transported over German territory and the German authorities must cooperate to give the necessary guarantees.

The Poles had no reason to trust the power-hungry Nazi dictator, but the price they paid as a result of noncooperation with the British and French governments' request for direct Polish negotiations with Germany regarding Danzig was a ghastly tragedy for the free world. The Communists at Moscow were the only victors.

13

THE CRUCIFIXION OF POLAND

I am impelled by my intense feeling of resentment to write in some detail about the abominable treatment of free and independent Poland, created with the help of Woodrow Wilson after World War I, and destroyed and turned over to Stalin and totalitarian communism by an American president at the Yalta Conference in 1945. This shocking double-crossing of Poland, the one nation which stood up to Hitler and the Nazis at the specific urging of FDR and the British, should be known not only to all free Poles, but to all free men and women everywhere.

I have described how Poland was pressured, pushed and goaded into war by promises of military support. It is time for the truth regarding the postwar crucifixion of free Poland by its deceitful and treacherous allies to be made clear to the American people. It was a cruel abomination—a stabbing in the back of 30 million freedom-loving people.

In relating this story of the tragic murder of a nation, I will first disclose my personal involvement. My great-grandmother, Susan Livingston, was married to Count Julian Ursyn Niemcewicz in 1800. He was one of the foremost Poles in history—poet, author, historian, soldier and statesman. He adopted his wife's only son by her former marriage, Peter Kean, from whom I am descended.

Whether that makes me part Polish by adoption is merely academic. Niemcewicz claimed that the adoption was for all time. Also, my wife, although of Russian-Georgian origin, had a Polish grandmother of the famous Chartoryski family and a Polish great-grandmother, Countess Potocki.

Among Roosevelt's pre-World War II dealings with Britain, France and Poland was a statement by Jerzy Potocki, the Polish ambassador in Washington, which was found among the Polish diplomatic files seized by the Germans at Warsaw. This was confirmed later by Mr. Potocki who was then living in South America. That statement was made after an extensive interview with Ambassador William C. Bullitt, FDR's key representative in Europe on January 16, 1939 when he was about to return to his post in Paris. It read as follows:

"It is the decided opinion of the President Roosevelt that France and Britain must put an end to any sort of compromises with the totalitarian countries. They must not let themselves in for any discussions aiming at any kind of territorial changes.

They have the moral assurance that the United States will leave the policy of isolation and be prepared to intervene actively on the side of Britain and France in case of war." This needs repetition again and again.

This is damning evidence of FDR's prewar interference, promise of intervention and positive opposition to any peace compromises in regard to Danzig, the main cause of the war. The Polish ambassador to France, Lukasiewicz, according to reports also taken from the Polish archives, complained to Ambassador Bullitt that the British policy exposed Poland to the risk of war without taking adequate preparedness measures. Bullitt is alleged to have told the Polish diplomat that he had used his special powers to request Ambassador Kennedy in London to take the matter up with the British government. I am convinced that the German propaganda agency and their foreign office would never have used the name of a living Polish ambassador unless they had the facts.

The following is taken almost verbatim from *The Struggle Against the Historical Blackout* by Harry Elmer Barnes, an able historian who can distinguish truth from propaganda.

There is conclusive evidence drawn from authentic Polish documents and Roosevelt's assurances to Anthony Eden on his visit to Washington in December 1938 and his statement to Edward Benes at Hyde Park in May, 1939, that the United States would surely enter any European war against Hitler, and also what we know of the *Tyler-Kent case*. If it were not for Mr. Roosevelt's pressure on Britain, France and Poland, his commitments to them before September, 1939, and the irresponsible antics of his agent-provocateur William C. Bullitt, there would probably have been no European war in 1939. Any European war that broke out in the years to come would have been a war of Germany against Russia. This would have fatally weakened the two great totalitarian powers and left the free western democracies in control of the destinies of civilization.

If Roosevelt and Churchill had really wished to deliver the world from the menace of totalitarianism, they had their God-given opportunity on June 22, 1941. England could have withdrawn from the war and made peace with Hitler on the most favorable terms. Hitler had no designs whatever on the United States, so we would not have been endangered by this turn of events. Then Hitler and Stalin would have fought each other into exhaustion. This is exactly what the Baldwin-Chamberlain foreign policy had originally envisaged. Mr. Truman, then a senator, strongly supported this policy, as did Senator Vandenberg and many others. It would have left the United States and England dominant powers in the world, and they might have kept it a predominantly free world.

It is well known that Churchill was never so elated as in the midst of war, especially if he were dramatically connected with such events. The eminent English publicist, F. S. Oliver, has written of Churchill: "From his youth up, Mr. Churchill has loved with all his heart, all his mind, and with all his soul, and with all his strength, three things: war, politics, and himself. He loved war for its dangers, he loved politics for the same reason, and himself he has always loved for the knowledge that his mind is dangerous—dangerous to his enemies, dangerous to his friends and dangerous to himself. I can think of no man I have ever met who would so quickly and so bitterly eat his heart out in Paradise."

Even Roosevelt's friendly biographers admit that until he was weighed down by physical illness in his last year, he had never been so happy as during World War II. In a letter to George VI, written after the fatal Casablanca Conference, Roosevelt wrote: "A truly mighty meeting . . . As for Mr. Churchill and myself, I need not tell you that we make a perfectly matched team in harness and out—and incidentally we had lots of fun together, as we always do."

In the light of the disasters to humanity which followed in the wake of his fun-making, the cynicism of Nero's fiddling during the burning of Rome pales in contrast. We see here a president very different from a Lincoln, bowed down with sorrow over the agonies of the Civil War.

The U.S. State Department issued in 1961 a volume containing the long-overdue secret papers documenting the Teheran Conference. Notes on the proceedings were taken by Charles Bohlen, then first secretary of the U.S. embassy in Moscow, FDR's interpreter, and later American ambassador to France. Roosevelt said that there was an election coming in 1944 and that he might be a candidate; he added "that there were in the United States some six to seven million Americans of Polish extraction and, as a practical man, he did not wish to lose their votes." He also said, "he certainly agreed with the views of Marshall Stalin in regard to Poland but hoped, however, that the marshall would understand for political reasons, he could not publicly take part in any such arrangement at the present time." Marshall Stalin replied that "he understood."

In short, this exercise in political hypocrisy was designed to hoodwink and deceive seven million people of Polish origin in the United States. It took eighteen years to expose the secret sellout of free Poland at the Teheran Conference. Immediately after FDR's fourth-term reelection, which had the support of most of the Polish Americans, he joined openly at Yalta in the dismemberment of Poland that was the first step in its subsequent communization.

President Roosevelt wrote a letter to a member of Congress, of Polish origin, in which he denied that any secret commitments were made by him at the Teheran Conference. It is a shocking example of the twisting and torturing of the truth for political purposes. The letter speaks for itself:

White House, March 6, 1941

Honorable Joseph Mruk
House of Representatives
Washington, D.C.

Dear Congressman:

I am afraid I cannot make any further commitment except what I have written to you before. There were no secret commitments made by me at Teheran and I am quite sure that other members of my party made none either. This of course does not include military plans which have nothing to do with Poland.

Sincerely yours,
Franklin D. Roosevelt

Polish freedom and independence were not only undermined but virtually destroyed at Teheran. FDR's letter is a cover-up, nothing more than a ruse and a cunning political trick to veil the truth of Poland's betrayal.

Lest some readers feel I am politically partisan, I quote from a book entitled *Defeat in Victory* by Jan Ciechanowski, who succeeded Jerzy Potoki as Polish ambassador to the United States during World War II.

I was frequently asked by election agents of the New Deal what I thought would be the most appropriate way to obtain the support of what they called "the Polish vote" for Roosevelt's re-election to a fourth term (in 1944).

I was repeatedly told bluntly by the New Dealers of the palace guard that the appointment of Ambassador Lane to replace Biddle as American ambassador to the Polish government on September 2, 1944, was not only a proof of the President's "abiding" interest in Poland but also a political move which they hoped would be reflected by the "Polish vote."

Ciechanowski writes further that in spite of all these maneuvers, the Polish-American Congress, representing most voters of Polish extraction, was still doubtful that Roosevelt was actively for a free and independent Poland until he saw Charles Rozmarek, head of their organization, in Chicago on October 18, 1944.

In that interview, Ciechanowski reports that Roosevelt "definitely promised" Rozmarek "to take active steps to insure Poland's independence."

.Whereupon the main Polish-language press and the Polish-American Congress came out for Roosevelt's reelection for a fourth term. This endorsement was not only very helpful in reelecting Roosevelt through the support of the Polish vote, but it had great influence on the voting of American citizens who came from the other nations in eastern Europe taken over by Soviet Russia.

The *Times-Herald*, Washington's independent newspaper, in an editorial entitled "How Roosevelt Double-Crossed the Poles," said: "The records show plainly enough that even as Roosevelt was promising the Poles one thing, he was assuring Stalin on the side by word and deed that it was all just campaign talk."

The details of how the truth came home to Ciechanowski and the Poles in general are chilling but worth every citizen's attention as a lesson in FDR's faithlessness and lack of character. Here is one fair sample, reporting a meeting after the election between himself and

Harry Hopkins who was even then on the way to see Stalin:

> Hopkins was in a jovial mood. He assured me that he would do his best, although it was no easy matter to oppose Stalin. He then added jokingly, "We have to think of other very important things." I asked him what things could be more important at this time than to lay the foundations for the United Nations collaboration in a secure postwar world on the basis of American principles (and the freedom of Poland). He laughed and answered in his humorously cynical way, "Why, we have to prepare the President's election campaign of 1948." Hopkins may have thought that was funny but he certainly was not joking. The only joke was on the Poles. Those still alive to receive Stalin's cruel mercies.

Mikolajczyk, the great Polish peasant leader, went to Moscow in 1945 to see Stalin. He raised the question of Polish boundaries at a meeting which Averell Harriman and Prime Minister Churchill attended. Let Ciechanowski tell the harrowing tale.

> At this point Molotov made a surprising statement. He said that he saw it was necessary to remind those present that at Teheran, President Roosevelt had expressed his complete agreement with the Curzon line as the Polish-Soviet frontier and regarded it as a just solution which should be satisfactory both to the Soviet Union and to Poland and that the president had merely added that, for the time being, he preferred his agreement on this point should not be made public.
>   Molotov . . . turned to Churchill and Harriman and challenged them to deny his statement . . . "because it appears to me," he said, "that Mr. Mikolajczyk is not aware of this fact and is still in doubt regarding the position of America on this subject."
>   Molotov paused dramatically . . . to see if anyone would take up his challenge, which no one did.
>   Look at the dates. Roosevelt had agreed, as Molotov said, to the Curzon line on December 1, 1943, but all through 1944 he was telling the Poles another story.

However you look at it, FDR betrayed free Poland and sacrificed its people on the altar of communism for his own inordinate ambition and friendship for Stalin. There is no question but that the great majority of Americans of Polish origin were confused and deceived by the shameful and false propaganda that emanated from the White House, depicting Roosevelt as the friend of Polish freedom against Stalin and world communism. The time has come for this agonizing reappraisal so that not only Polish-Americans, but all who believe in and love freedom should know the truth.

William H. Chamberlain, writing in the *Wall Street Journal,* November 18, 1960, regarding the disastrous concessions by FDR to Stalin at Yalta, said:

This policy was one of wheedling, cajoling, and appeasing the grim dictatorship of Joseph Stalin—by every possible means. This policy reached its logical and shameful climax at the Big Three Yalta Conference in February, 1945, when the western leaders handed Stalin the keys to eastern Europe and eastern Asia.

By the Yalta decision, the legitimate representative Polish government which maintained headquarters in London was thrown over and replaced by a regime completely dominated by Stalin's Polish Communist stooges.

The Soviet Union was given Japanese territory of North Sakhalin and the Kurile Islands and a stranglehold on Manchuria. Furthermore, the Yalta concessions made it possible for the Soviet government to give the Chinese Communists considerable aid in their successful effort to overthrow the Nationalist government.

It will always be a moral and psychological puzzle why those of authority and influence in the Roosevelt administration, after denouncing so vehemently, as wrong and evil, the appeasement of Hitler before 1939, saw nothing insidious or immoral in the appeasement of Stalin.

On the basis of existing historical records, the explanation of a policy that helped rivet Communist domination on much of Europe and East Asia lies in the fact that neither President Roosevelt or his chief adviser Harry Hopkins, had much knowledge of what communism was all about.

But Alger Hiss did. Harry Hopkins was a friend of Stalin and a fanatical associate of Roosevelt. Hopkins and Hiss were close advisers of Roosevelt at Yalta. The article by Mr. Chamberlain is quoted because he was an authority on Soviet Russia.

The crucifixion of the gallant, freedom-loving Poles, who stood up to Hitler at the instigation of Britain and FDR and who never had a quisling, is one of the greatest crimes of the war. The deplorable part played by Roosevelt in the betrayal of the independence and integrity of the young Polish republic and of freedom throughout eastern Europe is a sad and deplorable travesty of American principles. It is a heavy, tragic burden that only time may dissipate.

> The moving finger writes; and, having writ,
> Moves on: nor all your Piety nor Wit
> Shall lure it back to cancel half a Line,
> Nor all your Tears wash out a Word of it.

The Teheran and Yalta legacies unleashed the appalling and evil Communist Frankenstein on a war-stricken world. These secret meetings spawned the appeasement policies which eventually spread communism throughout Poland and eastern Europe, China, Korea, Vietnam. I listened, as the ranking Republican member of the House Foreign Affairs Committee, when President Roosevelt on January 11, 1944, made his State of the Union address to Congress, the same day that the Soviet Union broadcast its intention of taking possession of a Polish territory west of the Curzon Line. FDR ignored the Soviet broadcast and said almost nothing about the Teheran Conference, except that military plans for victory had been agreed on. He also told the Congress and the American people that there had been "no secret treaties or political or financial commitments." Naturally, the Congress and the people believed what the president said.

History, however, makes very clear that he misled and

tricked not only the Poles but the American people by making erroneous statements.

The political contest between economic free enterprise and socialism is important; but the main issue is the survival of political freedom against the worldwide Communist conspiracy trying to crush it.

President Roosevelt was alone responsible for secretly betraying Poland into the hands of Stalin and communism, for a repudiation of the freedom and democracy the American army was fighting for in World War II. It was a crime against humanity and the peace of the world.

Chief Justice Warren, a political liberal, once said, "Freedom is the most contagious force in the world, not communism. Freedom will eventually prevail everywhere, as the people will not remain slaves."

The spirit of freedom is still very much alive in Poland as well. Americans of Polish origin, dismayed by the communization of Poland, look forward to the time when Poland will again be free. The tragic betrayal of Poland will remain a stigma on the conscience of Americans until all freedoms, including freedoms of speech and religion, are restored.

The Polish army in September 1939, attacked on the west by the modernized German armed forces with innumerable tanks and airplanes, and on the east by hordes of Stalin's troops, fought bravely but was overwhelmed.

The British Foreign Office has just released, thirty years after the fact, a secret statement blaming the USSR for the murder of 4,000 Polish officers in the Katyn woods and 8,000 more throughout Russia: "We have in fact, perforce used the good name of England to cover up a massacre," a former British diplomat wrote in a confidential dispatch seen only by the British cabinet and King George VI. In short, the British deliberately covered up an abominable war atrocity—an atrocious crime that exceeded any German military brutality except the horrible extermination of the Jews in Polish gas ovens.

Sir Owen O'Malley, the British ambassador to Poland at the time, secretly reported the barbaric killing:

> If a man struggled, it seems that the executioner threw his coat over his head, tying it around his head and leading him hooded to the pit's edge, for in many cases a body was found to be thus hooded and the coat to have been pierced by a bullet where it covered the base of the skull.
>
> When it was all over the butchers seemed to have turned their hands to one of the most innocent occupations, smoothing the clods and planting little conifers all over what had been a shambles.

Stalin was responsible for the mass murder of 12,000 Polish officers and 30 million of his own people and Hitler for the mass murder of six million Jews and a million Poles and other minorities. Stalin outnumbered him five to one. The bloody murderer Stalin, responsible for the massacre at Katyn, appointed the Russian officials and judges at the Nuremberg Trials who condemned the German officers to death for starting a war for which Stalin was also to blame.

Communism will inevitably decline and disappear in the course of time as a world force, unless Moscow resorts to nuclear war in desperation. The symptoms of the decline and fall of communism are everywhere. In June, 1972, two young Lithuanians burned themselves to death as a protest against the tragic Communist oppression there. Dissent is gaining in Russia for freedom and civil rights, and is boiling over in Czechoslovakia, Hungary, Poland, Yugoslavia, Rumania, Lithuania and Latvia. Freedom will eventually prevail over Communist tyranny.

The Communist dictators are fearful of their own people and do not dare to give them civil rights. Like animals in a zoo, they live behind iron walls. If the Communists opened the gates of freedom, millions of the enslaved population would try to escape to free nations.

The Communist campaign against freedom and democracy in the free nations, including the United States, is full of sound and fury, but it is as futile as snowflakes in July, particularly in the United States whose people know that world communism is a hoax and fraud and a deadly conspiracy against freedom everywhere.

The ardent supporters of President Roosevelt might have had some alibis for his tricking the United States into war without the knowledge of the American people and in violation of the Constitution, *if* we had won the war for freedom and self-determination at the Yalta Conference. But to win the war and lose the peace was too high a price to pay for the lives of 300,000 American boys and 700,000 wounded. The tragedy is that the freedom of those very nations which Woodrow Wilson helped to create, Czechoslovakia and Poland, were turned over to Stalin and world communism.

The legacies of the Yalta Conference were Communist China, North Korea, Vietnam and Southeast Asia—and our long and disastrous wars in Korea and Vietnam.

14

THE ATLANTIC CHARTER

*A great hoax and fraud perpetrated
on free people everywhere*

It is more in sorrow than in anger that I am obliged to denounce the Atlantic Charter as primarily a propaganda gimmick against the totalitarian nations, Germany and Italy.

I was a fervent supporter of the Atlantic Charter originally and inserted it in the *Congressional Record* with words of praise and an enthusiastic endorsement. I now have to apologize for having been one of the many, many millions who fervently believed that this idealistic Anglo-American declaration sincerely advocated self-determination among all nations through the democratic process.

The free world was as much deceived as I was listening to President Roosevelt's State of the Union speech in January, 1941, in which he espoused freedom of speech, freedom of religion, freedom from want and freedom from fear. These immediately became known as the Four Freedoms and raised the hopes of oppressed people everywhere. Like most Americans, I accepted Roosevelt's perfidious words as the gospel truth.

Although millions of Americans believed that the Atlantic Charter, announced seven months later, pledged to support the Four Freedoms, *there is no reference to free speech or freedom of religion in the Atlantic Charter*. And the record now shows that this omission was made at the request of FDR to gain the goodwill and acceptance of Soviet Russia.

When I began a thorough research into the origin and composition of the Atlantic Charter, I was amazed to find that free speech and freedom of religion had been deliberately omitted. Robert Sherwood, in his book *Roosevelt and Hopkins*, states that the officials of the British government never regarded the Atlantic Charter as much more than a publicity handout. Roosevelt and Undersecretary of State Sumner Welles were anxious to have the Atlantic Charter glorify the war and its objectives in the eyes of the American people.

The Anglo-American declaration was received with enthusiasm by the American public. It was a well-organized and timed Roosevelt political coup, dramatic and appealing to all elements of our population. It contained no reference to our participation in the war, the issue uppermost in the minds of all Americans. Questioned by reporters, "Do you think we are any closer to entry in the war?" the president answered cryptically that "he would not say so."

Winston Churchill won three-quarters of his objectives at the Atlantic Charter meeting. He came, he saw, and he won everything except a declaration of war by President Roosevelt. Roosevelt would have been delighted to have done so, but he was far too clever to get out on a political limb on such an issue while 85 percent of the American people and 75 percent of the Congress were against military intervention. Churchill, however, did succeed in persuading the president to take an even stronger stand against Japan than he already had. Roosevelt had previously ordered an embargo on all trade with Japan. The embargo was strangling that highly industrial nation. The Japanese government, however, was determined to avoid war at all costs with the United States, as it realized our war potential.

Churchill did not place much stock in the Charter, but he knew it would be well received in America and, above all, he was sure that, as he wrote, "the fact alone of the United States still technically neutral joining with a belligerent power in making such a declaration was astonishing."

Churchill was one of the greatest orators in recent history, and he made every effort to influence American public opinion by masterful radio appeals. He proclaimed a crusade "of the good forces of the world against the evil forces." He cast such a spell with his oratory that the listeners forgot the long and bloody record of British conquests throughout the world, even including our own Revolutionary War. He naturally did not refer to the ousting of Soviet Russia from the League of Nations only a year or two previously for military aggression against Finland, or the fact that he had denounced Soviet Russia in the famous historic statement that "Communism rots the soul of a nation."

Right as he was about that, he erred completely when he said on February 29, 1945, just after the Yalta Conference, "I know no government which stands to its obligations more solidly than the Russian Soviet Government." At this, the well-known English naval historian, Captain Russell Grenfell, commented: "This must surely rank as one of the most serious political misjudgments in history."

Very shortly after Churchill's statement, Stalin began his steady and open repudiation of the pledges contained in the Atlantic Charter "to seek no territorial aggrandisement." He seized by force and violence the Baltic nations and began the process of taking over and communizing Poland, Czechoslovakia, Hungary and the Balkan nations.

One year after Churchill's speech about marshalling the good forces of the world against the evil forces, he made his famous speech at Westminster College at Fulton, Missouri on March 5, 1946, when he dramatically proclaimed, "From Stettin in the Baltic to Trieste in the Adriatic, an iron curtain has descended across the Continent . . . Police governments are prevailing in nearly every case . . . Communist parties or Fifth Columns constitute a growing challenge and peril to Christian civilization."

One of the most extraordinary events in the entire history of World War II was the fraudulent signing of the Atlantic Charter by the notorious Communist commissar of foreign affairs, Molotov. This travesty took place at St. James Palace, London, on September 24, 1941, and pledged the Soviet dictatorship to support the eight points of the Atlantic Charter. Some twenty-six other nations also officially endorsed the charter.

It might interest the reader to know a few of the main points in the text of the charter. "First, their countries [America and Great Britain] seek no aggrandisement, territorial or other. Second, they desire no territorial changes that do not accord with the freely expressed wishes of the peoples concerned. Third, they respect the right of all people to choose the form of government under which they will live; and they wish to see sovereign rights and self-government restored to those who have been forcibly deprived of them."

The fourth, fifth, seventh and eighth points do not affect the vital issues of self-determination. The Sixth point advocates "assurance that all the men in all the lands may live out their lives in freedom from fear and want." *There is no mention anywhere in the Charter of free speech or freedom of religion.*

The great mass of the American people, including most of the Congress, was deliberately deceived by FDR's radio speeches and White House propaganda into believing that the Atlantic Charter enshrined the Four Freedoms. This was the slogan or boiled-down version of the Atlantic Charter which swept the country. Such was the power of White House propaganda that the Four Freedoms were acclaimed by Republicans and Democrats as the objectives of the war—an utterly false and a gigantic fraud upon the public.

The Atlantic Charter was President Roosevelt's baby, conceived by him and Sumner Welles, undersecretary of state. Churchill was merely a foster father who made a few suggestions. But it was FDR's political project and was popular at the outset. It was Roosevelt's lawful child; he was morally bound to protect and defend it against all open and secret enemies. The principal enemy and violator of the provisions of the Charter wasted no time after the Yalta Conference in torpedoing it. The Communist torpedoes soon sank the Atlantic Charter without a trace. It had no protection from the lukewarm British government, and the American defense was too little and too late.

But what about its powerful father, FDR? Instead of drawing his mighty sword and rushing to his infant's defense, he fired a few blank shots and ran up the white flag. Later he issued innocuous and harmless propaganda protests that had about as much effect on Stalin's communization of eastern Europe as a New Jersey mosquito bite.

At the time of the Yalta Conference, the *New York Times* very properly said, "What both the British and American people wished to know is whether the Atlantic Charter still applies and if not, what takes its place as a standard of conduct and a frame of reference for the organization of victory."

Walter Lippmann, a well-known syndicated columnist on foreign affairs, discussing the Russian break with Poland, never even mentioned the murder by the Communists of thousands of Polish officers in Katyn forest, now a well established fact, but which then was the reason given for Russia's false denunciation of Poland.

Churchill, who had remained silent on Roosevelt's commitments at Teheran, adverse to Poland, finally on December 16, 1944, declared that if Poland did not cede to Russia voluntarily all territory east of the Curzon line, Britain would support Russia's demand.

The great cover-up or pattern of deception which was pursued before the war was continued at Yalta. Secret protocols were agreed to, which provided for Soviet domination of Manchuria, the Port of Darien, a naval base at Port Arthur and possession of the Kurile Islands and southern Sakhalin. Other covered-up agreements provided for three Soviet votes in the anticipated United Nations and for the use of German forced labor by Soviet Russia after the war.

Yalta was proclaimed by FDR as a victory for free governments everywhere, whereas it actually amounted to communizing Poland and all eastern Europe and, later, China.

FDR locked the secret protocols in the White House safe. They did not see the light of day until long after his death and even then they were revealed by Moscow, not Washington. The secret agreement on the Far East was disclosed by Russia in January, 1946. The protocol on forced German labor—the existence of which FDR denied—was revealed by Russia several years after Germany surrendered.

15

HOW THE UNITED STATES BECAME INVOLVED IN WORLD WAR II

The "unnecessary war"—the secret war ultimatum to Japan; how the American people were tricked into war

President Roosevelt's responsibility for goading the Japanese into war by sending a war ultimatum on November 26, 1941, demanding that the Japanese withdraw all troops from Indo-China, and China (Manchuria) is an historic fact, although a closely-guarded secret. The British cabinet was all for the appeasement of the Japanese prior to Hitler's invasion of Russia on June 22, 1941. After that it changed policy in a twinkling of an eye, as Churchill obtained FDR's promise that he would protect British interests in the Far East. Credit Churchill, Stalin, Owen Lattimore, Stimson and Lauchlin Currie with assists in getting the United States into World War II through the back door.

FDR's war ultimatum was deliberately withheld from Congress until after Pearl Harbor; Roosevelt was responsible for the war ultimatum. Secretary of War Stimson and Secretary of the Navy Knox were for forcing the Japanese to fight. As ardent interventionists, they favored the ultimatum and welcomed war with Japan, though both might have preferred several months' delay to be more adequately prepared in the Philippines and Pearl Harbor. Roosevelt and Stimson called it a "war ultimatum," according to Stimson's diary. All agreed that the ultimatum left Japan no alternative but war. That is how we got into the unnecessary and unwanted war in defiance of Congress, the American people, and the Constitution.

President Roosevelt insisted that Hull hand the ultimatum to the Japanese ambassador, Nomuro, the next day, November 26. The responsibility for the ensuing war and tragedy at Pearl Harbor was his alone, but was persistently covered up. Secretaries Hull, Stimson, and Knox, General Marshall and Admiral Stark, all presidential appointees, were the only men present at the White House meeting on November 25. They had a common aim: to involve the United States in war without the advice and consent of Congress or the knowledge of the American people. It was and still is the biggest cover-up in our history.

My interest is to cut through the tangled web that was so skillfully thrown around this infamous secret ultimatum and the attack on Pearl Harbor, so that the American people might know the truth at last.

By this time, most people may concur that pitiless scrutiny and exposure should be turned on the actions of those responsible for serving a secret war ultimatum on Japan.

Admiral Kimmel and General Short should have been exonerated of any charges of dereliction of duty or errors of judgment. They were, as Admiral Halsey truthfully said, made the "scapegoats and were the martyrs" to protect the higher-ups who were responsible for the death of 3,000 American sailors and members of our armed forces at the terrible tragedy at Pearl Harbor. Years later Admiral Kimmel did not mince words when he said, "FDR and the top brass deliberately betrayed the American forces at Pearl Harbor,"* and that "FDR was the architect of the whole

---

Newsweek, Dec. 12, 1966.

business. He gave presumably the orders that no word about the Japanese fleet movement was to be sent to Pearl Harbor, except by Marshall, and then he told Marshall not to send anything."*

The infamous war ultimatum was served on the Japanese ten days before Pearl Harbor and its immediate consequence was the Japanese air attack. The hulk of the sunken battleship *Arizona* is the tomb of 1,000 American sailors—a legacy of the ultimatum.

These young American sailors and soldiers killed at Pearl Harbor did not start the war—they just died in a war started by others. Franklin D. Roosevelt was not only the president, but the was commander in chief of all our armed forces, including the National Guard, commissioned in the federal service. For two years prior to Pearl Harbor, his every thought and act were designed to maneuver the United States into war against Germany.

Arthur Krock of the *New York Times* said to the president of the United States: "From the time of the quarantine speech in 1937 you have done everything possible to antagonize Japan and force it into the Axis . . ."

The alliance of Japan with the Axis powers was a bombshell to their opponents. Senator Nye declared, "Our foreign policy has succeeded in driving Japan into the arms of those who were the last ones we wanted her to associate with. Japan claimed it was due to the blunders of the United States State Department."

The Japanese would have done almost anything to avoid war with America. To protect their needed rice, rubber and tin supplies, they got permission from Pétain's Vichy government to take over control of Vietnam. Naturally if Holland had refused to supply them with oil, they would have gone into the East Indies to be assured of a supply which was vital to their existence. They had no design on the Philippines or on any of our possessions. But as a nation they could not exist without oil for their industries,

---

The New York Times, Dec. 7, 1966.

merchant marine and navy. Prince Kenoye, the prime minister, who was very peacefully inclined, repeatedly requested to come to Washington or Honolulu to meet with President Roosevelt. He was willing to agree to our terms to keep out of war on a *modus vivendi* but FDR refused to talk with the Japanese prime minister simply because he was determined to get into war with Japan, and through that, with Germany. The American ambassador in Tokyo, Joseph Grew, knew how much Japan wanted to maintain peaceful relations and urged such a conference. But FDR and his fellow ardent interventionists used ruses, dodges, and tricks to involve us in a totally unnecessary war. Arthur Krock of the *New York Times* blamed FDR's drastic embargo policies for creating a war crisis and for forcing Japan to fight the United States.

It is utterly preposterous and untenable to say that Britain could hold Hong Kong, Singapore, Malaya, North Borneo and her other possessions in the Far East, yet deprive Japan of the right to purchase needed rice, oil, rubber and other commodities. The Japanese would have signed any treaty and stopped any aggression to the south if they had been assured peacefully of buying rice and oil without which they could not exist as a first-class nation.

It is true Japan had been engaged in an undeclared war with China for four years, but it was also true that Soviet Russia had been the aggressor against Finland, Poland and the Baltic nations. We not only did nothing about it, but later allied ourselves with them. But Japan was willing to negotiate a withdrawal of its forces from China (not Manchuria) and also from Vietnam and agree not to move southward. What more could the United States ask from a powerful nation like Japan? Emperor Hirohito and Prime Minister Kenoye were willing to make incredible concessions to maintain peace.

Japan was a comparatively small nation of 80 million people, not quite as large as California, with very few natural resources and facing the constant threat of Soviet Russia, a ruthless neighbor. The emperor was a man of honor and peace who did his utmost to restrain the aggressive militarists around him.

The tragic war with Japan was unnecessary and neither side wanted it. It was a catastrophe for two nations that had much more to fear from communism than from each other. We not only gained nothing from the war, but lost a friendly China to the Communists.

Britain lost much more, as she had special interests and privileges in China and lost Malaya, Singapore, Burma, India and Ceylon.

Chiang Kai-shek was badly advised by Owen Lattimore in opposing the *modus vivendi* that called for the withdrawal of Japanese forces from China. That would have left Chiang Kai-shek in control of all of China. This was three years before the concessions made by Roosevelt to Stalin at Yalta. There would have been no reason for Stalin's Communist army, as our ally, to invade Manchuria. Chiang Kai-shek, as the friend of the United States, would have had all the arms and resources he needed to crush the Chinese Communist opposition.

American public opinion in 1940-41 was bitterly opposed to involvement in another world war. In a democracy, where free speech prevails, the voice of the people creates public opinion. The percentage was reduced from 97 percent to approximately 85 percent when Hitler invaded Poland due to massive consistent administration propaganda, remaining at that level until the attack on Pearl Harbor.

The question is often raised, what would have happened if we had not entered the war, that is, if there had been no Japanese bombing of Pearl Harbor? The question deserves a detailed answer. I am convinced that we could have easily made a peace treaty with Japan in which she would have agreed to a mutually friendly withdrawal from

China and Indochina in return for the right to trade with all nations in the Far East including the Philippines and Dutch East Indies.

The extensive memoirs of Secretary of State Cordell Hull are a treasure-house of historical information, although naturally highly slanted in covering up his responsibility and that of FDR for the war ultimatum that caused not only the war with Japan, but also with Germany and Italy. In referring to the war ultimatum it seems appropriate to have it preceded by the word "infamous," derived from Roosevelt's designation of the attack on Pearl Harbor as a date to live in infamy.

This epithet was acclaimed by all of us at the time and was repeated all over the world. The full story of the infamous ultimatum will be related in detail in this chapter. There never was, in the history of America, such trickery, deception and double-crossing of the American people.

The all-out war ultimatum, approved by FDR and presented to the Japanese ambassador Nomuro on November 26, 1941, demanded that Japan *withdraw all of its armed forces—army, navy, air force and even police—from China (Manchuria) and Indochina immediately*. Like cornered rats, the Japanese had no alternative than to fight. If they hadn't, their leaders would have had to commit suicide or be killed by their own people.

Hull's memoirs do not even mention the crucial November 25 meeting at the White House. According to Stimson's diary, the only question considered at this meeting was how to maneuver, incite and provoke Japan to fire the first shot. The next day Secretary Hull scrapped the *modus vivendi*, or truce for ninety days (which had been acceptable to Japan), and handed Ambassador Nomuro the infamous war ultimatum. It was not released until after Pearl Harbor, when it went unnoticed. Very few of the American people ever even heard of the war ultimatum. FDR, Secretary Hull, and Secretary Stimson were the main instigators but Secretary Knox, General Marshall and Admiral Stark were lesser collaborators. They all knew it would force the Japanese to attack immediately without warning.

It is only fair to the leading officers of the American armed forces to emphasize that even as late as November 26 they still counseled and cautioned against war. On the morning of November 26 there was a meeting of the Army-Navy Joint Board at which Admiral Ingersoll presented a series of arguments against precipitating a war.

Evidently the protest of the Army-Navy Joint Board had little effect on President Roosevelt and Secretary Hull. So on that afternoon, Hull, representing the president, abandoned all thought of a truce with Japan and rejected any idea of compromise or conciliation. With the full approval of FDR, he presented to Nomuro the demand that "the government of Japan withdraw all military, naval, air and police forces from China and Indochina."

Admiral Nomuro was accompanied by Saburo Kurusu, who had served as a consul in New York and had recently been the Japanese ambassador to Berlin. He was married to an American girl, which gave him an added interest in maintaining friendly relations between Japan and the United States. After he had read Hull's proposals, Kurusu asked if this were the American answer to the Japanese request for a *modus vivendi* or truce. Secretary Hull gave an evasive and virtually negative answer. Kurusu replied that the secretary's statement was "tantamount to meaning the end." It was obvious to Nomuro and Kurusu that this was a war ultimatum and that the next step would be war.

The undisputed fact is that even those Japanese militarists who had no love for the United States realized the tremendous potential strength of our country and wanted to avoid such a ruinous war if a peace with honor could be found. They were willing to make unprecedented concessions and to accept virtually all our terms in the proposed *modus vivendi*, which included a ninety-day truce. Secretary Hull for eight months had been stringing Ambassador Nomuro along, stalling for time to permit our army and navy to strengthen their defenses in the Philippines and in our other Far Eastern possessions. Hull in his memoirs made it very clear that he was playing for time at the request of both the army and the navy. His dilatory tactics finally became apparent to the Japanese cabinet, which set November 29 as the final day for ending negotiations. Hull knew definitely that the showdown on peace or war had been reached through the intercepted Japanese messages to Nomuro, as we had broken the Japanese code.

Hull had been working on a *modus vivendi* which would not only have postponed the war, but might have averted an unwanted, unnecessary, costly and bloody war with Japan completely. President Roosevelt received protests from Churchill and Chiang Kai-shek. FDR's administrative secretary, Lauchlin Currie, friendly to the Communists, received an urgent cable from Owen Lattimore, another apologist for communism. Lattimore had been appointed by Roosevelt as an adviser to Chiang Kai-shek. Naturally Soviet Russia was opposed to any peace terms and favored war between the United States and Japan.

Churchill realized, as did Roosevelt, that if we became involved in war with Japan it would automatically bring us into war with Germany. Consequently, the *modus vivendi* was scrapped.

Roosevelt used his tremendous presidential powers to deceive the American public and succeeded in keeping the existence of the war ultimatum a secret from everyone, including all members of Congress, until after Pearl Harbor. It was a conspiracy of silence. Later the administration refused to institute a nonpartisan, impartial court-martial of Admiral Kimmel and General Short, *at their own request*, to ascertain the true responsibility for the Pearl Harbor disaster. It was denied by the Roosevelt administration because it would have exposed FDR's ultimatum and likewise his responsibility for provoking the war secretly.

Although the Congress was totally ignored, and only a handful of Americans in the cabinet knew of the existence of the war ultimatum, Winston Churchill and the British high command were kept informed of every move.

FDR secretly maneuvered us into war. The responsibility for the deadly blow to the U.S. navy was his, as well as the deaths of 3,000 American sailors at Pearl Harbor—America's greatest naval defeat and disaster.

The tragic fact is that few Americans know about FDR's ultimatum to Japan. It is still America's greatest and best-kept secret, part and parcel of the perpetuation of the Roosevelt myth, and the greatest cover-up in American history.

FDR deliberately goaded Japan into war just as he secretly betrayed the freedom of Poland at Teheran.

It may be years before all the well-hidden secret actions of former President Franklin D. Roosevelt in his quest for war, long withheld from the American people, will become common knowledge. Some of his 1,700 communications with Winston Churchill, dating back two years before our entrance into the war, have still not been made public.

The facts regarding the decoding of the Japanese "eastwind" message were so carefully covered up or destroyed at the time that it may be impossible to unravel them for the sake of historical accuracy.

FDR knew that his war ultimatum would provoke Japan to fight, and that is exactly what he planned and what he wished. Hull, Stimson, Knox, General Marshall and Admiral Stark also knew that the ultimatum had been sent, and expected that the Japanese would attack without warning. They were the prime warmakers under FDR's leadership.

There were some ardent Anglophiles who believed it was America's function on any and all occasions to pull the chestnuts out of the fire for the British Empire. Just why Great Britain should have the unquestioned right to maintain numerous possessions in the Far East while Japan should be restricted by us, unable to even buy rice, oil, rubber, tin, and other commodities in nearby nations, is still an unsolved paradox.

The Japanese are a very sensitive, proud, courageous

race imbued with a high sense of loyalty, honor and patriotism. Thirty-five years earlier, the Japanese navy had destroyed the Russian fleet, and its army had driven the Russians out of Manchuria. At the time of our drastic war ultimatum, the Japanese, after four years of war, controlled the seacoast, most of the large cities and a large part of China, and all of Manchuria and was the most powerful nation in the Far East.

Today, Japan has become our best and most reliable friend in the Orient, whereas Soviet Russia, our former ally, has become our foe and an enemy of freedom throughout the world. The destinies of the United States and Japan are now linked together not only by bonds of friendship but by principles of freedom and democracy. The Japanese fought bravely to the end. Let us hope that there will never be another war between us, but that we will march forward, as two great nations, to preserve the freedom, the independence and the sovereignty of both of our countries for eons of time. The entire world should know that we will keep our agreement for the defense of Japan if attacked. I was heartened when the *New York Post* on April 14, 1971, ran a picture of Norman Mineta, who as a child spent two years in a Japanese war relocation camp in the United States, accepting congratulations with his Japanese wife after winning an easy victory in the San Jose, California, mayoral race. He is the first Japanese-American to be elected mayor of a major American city.

Secretary of War Henry L. Stimson held chauvinistic views and unconstitutional beliefs that FDR had the right to involve the United States in war without the consent of the Congress and by any devious methods he determined.

If any president, by trickery, secrecy and without the consent of Congress, involved the United States in war, he should be impeached. On November 28, 1941, two days after the ultimatum, Secretary Stimson discussed with FDR measures which might be taken against Japan. Evidently the president was not absolutely certain that the previous ultimatum would cause the Japanese to fight immediately. He wanted to know if anything was to be done "to make something in the *nature of an ultimatum again*, stating a point beyond which we would fight or to fight at once." Note the use of "ultimatum again."

Secretary Stimson favored the latter alternative, to fight at once. Both Stimson and Roosevelt were determined to get into war with Japan even if we had to fire the first shot. Neither seemed to give a continental about American public opinion, the Congress, or the Constitution.

Stimson was a longtime Japanese-hater. As secretary of state in 1931 in the Hoover administration, he had to be restrained by President Hoover from starting a war over Manchuria. FDR and Churchill wanted war with Japan in order to get into war with Germany. I repeat what Stimson said was Roosevelt's suggestion, "to make something of a nature of an ultimatum again, stating a point beyond which we would fight." This doubly proves that Roosevelt himself knew that the proposal of November 26 was a war ultimatum, but not having heard from Japan immediately, was even considering sending a second ultimatum.

The first ultimatum was enough, and all six collaborators felt sure of it at the time. It succeeded in getting us into war with Japan which inevitably brought Italy and Germany into it in a few days, a cost to the United States of 400 billion dollars and a million casualties.

The Roosevelt-Hull ultimatum reached the emperor's palace on the morning of November 27 while a liaison conference was in session. It was immediately recognized as a war ultimatum. It called for Japan to immediately "withdraw all military, naval, air, and police forces from China and Indochina, to support no other government or regime in China except Chiang Kai-shek," and, in effect, to abrogate the tripartite pact.

The Japanese construed China to include Manchuria, which they had no intention of giving up. If Hull had not meant "Manchuria" under the term "China," he should have made it clear at the time, not in an alibi afterwards. But Hull told Secretary of War Stimson the next day, "It is now in the hands of the army and navy."

It required no profound knowledge of Japanese history, institutions and psychology to warrant three conclusions respecting the ultimatum. First, that no Japanese cabinet, liberal or reactionary, could have accepted its provisions as a basis of negotiating a settlement without incurring the risk of immediate overthrow. Secondly, that our State Department knew that the drastic ultimatum could not be accepted by the Japanese government as a program for renewed conversations "looking towards the maintenance of peace in the Pacific." And thirdly, both President Roosevelt and Hull knew that the delivery of the war ultimatum to Japan would cause open warfare to begin without any declaration of war.

16

THE TRAGEDY OF PEARL HARBOR

*The silence of the conspirators to make
Admiral Kimmel and General Short
the scapegoats to protect themselves*

All Americans, including myself, joined President Roosevelt in denouncing the attack on Pearl Harbor by the Japanese as a Day of Infamy. Every American was shocked by such a dastardly, unprovoked attack. They were bitter, angry and mad at this outrageous, undeclared war sneak attack. All Americans regardless of partisanship wholeheartedly supported the president's Day of Infamy speech as we had no thought or idea then that he had planned and tricked us into a war, opposed by eighty-five percent of the American people.

President Roosevelt called the attack on Pearl Harbor the Day of Infamy and all Americans applauded and acclaimed him. We naturally believed him that it was an outrageous attack by the Japanese in the midst of peace negotiations. Not a single member of Congress, Democrat or Republican, had the faintest idea of the existence of President Roosevelt's war-provoking ultimatum handed to the Japanese Ambassador Nomura at the State Department by Secretary Hull on the afternoon of November 26, 1941, ten days before the attack on Pearl Harbor. It was a well-hidden conspiracy by FDR's war cabinet that met at the White House on November 25th, consisting of Secretary of State Hull, Secretary of War Stimson, Secretary of the Navy Knox, General Marshall and Admiral Stark. The only issue discussed at this meeting was how to maneuver, provoke, and force Japan to fight and fire the first shot. This secret conspiracy resulted in the issuance of the infamous war ultimatum in defiance of the Congress and the American people, and in violation of the Constitution.

As ranking Republican member of the Committee on Rules, I opened the debate on Monday, December 8th, 1941, for the declaration of war resolution against Japan. My speech was not only the first one, but it was also the first speech ever delivered over the radio in the House of Representatives.

I am ashamed of that speech today as I now know about Roosevelt's infamous war ultimatum that forced Japan's leaders to fight. And if they hadn't, they would have been shot by their own people. At that time I did not mince words and was proud of my remarks which were acclaimed in the House and over the radio to an estimated twenty-five million Americans. Here is my speech as then delivered for what it is now worth:

DECLARATION OF WAR
An Appeal for National Unity in America
and for War to Final Victory
Declaration of War Speech
of
Hon. Hamilton Fish
of New York
In the House of Representatives
Monday, December 8, 1941

MR. FISH. Mr. Speaker, it is with sorrow and deep resentment against Japan that I rise to support a declaration of war.

I have consistently opposed our entrance into wars in Europe and Asia for the past 3 years but the unwarranted, vicious, brazen and dastardly attack by the Japanese Navy and Air Force while peace negotiations were pending at Washington and in defiance of the President's eleventh-hour personal appeal to the Emperor, makes war inevitable and necessary.

The time for debate and controversy within America has passed. The time for action has come.

Interventionists and noninterventionists must cease criminations and recriminations, charges and countercharges against each other, and present a united front behind the President and the Government in the conduct of the war.

There can be only one answer to the treacherous attack of the Japanese, and that is war to final victory, cost what it may in blood and treasure and tears. This unprovoked and senseless aggression by the Japanese armed forces upon our possessions must be answered by war.

Although I have consistently fought against our intervention in foreign wars, I have repeatedly stated that if we were attacked by any foreign nation, or if the Congress of the United States declared war in the American and constitutional way, I would support the President and the administration to the bitter end.

Whom the gods would destroy they first make mad. The Japanese have gone stark raving mad and have by their unprovoked attack committed military, naval and national suicide.

I shall at the proper time volunteer my services as an officer in a combat division, as I did in the last war, preferably with colored troops.

There is no sacrifice too great that I will not make in defense of America and to help annihilate these war-mad Japanese devils.

Now that we are to fight let us go in with our heads and chins up in the American way, and let us serve notice upon the world that this is not only a war against aggression and in defense of our own territories, but a war for freedom and democracy all over the world, and that we will not stop until victory is won.

I appeal to all American citizens, particularly to the members of my own party, and to noninterventionists, to put aside personal views and partisanship, and unite behind the President, our Commander-in-Chief in assuring victory to the armed forces of the United States.

> Our country! In her intercourse with foreign nations, may she always be right, but right or wrong, our country!

FDR's Day of Infamy speech on Dec. 8, 1941, asking Congress to declare war omits all reference to his war-provoking ultimatum, ten days before the attack on Pearl Harbor. It deliberately deceived all members of Congress, Democrats and Republicans alike, when he said the United States was still in conversation with its government and its emperor, looking toward the maintenance of peace in the Pacific. No member of Congress knew about FDR's war ultimatum, or of his receipt of the decoded Japanese answer, the evening of December 6th, when he turned to Harry Hopkins and said that this meant war. This is exactly what he wanted and expected, but strangely, although he was commander and chief of our armed forces, he did little or nothing about it. It was his duty to immediately call the Secretary of War, the Secretary of Navy and General Marshall and Admiral Stark. The only thing that is known is that he did call Admiral Stark who was at the theatre and so did not reach him. There is no record that he ever communicated that night with any of the prominent navy or army officers. The record shows that FDR knew from the decoded answer that it meant war more than fourteen hours before the Japanese attack on Pearl Harbor and did nothing about it, except in his Day of Infamy speech to start the spread of the greatest cover-up in history which continued for many years. Quoting FDR, "Indeed one hour after the Japanese air squadron had commenced bombing Oahu, the Japanese Ambassador to the United States and his colleague delivered to the Secretary of State a formal reply to a recent Message" (FDR's war ultimatum). As pointed out, the Japanese decoded answer was known to FDR fourteen hours before, and presumably, to Hull, Stimson, Knox, Marshall, and Stark. If they were not notified, FDR is responsible. The big cover-up got a good start wrapped up in a well-publicized and universally acclaimed Day of Infamy speech to Congress because not one member knew of the existence of FDR's war-making ultimatum. My speech represents clearly how effective FDR's cover-up and omission of his drastic war ultimatum were and how the American people were deceived.

Roosevelt's Day of Infamy has been turned into hypocrisy, deceit and ashes by the searchlight of truth on the causes, events and results of the war. Talking of results, history has made it very clear despite our terrible losses, greater than in any war we have ever been in; despite the fact that the gallantry of our soldiers turned the tide of defeat into victory for freedom and democracy—that victory was lost at Yalta when half the world was made safe for Stalin and communism.

As a result of the concessions to Stalin in eastern Europe and China, within four years a total of six hundred million people went under the yoke of communism. That was the price we paid for being tricked into war which the American people did not want. There was no valid reason for the infamous war ultimatum. Oh, what a tangled web we weave, when first we practice to deceive—the American people. The tragic part of this unnecessary war was that the Japanese government and people, as reported consistently by our Ambassador Joseph Grew, a career diplomat of high integrity and intelligence, did not want war and we certainly did not want war with Japan. The rabid internationalists, however, believed that it was our manifest duty and mission to police the world, almost single-handed, no matter what the cost in lives and treasure, and against the will of an overwhelming majority of the American people and the Congress of the United States.

Many books and thousands of pages by investigating committees are available to all historians and students about the Pearl Harbor tragedy. One thing is certain—that the Roberts Commission appointed by the president immediately afterwards was a specially selected committee by those who had been instrumental in sending the war-provoking ultimatum to Japan on November 26, 1941, ten days before the attack. Most of the testimony taken by this commission has been repudiated by the army, navy and congressional committees and tends to show that Roosevelt, Stimson and Knox who were responsible for the appointees, sought *to cover up their part in tricking the American people into war* and not informing the Hawaiian commanders of the war ultimatum or of the Japanese coded messages. The separate army and navy investigations and reports exonerated Admiral Kimmel and General Short of dereliction of duty and placed the blame squarely on Secretary Hull, General Marshall and Admiral Stark for not notifying Admiral Kimmel and General Short of the imminence of war on the morning of December 6.

These army and navy reports were held up by War Secretary Stimson and Navy Secretary Knox for some time, until public opinion finally forced their publication. Both the army and navy boards should be commended for the courage they demonstrated in their investigations, which placed the blame on the higher-ups in Washington. Secretaries Stimson and Knox only escaped condemnation because of their respective positions as secretaries of war and navy, as did President Roosevelt, their commander in chief.

Stimson was furious and tried to have the report amended by placing some of the blame on Congress—totally false. The Congress and the American people had nothing whatever to do with the war ultimatum or with not notifying the army and navy commanders at Hawaii before the attack on Pearl Harbor.

FDR and Knox were by that time dead, but Hull, Stimson, Marshall and Stark were alive. Stimson was more to blame than anyone, except the president and Hull, for the drastic war ultimatum. He even advised Roosevelt that if the Japanese did not attack, we should do so immediately.

Naturally when the army report condemning Hull and Marshall was publicized throughout the country, Stimson rushed to their defense (actually to his own defense as he was equally to blame). Why? Because it was absolutely necessary to hide from the public their part in the secret war-provoking ultimatum.

Roosevelt was the main instigator and firebrand to light the fuse of war, abetted by the five members of his war cabinet. They were all sure that the Japanese would start the war by an undeclared strategic attack, but none knew where or when they would attack, whether at Singapore, Thailand, Dutch Indonesia (for oil), Hong Kong, the Philippines, Midway, Guam or Pearl Harbor.

Roosevelt, through his numerous campaign pledges and also by the plank of the Democratic national platform against intervention, had tied himself in unbreakable peace knots. There was only one way out—to provoke Germany or Japan into attacking us. He tried in every way possible to incite the Germans to attack, but to no avail. The convoy of ships, and the shoot-at-sight order, were open and brazen efforts by the president to take the country into war against Germany, but Hitler avoided the lure.

Why did General Marshall and Admiral Stark delay in sending messages to the American Hawaiian commanders immediately after the ultimatum was issued, especially as soon as they knew of the intercepted Japanese repudiation of the ultimatum either the evening of the December 6 or the morning of December 7? Did Roosevelt contact General Marshall on the evening of December 6? And if not, why? Admiral Stark was at the theater when the information reached the president. Both Marshall and Stark were prowar and joined Secretary Stimson and Secretary Knox in a strange silence, still unaccounted for. Why did they not notify Kimmel and Short of the repudiation of the ultimatum and that Pearl Harbor might be attacked by Japan immediately?

The delay and virtual refusal to inform our Hawaiian commanders is inconceivable, except as a part of a deceitful and concerted scheme of silence.

I have read numerous books and reports of hearings before Congress, and they have always ignored the implications of the war ultimatum. After all, FDR was the recognized head of the Democratic party and his responsibility for issuing the ultimatum would have been equivalent to holding him responsible for the disaster at Pearl Harbor, which of course he was.

If the American people had known that they were deliberately tricked into a foreign war by Roosevelt in defiance of all his promises and pledges, there would have been political bombs exploding all over the United States, including demands for his resignation or impeachment.

FDR, and probably Secretaries Hull, Stimson, and Knox, General Marshall, and Admiral Stark had in their possession before December 7 intercepted messages from the Japanese government to its representatives in Washington and elsewhere that indicated that war would break out immediately. It is well known that President Roosevelt had such information at the White House by ten o'clock in the evening of December 6. He was then talking with Harry Hopkins when an officer brought in the first thirteen parts of the intercepted messages which were to be delivered to Secretary Hull. The president read the messages, turned them over to Hopkins to read and said, *"This means war."* Actually, outside of trying to telephone Admiral Stark who was at the theater, and deciding not to interrupt him there, he did nothing about it, or if he did, it is unknown to history. Certainly the commander in chief of our armed forces had the greatest responsibility of all to immediately notify the secretary of war, the secretary of the navy, General Marshall and Admiral Stark, and order them to notify Admiral Kimmel, General Short and other far eastern commanders immediately. This, however, was not done. The tragedy of Pearl Harbor rests with FDR, not only because of the infamous war ultimatum, but for not making sure that Kimmel and Short were notified of the Japanese answer to the ultimatum. Subsequently Short and

Kimmel were smeared and dismissed, presumably in order to clear President Roosevelt and his war cabinet of their responsibility.

Rear Admiral Robert A. Theobald (U.S.N. Retired) published a very carefully documented book, *The Final Secret of Pearl Harbor*, regarding the attack. In this book he confirmed that Roosevelt started the war. He also claimed that FDR assisted in the secret plans of leaving Pearl Harbor open for a surprise attack by not telling Admiral Stark and General Marshall to warn Admiral Kimmel and General Short of the contents of the decoded Japanese messages about the location of American warships in Pearl Harbor and the final answer to his war-provoking ultimatum.

Secretaries Stimson and Knox, both so anxious for war, did nothing. Their official spokesmen, General Marshall and Admiral Stark, likewise remained silent regarding the ultimatum. All of them, from the president down, refrained from sending direct warnings or seeing that they were sent to Admiral Kimmel and General Short. Secretary Hull apparently did nothing either, and he must have known of the intercepted messages of December 6. He was probably the first to receive such messages, and may have been the one who sent the intercepted reply to the ultimatum to FDR.

Although Hull is to blame, next to FDR, he had no direct responsibility for notifying the Hawaiian commanders. However, he should have informed Stimson and Knox immediately, and he may very well have done so. But Hull was also one of the collaborators bound to silence and was as much involved as anyone.

The record indicates that all remained silent, and did nothing to notify the Hawaiian commanders. That being so, they were as responsible as the president for the Pearl Harbor tragedy and terrible losses.

Admiral Theobald asserted definitely that Marshall was not out riding on the morning of December 7, but was in Admiral Stark's office discussing the decoded Japanese answer to the ultimatum. When Stark offered to notify Admiral Kimmel, Marshall said that he would do it, which he proceeded to do later on, with a belated message, received long after the attack. Under the circumstances, General Marshall's stupidity or his deliberate silence is incomprehensible unless he was acting on orders from President Roosevelt, as Admiral Theobald claims he was.

Admiral Kimmel and General Short, according to Admiral Halsey, were scapegoats, sacrificed on the political scaffold in order to protect the guilty parties. The president appointed the Roberts Commission to investigate Kimmel and Short, but not his own infamous secret ultimatum.

President Roosevelt made sure that the records would not disclose his war ultimatum by appointing Supreme Court Justice Owen Roberts, a Republican. He was just as outspoken a prowar zealot as Stimson and Knox and an advocate of "Union Now." He was recommended by Stimson to serve as chairman of the commission. Knox and Stimson recommended the army and navy personnel of that commission. Naturally the tragic war ultimatum was hushed up, and the entire responsibility for the disaster at Pearl Harbor was placed on Admiral Kimmel and General Short.

Admiral Halsey, one of our greatest fighting admirals and one of the three senior commanders of the Pacific Fleet serving under Admiral Kimmel at Pearl Harbor, had this to say in a foreword to *The Final Secret of Pearl Harbor*:

Had we known of Japan's minute and continued interest in the exact location and movement of our ships at Pearl Harbor as indicated in the "magic messages" (which were never sent to Admiral Kimmel) it is only logical that we would have concentrated our thought on meeting the practical certainty of an attack on Pearl Harbor . . . If the magic messages had been known to us, there can be no doubt that a 360-degree search would have been ordered and maintained to the breaking point of material and personnel.

I have always considered Admiral Kimmel and General Short to be splendid officers *who were thrown to the wolves as scapegoats* for something over which they had no control. They had to work with what they were given, both in equipment and information. *They are our outstanding military martyrs.*—William F. Halsey, Fleet Admiral, U.S. Navy, Fishers Island, September 1953.

This testimony of one of our greatest war heroes makes it very clear that Admiral Kimmel and General Short were not alerted after the war ultimatum was sent to Japan, and even more important, not told that Japan repudiated the ultimatum.

Admiral Kimmel, referring to *The Final Secret of Pearl Harbor*, said his studies have caused him to conclude "that we were unready at Pearl Harbor because of *President Roosevelt's plans that no word be sent to alert the fleet at Hawaii* . . ."

Kimmel was emphatic that the "individuals in high positions in Washington who willfully refrained from alerting our forces at Pearl Harbor, should never be excused." Later he denounced FDR as being responsible.

President Roosevelt evidently did not want to take any steps that might prevent an attack by the Japanese, because if the Japanese knew in advance that we had been warned and were prepared, the attack on Pearl Harbor would have been called off.

Kimmel and Short, as longtime distinguished officers in our armed forces, were entitled to a court-martial. This was consistently denied them. The administration knew that in an impartial court-martial both officers would subpoena witnesses and cross-examine them and that the whole truth about the war ultimatum would be brought out.

On June 5, 1944, speaking in the House of Representatives, I said that there had already been too much delay and shadowboxing by the Roosevelt administration to avoid telling the whole truth to the American people and, more important, in holding those responsible for the Pearl Harbor disaster strictly accountable:

Mr. Speaker, I propose to read an editorial taken from the *World Telegram*, a Scripps-Howard paper in New York. If I should use the same words someone might accuse me of making a political speech or injecting politics into our war efforts. This paper is one of the largest in the city of New York, and the same editorial was probably circulated widely over the country. It is entitled "Kimmel, Short, Roosevelt, Hull." Mr. Speaker, the administration should have held the Pearl Harbor court-martial long ago. The editorial stated, "The administration is plainly resolved to postpone the Pearl Harbor trials until after the election. The Japs have long known exactly what they did to us in that most disgraceful disaster ever suffered by American arms. To hold the trials now would tell them nothing they don't know already.

"But it is widely believed that the trials would force to light evidence connecting high Washington officials with orders to Kimmel and Short to take the No. 1 alert (readiness for sabotage from within) instead of No. 3 (readiness for anything) which might have turned Pearl Harbor into a victory for us and shortened the Pacific war. These orders might have been urged by Mr. Hull, or sent by Mr. Roosevelt.

"If such orders were sent (alert No. 1), the administration is determined to keep the American people from knowing who sent them until after the election. Politics and politics alone is the cause of this procrastination."

Mr. Speaker, those are not my words. They are from an editorial in one of our largest newspapers, a more or less nonpartisan paper that reflects, I believe, public sentiment throughout the United States.

But the real issue of the Roosevelt war ultimatum was not known then and is still the best-kept secret in American history

The Roberts report was so slanted and outrageous that public opinion demanded further investigation. A congressional committee was created consisting of Senators Barkley, George and Lucas (Democrats), and Senators Brewster and Ferguson, Republicans; Representatives Cooper, Clarke, and Murphy (Democrats) and Gerhart and Keefe (Republicans).

Two of the three Democratic members of the committee, Senators Barkley of Kentucky and Lucas of Illinois, were both candidates for the vice-presidency. FDR was not only the leader of the Democratic Party, but controlled the Democratic national organization that nominated the presidential candidates.

The following well-known ditty fits the political situation confronted by the Democratic members of the congressional investigating committee:

> Mother, may I go in to swim?
> Yes, my darling daughter.
> Hang your clothes on a hickory limb.
> But don't go near the water.

The "water" here was FDR's secret war ultimatum. The composition of the Democratic majority was part of the cover-up of Roosevelt, come hell or high water. Naturally Senator Robert Reynolds, chairman of the Military Affairs Committee or Senator David Walsh, chairman of the Naval Affairs Committee, were not on it; they were both outspoken noninterventionists and would have conducted an impartial investigation that let the chips fall where they may. Three out of the four Democratic investigating committee members came from the South and were ardent Roosevelt followers in both war and peace. The fourth from the North, was a politically ambitious candidate for president or vice-president who naturally followed the Roosevelt line. However, the Congressional Joint Investigating Committee was fair in repudiating the actions of the Roberts Commission in finding Kimmel and Short guilty of dereliction of duty. This was changed into failure of the commanders in errors of judgment. To this extent, they lifted the stigma of dereliction placed on the officers by Roosevelt's Roberts Commission. Two Republican members of the House, one of whom wrote a separate report, were defeated for reelection in their congressional districts. The prowar interventionist

Democrats on the Committee did everything they could to protect Roosevelt and the members of his war cabinet. The real key to the Hawaiian disaster, the infamous war ultimatum, was swept under the rug.

Senator Brewster of Maine and Senator Ferguson of Michigan, members of the Congressional Investigating Committee, signed a minority·report placing the blame for the Pearl Harbor tragedy squarely on Roosevelt, Hull, Stimson, Knox, Marshall and Stark. But Admiral Kimmel's demand for a court-martial, supported by a congressional resolution, was sidetracked by the administration.

Speaking in Congress on June 5, 1944, I made specific predictions which have been verified and borne out by subsequent events:

MR. FISH: Mr. Speaker, Admiral Kimmel has demanded a free and ·open trial, and I am sure, knowing General Short as I do, having served on his staff in the 1940 maneuvers held in northern New York State, that he is the type of man who would like to have a free and open trial immediately. However I do not believe that this court-martial will ever be held in spite of a congressional resolution or anything the Congress does or says, at least until after election, and then there is some uncertainty of its ever being held until a new administration takes over at Washington.

MR. SHORT: If it is not held it will not be the fault of Congress if we pass this resolution.

MR. FISH: That is true. I want to make another prediction. If the administration holds a trial and Admiral J. O. Richardson is called as a witness, the public will find out that he protested placing our warships in Pearl Harbor, where they could be picked off like a lot of sitting ducks, as they were on the seventh of December 1941. Admiral Richardson was in command of the Pacific Fleet and was removed from office because he resisted the orders from President Roosevelt to take his fleet into Pearl Harbor and was succeeded by Admiral Kimmel. I think the American people will be surprised and shocked if Admiral Richardson ever appears before a court-martial and testifies to the whole truth, which he will be required to do as a witness. That is the kind of information the American people want and are entitled to, but probably will never get.

FDR was evidently thinking of getting into war with Japan as far back as October 8, 1940, when he told Admiral Richardson, then in charge of the fleet at the Hawaiian base, that sooner or later the Japanese would make a mistake and we would enter the war. That was a year and two months before Pearl Harbor, and shows that Roosevelt was already considering a war with Japan as a means of getting into World War II.

At the Atlantic Conference, August 1941, President Roosevelt conferred with Prime Minister Churchill regarding an agreement to protect the British interests in the Far East; the proceedings have never been released to the American public. Churchill's statement to Parliament on January 27, 1942, verified this agreement: "The probability since the Atlantic Conference at which I discussed these matters with President Roosevelt, that the United States *even if not herself attacked would come into the war in the Far East* and thus make victory sure, seemed to allay some of the anxieties."

Secretary Stimson was so anxious to get into war that he conjured up limitless war powers for the president in defiance of the Congress and the Constitution. He claimed that the president had power to inform a foreign government that if terms he determined were not accepted and obeyed that the president had power to order war on any government without any declaration of war by Congress. The legality of Stimson's views was distorted at best; such claims ignored the Congress and the Constitution completely.

The Congress under the Constitution provides for our national defense and has the sole power to declare war, but the Constitution does not state that a president can use any pretext he wants to secretly trick the American people into war.

The reports of both the army and navy boards are a living testimony of the high character, integrity and honor of our army and navy officers. All members of these boards knew they were jeopardizing their own careers by telling the truth, and blaming those responsible in Washington, in direct opposition to their superior officers, the secretaries of war and navy.

What has impressed me in reading and studying the testimony in most of the investigations and particularly their recommendations, is that those naval officers who were present at Hawaii and who knew the situation firsthand have been the most outspoken in support of Admiral Kimmel and in blaming their superiors General Marshall and Admiral Stark in Washington.

Admiral Halsey said in his foreword to Admiral Theobald's book, *The Final Secret of Pearl Harbor*, that every American who believes in fair play should read it. The thesis of Admiral Theobald's book is that FDR alone was responsible for the helplessness of the Pacific Fleet and the unpreparedness at Hawaii, not Admiral Kimmel and General Short. Admiral Theobald was at Pearl Harbor on the fatal day and like most naval officers, he is of unimpeachable character and integrity. Admiral Halsey also did not mince words when he stated in the foreword, "We were sadly deficient in long-range scouting planes. The only army planes available were B-18's. These planes were slow, short legged, and unfitted for overseas scouting."

FDR in an address to the nation said: "I tell you the blunt fact that the German submarine fired first upon the American destroyer without warning and with deliberate design to sink her."

The Senate Committee on Naval Affairs headed by Senator Walsh of Massachusetts cross-examined Admiral Stark and discovered that FDR's statement was completely erroneous. The American destroyer *Greer* had trailed the German submarine for three hours, reporting its position to a British plane which finally attacked with depth charges. The submarine had fired at the *Greer* only after the plane departed to refuel and the *Greer* had actively continued the hunt alone. It was at the time of the attack on the *Greer* that FDR issued the "shoot first" orders. The report of the Naval Affairs Committee was not issued until much later.

The alleged attack on the SS *Kearny* was likewise deceptively presented to the American people.

The fact is that the *Kearny* had dropped depth bombs on a German submarine which later retaliated. These are merely examples of FDR's attempts to mislead and misrepresent the facts and thereby stir up an emotional flame of hatred against the Germans, all of which was a part of his consistent campaign of deception.

Roosevelt two months before Pearl Harbor issued orders to shoot at sight at German ships and submarines. But Hitler ordered his navy to avoid attacking American vessels and only to defend themselves. This ruined FDR's plans to provoke Germany. Consequently Japan was made the scapegoat and war target. Admiral Stark, then chief of Naval Operations, in reply to a question before the Joint Congressional Committee investigating the naval disaster at Pearl Harbor said:

Technically, or from an international standpoint, we were not at war, inasmuch as we did not have the right of belligerents, because war had not been declared. But actually, so far as the forces operating under Admiral King in certain areas (European zone), it was against any German craft that came inside that area.

A combination of Admiral Stark's testimony and the infamous ultimatum to Japan proves beyond any reasonable doubt that FDR sought to get us into war, and finally succeeded.

The intense pro-Roosevelt apologists may try to defend his un-American, undemocratic and unconstitutional methods of provoking war. They will probably say that the end justifies the means and he knew best what was in the interests of the nation. That doctrine is a total repudiation of our democratic institutions and representative and constitutional form of government. It violates Lincoln's "government of the people, by the people and for the people." It turned to ashes the principles and policies of neutrality and peace established by Washington, and upheld by Jefferson, Jackson and Theodore Roosevelt. It makes a joke of the great consitutional speeches and legacies of Hamilton, Madison, Jay, Marshall, Clay and Webster. FDR's clandestine foreign policy spurned the Congress and created a near dictatorship. It disavowed our Declaration of Independence, which repudiated the divine right of any one man to declare war.

If Secretary of War Stimson had not kept a diary, this conspiracy might never have been discovered. An entry in his personal diary in his own handwriting on November 25, 1941, relates how he, Secretary Hull, Secretary Knox, General Marshall and Admiral Stark were called to a special meeting at the White House by President Roosevelt on November 25, 1941. At this meeting, Roosevelt did not mention the European war. All that was discussed, according to Stimson's diary, was how to goad and maneuver Japan to fire the first shot. I defy anyone to deny it or submit proof to the contrary.

Secretary Stimson's diary was left to Yale University where it is available for research work and for inspection. Professor Tansill's well-documented book *Back Door to War* is available in most public libraries. The eminent American historian Charles A. Beard's book *President Roosevelt and the Coming of the War, 1941* stresses the tragic story of how we became involved in World War II. These and numerous other books on Pearl Harbor and the loss of our war objectives at the Yalta Conference verify the details of the whole tragic story. I recommend them for further reading, particularly *The Final Secret of Pearl Harbor* by Rear Admiral Robert A. Theobald. Some extracts from this book showing the American moves which led to the Japanese attack, are herewith included.

President Roosevelt's conversation with Admiral Richardson in October 1940 indicated his conviction that it would be impossible without a stunning incident to obtain a declaration of war from Congress.

Despite the conditions of undeclared war which existed in the Atlantic during the latter half of 1941, it had long been clear that Germany did not intend to contribute to the creation of a state of formal war between her and the United States. The stoppage of Philippine exports to Japan via executive order on May 29, 1941;

The freezing of Japanese assets and the interdiction of all trade with Japan by the United States, Great Britain, and the Netherlands, on July 25th, 1941.

The termination of the Washington Conference of Nov. 26, 1941, when Secretary Hull handed Admiral Nomura the famous war provoking ultimatum, unknown to Congress or to the American people until after the attack on Pearl Harbor.

President Roosevelt and his military and naval advisers were well aware that Japan invariably started her wars with a surprise attack synchronized closely with her delivery of a declaration of war.

The retention of the fleet in Hawaii, especially after its reduction in strength in March 1941 could serve only one purpose, an invitation to a surprise Japanese attack.

The denial to the Hawaiian commanders of all knowledge of magic was vital to the plans of enticing Japan to deliver a surprise attack upon the fleet at Pearl Harbor.

Everyone familiar with Japanese military history knew that her first acts of war against China in 1894 and Russia in 1904 have been surprise attacks against the main fleets of those countries. The only American naval force in the Pacific that was worth the risk of such an operation was the fleet in Hawaiian waters.

A Tokyo dispatch to the Japanese Embassy at Washington on Nov. 28th definitely stated that the Japanese Government considered that the American note of the 26th had terminated all possibility of further negotiations.

The Japanese code destruction messages of December 1st and 2nd meant that war was extremely close at hand.

With the distribution of the pilot message at three P.M. on Saturday, Dec. 6, the picture was complete for President Roosevelt and other recipients of "magic."

Never before in reported history had a Field Commander been denied information that his country would be at war in a couple of hours and that everything pointed to a surprise attack upon his forces shortly after sunrise. No naval officer on his own initiative would ever make such a decision as Admiral Stark thus did.

That fact and Admiral Stark's decisions on that Sunday morning even if they had not been supported by the wealth of earlier evidence, would reveal beyond question the basic truth of the Pearl Harbor story, i.e., that these Sunday messages and so many earlier ones of vital importance to Admiral Kimmel's exercise of his command were not sent because Admiral Stark had orders from the President which prohibited that action.

This deduction is fully supported by the Admiral's statement to the press in August 1945 that all he did during the pre-Pearl Harbor days was done on order of higher authority, which can only mean, President Roosevelt. The most arresting thing he did during that time was to withhold information from Admiral Kimmel.

Speech of Hon. Dewey Short (Republican) of Missouri in the House of Representatives on November 28, 1944, three years after the attack on Pearl Harbor.

Mr. Speaker: Truth tho crushed to earth will rise again and like murder tho it hath no tongue will speak in a most miraculous way. The American people have not been told the truth about Pearl Harbor. They want to know the truth and are entitled to know it in the name of both the living and the dead. Some day we will know it, and though from my exasperating and painful experience with this particular matter, I dare not prophecize when, but I repeat, sir, some day we will know the complete story and the whole truth about the most painful and disgraceful defeat of our armed forces in the annals of our country.

And when the complete story is told and the whole truth known, the American people will be shocked, angered, and grieved—deeply grieved and sorely wounded. Perhaps we shall have to wait for future historians to place the responsibility for this most tragic chapter of our nation's history but that does not relieve us from at least attempting to do our duty now. We certainly should assert every effort to prevent a replica of the Dreyfus case in the United States with all its unfortunate implications.

17

GENERAL OF THE ARMY DOUGLAS MacARTHUR

Our greatest general and administrator

No American knew more about the critical and dangerous Chinese situation than General Douglas MacArthur who lived in the Far East for fifteen years and understood its problems far better than Marshall or Acheson (who made only short visits there), or Presidents Roosevelt and Truman, who had no experience in dealing with Asians.

General MacArthur was no paragon of virtue, no Sir Galahad in quest of the holy grail. He was a highly intelligent, able, patriotic American who placed the interests of his country first in peace and war. He also had wide experience as a commanding general and as an administrator both in the Philippines and Japan, who fearlessly meant what he said and said exactly what he meant, based on his wide knowledge.

It is a disservice to Americans, irrespective of partisanship, to attempt to smear, defame, or impeach his honor and the truth of his statements. MacArthur is dead, but his living words will endure long after his envious critics have passed into oblivion.

In writing about the appalling situation in China just

"Mac" greets "Ike" at Atsugi Airport, Japan, in 1946. (Acme Photo)

MacArthur signs Japanese formal surrender on "Big Mo," 1945. (Acme and Kaufmann & Fabry)

after the end of World War II, MacArthur said, "Marshall's decision to withhold previously pledged American support was one of the greatest mistakes ever made in our history. At one fell blow everything that had been laboriously built up since the days of John Hay was lost."

This ghastly blunder of Marshall's on the advice of the Communist-appeasers in the Far Eastern division of our State Department and such others as Acheson, Lauchlin Currie, Owen Lattimore, Harry Dexter White, John Carter Vincent and Vice-President Henry Wallace, resulted in undermining and defeating Chiang Kai-shek and turning China over to our Communist enemies. It was a tragic blunder that may well cause the death of millions of young Americans in a future war—God forbid.

General MacArthur, General Wedemeyer, General Chennault and General Hurley all protested against General Marshall's ruinous appeasement policies toward the Chinese Communists, which resulted in destroying our Chinese Nationalist friends and making China safe for communism.

When the anti-Communist forces were finally defeated in China in 1949, they retired to Formosa. There are today roughly 500,000 friendly anti-Communist Chinese soldiers on the island of Formosa. These soldiers represent, together with the South Korean army, a sizable anti-Communist Asian military force that may play an important part within the next ten years in the fight to preserve freedom against the spread of Chinese communism. The United States must under no circumstance forget that these well-trained and equipped armies in Formosa and South Korea are our most dependable allies in the Far East.

China has its hands full protecting itself against a war with Soviet Russia, which may continue to threaten China for years to come. We have binding military commitments to Japan and the Philippines, and indirectly with Australia and New Zealand. Of all of our commitments, that with Japan is the most important.

General MacArthur, Admiral Nimitz and many American scientists publicly stated that they believed the unleashing of the American atomic bombs was unnecessary. The destruction of the two Japanese cities and the incineration of 120,000 defenseless people was a ghastly blunder, and one of the greatest atrocities in World War II. If the bomb had to be used, it should have been tried out on some small fortress island or on a forest as a warning of its destructive nuclear power to the Japanese government.

Japan had been trying to surrender for months through the offices of the Soviet government. Stalin deliberately withheld the peace offer for his own selfish purposes.

At the time the atomic bombs were ignited over Nagasaki and Hiroshima, the U.S. had the greatest navy and air force in the world and our country was impregnable to attacks. After the use of atomic bombs and their ultimate development by Soviet Russia, we became almost naked and defenseless against long-distance nuclear missiles. It amounted to a retribution of justice. Both the United States and Soviet Russia today live in constant fear of the possibility of nuclear war, and we must consistently strengthen our nuclear defenses so that no nation will dare to attack us.

We have a duty in the Far East to help protect South Korea, Taiwan, Japan, the Philippines, Indonesia, Australia, and New Zealand by maintaining a powerful navy in the Pacific. But we must not involve American land forces through commitments on the Asian mainland. General MacArthur, Senator Taft and others warned against it many years ago, and we learned a tragic lesson in South Vietnam. We cannot afford such a policy and preserve our economy at home. The American people do not want to be involved in continuous wars increasing our national debt and playing into the hands of the Communists at Moscow who have long hoped to undermine our financial stability.

The Formosa situation is so important that it should be understood by all Americans. On December 23, 1949, Secretary of State Dean Acheson sent the following secret memorandum to all overseas State Department officials, telling them to prepare for the fall of Formosa, to pass the word that no aid would be sent to the anti-Communists on Formosa. When the memorandum was made public, Acheson admitted he was responsible. The message said:

American criticism of American policy over Formosa had come largely because of a mistaken popular conception of its strategic importance to the United States in defense in the Pacific. The loss of the island is widely anticipated and the manner in which civil and military conditions there have deteriorated under the Nationalists adds weight to the expectation. All available material should be used to counter false impressions that the retention of Formosa would have saved the Chinese Nationalist government or that its loss would seriously damage American interests.

Formosa is exclusively the responsibility of the Chinese Government. Formosa has no special military significance.

General MacArthur discussed the military significance of Formosa in a message to the national encampment of Veterans of Foreign Wars. After first outlining our chain of Pacific island defenses, he had this to say:

The geographic location of Formosa is such that in the hands of a power unfriendly to the United States it constitutes an enemy salient in the very center of our defense perimeter, 100 to 150 miles closer to the adjacent friendly segments—Okinawa and the Philippines—than any point in continental Asia.

Formosa in the hands of such a hostile power could be compared to an unsinkable aircraft carrier and submarine tender ideally located to accomplish offensive strategy and, at the same time, checkmate defensive or counteroffensive operations by friendly forces based on Okinawa and the Philippines.

This unsinkable carrier-tender has the capacity to operate from ten to twenty groups or types ranging from jet fighters to B-29 type bombers as well as to provide forward operating facilities for short-range coastal submarines.

In testifying before the Russell Committee on May 3, 1951, MacArthur as usual was consistent. He said:

I believe that from our standpoint we practically lose the Pacific Ocean if we give up or lose Formosa . . . Formosa should not be allowed to fall into Red hands.

In 1950 the North Korean Communist army invaded South Korea, overwhelmed its army, and marched to the tip of the peninsula. President Truman wisely decided to intervene and obtained the support of the United Nations including all the major nations except Soviet Russia. He immediately appointed General MacArthur as commander of all the U.N. forces to drive the Communists out of South Korea, which he proceeded rapidly to do. He outflanked the Communist invaders by using our navy to land his troops at Inchon in the north on September 15. This was a difficult but perfectly executed maneuver, extremely bold and audacious, and highly successful. The British Chiefs of Staff minced no words in their message to the general: ". . . one of the finest strategic achievements in military history."

The enemy was cut off and surrounded and its remaining forces were driven out of South Korea and back to the Yalu River. President Syngman Rhee returned to his palace in Seoul. In November the Communist dictator Mao sent a quarter of a million Chinese soldiers across the Yalu, beginning, as MacArthur said, a new war. This was a real surprise attack—without warning or declaration of war. Some people at the time attributed this surprise attack to a failure of American army intelligence, but on a closer look, they saw why the Chinese Communists could take the chance. They could have been demolished by U.N. attacks on their bases behind the Yalu, by heavy bombing with blockbusters which MacArthur wanted to use. But he had orders not to attack these bases or the bridges, and the Chinese acted as if they knew it. The fact is that they did know.

In an interview with reporters Jim Lucas and Bob Considine in 1964 (revealed two days after the general's death) he said that the enemy knew every official dispatch within forty-eight hours. Apparently the U.N. secret plans, policies, and strategic information were relayed from our government via the British government to the enemy through the two highly-placed British spies, Burgess and MacLean. So the Chinese Communists knew in advance that they could launch a massive attack on our forces with impunity from bases in a privileged sanctuary. In preparing to meet the attack MacArthur was hamstrung by an order not even to fly his planes within twenty miles of the border. This was part of the appeasement policy of President Truman and Secretary Acheson.

It was done at the instigation of the British, who had not only recognized Red China, but were shipping war materials to Hong Kong that would help the Chinese Communist forces in Korea. It is inconceivable that our State Department did not demand that our allies in Korea should stop the shipment of all supplies to Red China for the duration of the Korean War.

MacArthur talked back, and the Joint Chiefs of Staff gagged him. He made a trip to Wake Island for a conference with President Truman. The stalemate and the slaughter went on. Finally MacArthur proposed a truce, which Washington considered its prerogative. There were implications that if the Reds did not accede, MacArthur might order his air force to bomb the military installations beyond the Yalu. The Republican leader of the House, Joe Martin, wrote the general, asking his views, and read his reply to the House. Among other things, he advocated bringing the Nationalist Chinese into the war.

President Truman resented MacArthur's outspoken public statement, his advocacy of bombing Chinese rear bases and the world-famous slogan, "There is no substitute for victory."

To make his and the U.N. policy clear against bombing the Chinese Communist supply lines, as necessary to achieve victory, President Truman on April 11, 1951, abruptly relieved the five-star general of all posts of command in Korea and Japan. In doing so, he had the approval of Winston Churchill, Dean Acheson, George Marshall and undoubtedly the blessings of Joseph Stalin and Mao, the Red Chinese Communist despot. That was his reward for having driven the Communists out of South Korea and wanting to drive the Chinese Reds out of North Korea and for having defeated Japan with the help of Admiral Nimitz and his victorious navy.

Hearing the news on the radio, MacArthur never turned a hair. He simply prepared to obey orders and return to the United States. He was seventy-one years old and had "served with exceptional strength and valor" (Truman's words in 1964) for over half a century. Few can ever forget the moving picture of the man, still straight as an arrow, as he strode (he never walked) to his embarkation from Japan. "Jeanie," he said to his wife, "we're going home."

The Japanese were shocked and gave MacArthur a tremendous ovation on his departure from Japan. Our former enemies honored and paid tribute to him then, and still do even after his death, and so do the people of the Philippines.

In the United States, MacArthur's welcome was wild. There were ticker-tape parades and an address before a joint session of Congress:

In war, there is no substitute for victory. . . . Why, my soldiers asked of me, surrender military advantages to an enemy in the field? I could not answer. . . . 'Old soldiers never die, they just fade away.' And like the old soldier of that ballad, I now close my military service and just fade away—an old soldier who had tried to do his duty as God gave him the light to see that duty . . . Goodbye.

Most Americans, irrespective of party, thundered their applause for our greatest general and administrator. Long after MacArthur had been dismissed by President Truman, General Mark W. Clark, who succeeded him in Korea, testified before a congressional committee: "I was not allowed to bomb the numerous bridges across the Yalu River, over which the enemy constantly poured his trucks, his munitions and his killers." General James Van Fleet also testified, "My own conviction is that there must have been information to the enemy from high diplomatic authorities that we would not attack his home base across the Yalu."

MacArthur was right. In war, there is no substitute for victory except appeasement; and Britain wanted to appease Red China.

Arthur M. Schlesinger, Jr., found fault with MacArthur for having been, as he alleges, dominated by his mother. He sought to prove that "the overhanging sense of maternal pressure accounts for his having nausea and for having vomited on the steps of the White House after a violent argument with President Franklin D. Roosevelt over the army budget, which FDR was cutting by 51 percent. MacArthur, then Chief of Staff, was enraged and argued fiercely, telling the president that he would be blamed by the dying soldiers in the next war. He realized he had been too outspoken and apologized before leaving."

Most people will disagree with Mr. Schlesinger's farfetched remarks connecting maternal pressure with MacArthur vomiting at the age of fifty-three. General MacArthur showed the courage of his convictions, which were both sound and wise in favor of preparedness in the 1930s, by standing up to the president at the risk of being removed as chief of staff. It was the same courage beyond the line of duty for which MacArthur received the Congressional Medal of Honor on the field of battle. That he vomited after the tense interview with the president does not lessen one jot or tittle his courage or involve any parental overtone. Perhaps a little more courage and a bit of vomiting by some top echelons in our armed forces, in defense of preparedness, might serve the best interests of the nation. I know nothing about Mr. Schlesinger's war record, if he had any, but it may not qualify him to berate a man who won the Congressional Medal of Honor and many other war decorations for personal bravery on numerous battlefields.

Field Marshall Viscount Montgomery, of Alamein fame, after reading and reviewing General MacArthur's book, *The Reminiscences*, wrote in *The* (London) *Times*, "I have always considered General MacArthur to be the greatest soldier produced by the United States in the Second World War. I am confirmed in that opinion after reading his book. It gives one a picture of a soldier who was a complete master of his profession, who always knew exactly what he wanted to do and then did it."

Lord Montgomery, after pointing out that MacArthur had refused to allow Soviet forces to have any part in the occupation of Japan, declared: *"I have always firmly believed that it is due to MacArthur that the Japanese did not turn over to communism."*

The *Daily News* in New York ran a main editorial in which it called *The Reminiscences* to be "one of the greatest, moving and most beautifully written books on war, peace, history, politics, persons and places which we have read in years. It is the story of one of the greatest military careers in U.S. history; the autobiography of a man whom ex-President Hoover called 'the greatest general and one of the greatest statesmen the United States has yet produced'."

Perhaps it is true that MacArthur loved rhetoric. He excelled in making exceedingly moving speeches, generally without notes. Generals are not expected to be orators, but MacArthur ranked with the greatest American orators in the last half-century. His farewell address to Congress and his farewell address at West Point will be remembered long after his petty and intolerant critics are forgotten. MacArthur, if he were alive, would reply to such critics, "shoo fly, don't bother me."

MacArthur had a brilliant mind and planned his statements carefully. He knew how to present the facts in glowing terms. None of his radical or Communist censurers will be able to change a single line, or to undermine the faith of the American people in his spoken and written word, or destroy his glorious record as the conqueror of Japan and as our greatest general and administrator.

As pro consul in Japan, he was worshipped on almost equal terms with the emperor. He alone with compassion and dynamic masterful leadership turned Japan from a deadly enemy into one of our few friends in the Far East other than Taiwan, South Korea, and the Philippines.

MacArthur is likewise loved and admired as the savior of the Philippines, where he spent many years. Who cares if Douglas MacArthur loved glory and was proud of his own achievements and his own historic record? That record is part and parcel of American history and no Communist or radical columnist can detract one iota from it. It is a glorious record of courage, steadfastness of purpose, integrity, honor, faith and patriotism unsurpassed by any president or any other American since the turn of the century.

18

MY RECEPTION FOR WINSTON CHURCHILL

Appraisals and reappraisals

In 1943, in the midst of the war, Winston Churchill came to Washington and stayed at the White House. At that time I was the ranking Republican member of the Foreign Affairs Committee of the House of Representatives.

FDR was the most partisan president in American history, and rarely if ever invited Republican members of Congress to meet such distinguished foreign guests as Winston Churchill. It occurred to me that it might be proper and constructive to have Churchill meet the top Republican senators and representatives. These minority members represented what in England would be called "the loyal opposition." Furthermore, the Republicans might in the next election win control of Congress. Then it would be in the best interests of the war effort for the Republican leaders to have some acquaintance and contact with Churchill.

I discussed the matter with Joe Martin, Bob Taft and Senator Arthur Vandenberg, and they agreed that it would be advisable and helpful. I telephoned my wife and asked her to engage the big reception room in the Sulgrave Club in Washington for Saturday at 5 P.M. for the proposed meeting with Winston Churchill. But I told her that there would probably be no such party and explained that I would tell her about it later that day. I knew how vindictive FDR was and that he would object to such a meeting with Churchill, but nevertheless I proceeded with the arrangements. First I telephoned Lord Halifax, the British ambassador whom I knew personally, having met him in London in 1939 when he was foreign minister, and I, president of the American interparliamentary group to the Oslo conference. I explained the desire of the loyal opposition to meet Churchill and asked him to invite the British prime minister to meet with us at a reception at the Sulgrave Club that Saturday. The British ambassador was most friendly and cooperative and said he thought it was an excellent idea. I then telephoned Secretary of State Hull, an old friend with whom I had served in the House for many years. He approved of the reception, as I knew he would, and said he would cooperate in every way. I telephoned him really because it was part of the official etiquette to do so. He was very cordial and said, "Young man, I wish you would telephone me more often."

I replied, "Mr. Secretary, if you will call me young man I was then 54 I will telephone you every morning."

The next morning Ambassador Halifax telephoned me and said the prime minister felt, as he was staying at the White House, that he should not accept any outside invitations, but wanted to know what I thought if he gave a similar reception at the British embassy at the same time on Saturday. I naturally agreed as I had anyhow anticipated the hidden hand of FDR.

The only change proposed by Churchill through the ambassador was that the reception should be bipartisan, five Republicans from the House and Senate and the same number of Democrats. When I spoke to Speaker Rayburn he suggested that I ask ten more, equally divided, from the House. I rang up Ambassador Halifax and he agreed immediately. Speaker Rayburn invited the Democrats and I invited the leading Republicans from the House and the Senate, all of whom accepted.

We met on schedule on the lovely lawn of the British embassy. The prime minister was a few minutes late. He came strolling down the lawn quite informally and in good spirits, perhaps after a few well-deserved drinks of brandy at the end of a hard day's work and numerous conferences. Each member of the Senate and the House shook hands with Churchill and introduced himself. We then formed a sort of semicircle around him. Speaker Rayburn asked me if I thought the prime minister would be willing to speak to our bipartisan group, whereupon I asked him to do so. Then this magnificent orator and heroic war leader launched into an interesting account full of pathos about his mother who was an American, and about the close ties existing between the two nations in the battle for freedom against German militarism and its ruthless dictator. He spoke eloquently for almost twenty minutes. When he finished amidst the applause, Senator Vandenberg stepped up to him and said, "Mr. Prime Minister, if you will only stay over here we will nominate you for president on the Republican ticket and elect you." Churchill chuckled and said, "Senator, I will take your suggestion under advisement."

What If Churchill Hadn't Been There?
(An Answer to Winston Churchill's Son.)

The above question is the title of a fantastic story published by Randolph Churchill, the son of the great war leader. It assumed that if his father had never lived, Hitler would have conquered England and the world, including the United States. This is carrying the Churchill legendary myth beyond the bounds of reason and reality. Without disparaging Churchill for his patriotic fortitude, courage, determination and magnificent leadership when France fell in 1940, there are several vital facts utterly ignored or omitted in his son's acclaim of his father.

Many students of history believe that Churchill was responsible for the loss and break-up of the British Empire he had pledged to defend and maintain as prime minister.

First, the war-provoking Danzig issue might have been peacefully settled and England and France might not have been involved in the disastrous war with Germany if Churchill and FDR had never lived. Hitler and the Nazis would in all probability have fought Stalin and the Communists instead of France and England. Secondly, the Battle of Britain was won by the gallantry of the British and Polish volunteer aviators and by the strength of the British navy—not by any one man. Churchill's tribute to the glorious achievements of the Royal Air Force in its defense of England in 1940 is justly famous: "Never in the field of human conflict was so much owed by so many to so few." Night and day, greatly outnumbered, the British air force valiantly and successfully fought off the continuous German bombing raids. The English Channel, protected by the British navy, has been for centuries the palladium of Britain—an impassable barrier to the great Spanish Armada in 1588, to Louis XVI in 1779, to Napoleon Bonaparte, and finally in World War II to the German army that had conquered France. Students of history will credit the impassable channel, the British navy and the Royal Air Force for preventing and dooming a German military invasion as sheer suicide.

Many Americans still believe that our shipments of huge quantities of military equipment—fifty destroyers, many thousands of field and machine guns, and other much-needed war supplies—helped to defend and safeguard England and the channel. It detracts nothing from the valor of the Battle of Britain to point out that Hitlerism and Nazism are dead, not because of Churchill who was driven out of France at Dunkirk, but because of the far larger and more powerful American and Russian armies, equipped with a vast number of modern American tanks and airplanes.

The United States has never militarily depended on any nation since it won its freedom until the advent of nuclear weapons. For more than 100 years it has been invincible against invasion from all the armies of Europe and Asia. It had a navy three times the size of the German navy at the outset of World War II and a much larger air force soon after it entered the war. The Atlantic and Pacific oceans serve as America's impassable barriers and are much larger and wider than the English Channel. It is sheer stupid propaganda to speak of Hitler's conquering the United States, when our navy was far more powerful than the Nazi navy, and even more important, we were about to unleash the atomic bomb.

There will always be an England and there will always be a United States, as long as the channel and the oceans exist—unless they become involved in a nuclear war which would bring death, dust and destruction to the six continents.

On August 4, 1914, Earl Grey said, "The lamps are going out all over Europe; we shall not see them lit again in our lifetime." That remark was only partly true then but it does describe the aftermath of World War II. With communism dominating half the world and nuclear missiles threatening us all, the lights are dimmer; an overt act of aggression might unleash a nuclear war that would extinguish lights everywhere.

But I have stated my belief that if Churchill and Roosevelt had never lived, there would have been no war alliance between Hitler and Stalin on August 23, 1939, the prelude to the Polish invasion and World War II. The Danzig issue would probably have been settled by arbitration and peaceful means.

Furthermore, even after England and France entered the war, both could have negotiated a peace treaty with Hitler to withdraw his troops to the Rhine, giving him a free hand to invade Soviet Russia, his continuous obsession. Churchill rejected this idea both before and after Hitler attacked Soviet Russia on June 22, 1941, very probably because he had the assurance of his friend FDR that the United States would soon be in the war. And so we were, in less than six months.

Lloyd George and many English Conservatives favored letting the two ruthless dictators fight it out to mutual exhaustion. This would have been in line with the original Baldwin-Chamberlain policy, which had numerous supporters in the United States, including Senator Harry S. Truman, Senators Vandenberg, Taft, Wheeler, Clark of Missouri, and myself. We felt that, otherwise, the Communist vultures would swoop down and seize the bloody remains of a large part of eastern Europe.

But Churchill refused all such offers. As a result, a large part of the British Empire was lost at a frightful sacrifice of the lives of its finest British youth, its resources, its allies' massive casualties—all for a final Communist victory at Yalta.

What Churchill called the "enigma" of communism was the only victor, and his famous victory sign turned into ashes as Stalin's armies marched into Warsaw, Prague, Budapest, Vienna, Dresden, Leipzig and Berlin. Soon eastern Europe and all of China were communized. This is the verdict of history: The Yalta legacies to Stalin and world communism are still marching on as a threat to the British Commonwealth and to free nations everywhere. Britain lost India, Burma, Singapore, Ceylon, Aden, and Malta, and her influence in Egypt, Greece, Palestine and parts of Africa.

History is very cruel to good intentions, and I am sure that Churchill had the best intentions. However, half a dozen times during the war, and actually before any real fighting occurred in France, he could have secured a negotiated peace that would have saved millions of young lives and most of Europe from conquest in a disastrous war. Such a war could have been diverted by letting Hitler and Stalin fight it out to self destruction. The lives of 3 million of the youth of Europe (and that includes not only England, France, Belgium and their allies, but Poland and the Baltic and Balkan nations) was too high a price to pay for Danzig and for maintaining the archaic British balance-of-power policy.

19

THE DEPLORABLE DECEPTION DURING 1944 ABOUT THE HEALTH OF A MENTALLY AND PHYSICALLY SICK PRESIDENT

Some contemporary accounts

One of the most tragic cover-ups in the entire Roosevelt administration had to do with the president's health in 1944, and during the Yalta Conference in February 1945, until his death the following April. His obvious physical deterioration was noted by almost everyone he came in contact with. Many of them were so shocked that they put their views in writing at the time. Every member of his family must have known about it. But the American electorate did not.

President Roosevelt probably never recovered from the illness he contracted at the Teheran Conference in December, 1943. This tragic deception over the status of his health during all of 1944 was one of the most unjustifiable, cruelest and most dangerous of all the political tricks and stratagems ever used to deceive the American people.

Roosevelt persuaded himself into believing that he was indispensable. That and his lust for power impelled him, despite his mental and physical deterioration, to keep his illness secret from the Democratic delegates who nominated him. To do this, he had to have a certificate of health from Vice Admiral Ross T. McIntyre, surgeon-general of the navy and Roosevelt's personal physician. McIntyre was appointed by FDR, had received numerous favors from him, and was his friend and admirer. He knew that the president had serious heart trouble and had secretly arranged for a heart specialist to be assigned through the navy to remain with the president constantly. He also had ordered the president not to work more than four hours a day. That alone was enough to disqualify him from seeking reelection as president. The presidency is, of course, exacting and strenuous, necessitating very long hours. It definitely requires that the president be in sound health.

Vice Admiral McIntyre knew the long and trying daily presidential schedule. Nevertheless, for reasons known only to him, he is quoted by Gene Perkins in *Life* magazine, July 21, 1944, during the presidential campaign: "The President's health is excellent. I say that unqualifiedly."

At the end of the Teheran Conference, December 1943, where he contracted an illness, Roosevelt returned to Hyde Park for the Christmas holidays. The precise nature of his illness at that time is still unknown to the public. Vice Admiral McIntyre said it was influenza which left an irritating bronchial inflammation, causing coughing spells that racked him, and that he showed a definite loss of his usual ability to recover. After Christmas he returned to Washington, still suffering from the bronchial irritation. By April it was necessary for him to go in search of sunshine in the south. He did not return until May 10. The record indicates that throughout the entire year of 1944 he was deteriorating. Nevertheless, he planned for his fourth term nomination despite his dwindling energies.

In 1936 Garner had said to his intimates, "Roosevelt will run for a third term and a fourth term. He will never leave the White House unless he is removed by death or defeat." Roosevelt was now concerned with the problem of frustrating both these enemies.

FDR was a sick man, but still clutching at the power that had become a part of his being. The Empress Theodora, wife of Justinian, said, "We must all die sometime, but it is a terrible thing to have been an Emperor and to give up an Empire before one dies." Roosevelt had no intention of giving up his power.

When FDR got back to Washington, Vice Admiral McIntyre called in two specialists. They found a moderate degree of arteriosclerosis. They found some changes in his cardiograph tracings, cloudiness in the sinus and bronchial irritation. But McIntyre continued to persist in stating that the president was in excellent health, which of course was misleading, and untruthful. McIntyre was a naval doctor in 1932 and was recommended to Roosevelt as the White House physician by Admiral Grayson. McIntyre was an eye, ear and nose specialist. He got along famously with FDR who appointed him to the rank of admiral and made him head of the naval hospital services.

In spite of Dr. McIntyre's public statements regarding FDR's good health, his heart specialist, Dr. James E. Paulling, established a strict routine for the president. He was to get ten hours of sleep, be allowed two hours to work in the morning and two in the afternoon, and cut down from thirty to five cigarettes a day; he was to have forty-five minutes of massage and violet ray treatments every day. In addition he was to rest one hour in the afternoon, lie down before dinner, and take vitamin injections. This was not precisely a schedule for a sound and healthy president by a top, experienced consultant.

In August, 1944, Roosevelt suffered a slight heart seizure at the Bremerton shipyards in Washington on his return from Hawaii. While reading a speech at the shipyards the president became confused and for a moment drew a blank. His words were unintelligible. What apparently happened was that he had a minor stroke. Grace Tully, his secretary, is quoted as having said that she was worried when the president dozed over his mail. In chats with political friends he frequently "drew a blank" as they listened.

Abashed he would have to ask what he had been talking about.

John Gunther after witnessing the 1944 inauguration ceremonies said, "I was terrified when I saw his face. I felt certain that he was going to die. All the light had gone out underneath his skin. It was like a parchment shade on a bulb that had been dimmed . . . the muscles controlling the lips seemed to have lost part of their function."

Roosevelt met Chiang Kai-shek and his highly intelligent and lovely wife at Cairo just before the Teheran Conference at the end of 1943. Afterwards she said she was shocked by the president's looks during the Cairo Conference. She thought he had fallen off considerably and looked quite ill.

Churchill, too, was reported to have said he noted signs of deterioration in the president. The faithful Admiral McIntyre was annoyed by these reports and stated that he completely disagreed with them.

Jesse Jones, former secretary of commerce and head of the Reconstruction Finance Corporation, stated in his book *Fifty Billion Dollars*, "I shuddered at the thought of the president, weakened mentally and physically as he obviously was, leaving that week for Yalta to meet Stalin and his hordes." According to this great Texan, "Roosevelt was determined to go to the Yalta Conference but he was in fast-failing health, weakened in mind and body, and went to Russia in the dead of winter to meet Stalin at Yalta. *There he made further commitments from which our country and the rest of the non-Communist world may never recover.* A few months later he was dead—his ambitions unattained."

Secretary of State Cordell Hull:

Secretary Hull was mad at de Gaulle and the Free French for the unauthorized occupation of Saint Pierre and Miguelon, French islands near the mouth of the St. Lawrence River. He was even on the verge of resigning over it. But Hull did not resign easily. For years he clung to the high office of secretary of state despite being constantly ignored by FDR in favor of Undersecretary Sumner Welles and Secretary of the Treasury Henry Morgenthau. Harry Hopkins, the alter ego of the president, replaced Hull at the Quebec Conference, the Atlantic Conference, the Teheran and Yalta conferences. Hull was constantly publicly humiliated, but the consummate politician FDR played Secretary Hull with a big political lure, promising that he would be his successor to the presidency.

Hull fell for the trap and continued in office, and while the president was offering Hull this political bait, he was telling his friends that Hull was too old and took too long to reach decisions. Finally, because of ill health, Hull was obliged to resign. Roosevelt sent Admiral McIntyre to Hull urging him not to resign. This is only important historically, since Hull was unmistakably a very sick man and knew it. However, McIntyre, who consistently proclaimed FDR's good health even while he knew the president was deteriorating rapidly, was sent to Hull to urge him to continue in office. Evidently McIntyre was also a political emissary of the president. The interesting thing about Secretary Hull's resignation on account of his health was that the president did not even consult him about his successor, who was recommended and virtually selected by Harry Hopkins. He was Edward Stettinius who had few qualifications and was almost unknown to Hull. His chief asset was that he could be easily influenced by the president and Harry Hopkins, who were running the show. Stettinius' report on the Yalta Conference reads like a fairy tale, with FDR as Prince Charming, or as a fairy godmother for Stalin and communism.

James Farley wrote in his memoirs that he visited Secretary Hull at the naval hospital at Bethesda, Maryland, shortly after FDR's death. They talked mostly about the late president. Hull said,

I last saw him shortly before he went to Warm Springs just before his death. When he came in to see me I was shocked by his appearance. He looked like death. He mentioned that he was not feeling well. I asked him what was the matter, and he said it was a sinus condition which caused him to have repeated nausea. [Farley asked Hull what they talked about.] He told me about the Yalta Conference. He was general and vague. Now and then he lost the thread of the conversation. He said Churchill was a garrulous old man and talked 90 percent of the time and that only 10 percent of the time was taken by Stalin and himself.

In our evaluation of President Roosevelt, Cordell Hull and I agreed that he was a sick man at Yalta and should not have been called upon to make decisions affecting this country and the world. Physical illness, we knew, taxes the mind and left him in no state to bargain with such hard bargainers as the Russians and such astute diplomats as the British.

Senator George McGovern a month after his unsuccessful presidential campaign called the Thomas Eagleton affair the saddest part of it. He questioned the Missouri senator's decision to accept the vice-presidential nomination without first divulging his serious mental history. "I thought I was acting in the national interest," McGovern said, "because I thought that the presidency was the one office where a serious illness should be a decisive condition."

The following extract from a presumably confidential letter to the president from his wife dated December 4, 1944, illustrates FDR's long personal domination of the State Department. "It does however make me nervous for you to say that you do not care what Jimmy Dunne thinks, because he will do what you tell him to do, and that *for three years you have carried the state department and you expect to go on doing it*. The reason I feel we cannot trust Dunne is that we know he backed Franco and his regime in Spain."

FDR's wife, Eleanor, wrote him her congratulations on his "colossal diplomatic service at Yalta." She was unaware, as the rest of the American people were, regarding the secret commitments made in the Yalta agreements.

Churchill said that FDR's face had a transparency and a far-away look in the eyes.

General MacArthur disliked leaving his important battle operations to come to Honolulu for what he thought was a political showcase as part of FDR's campaign for reelection in 1944. The general inquired politely, "Mr. President, do you think you are going to have a hard time against Dewey in November?"

Roosevelt grinned and replied, "I will beat that little son of a ——— in Albany if it's the last thing I do."

But MacArthur was convinced during this meeting that FDR was dying. When he returned to his headquarters in the Far East he told his wife Jean, "The president will be dead within six months." He was only two months off.

Admiral King saw the president when he went aboard the *Quincy*. He told Harry Hopkins that he was shocked at the state of FDR's health and noted the deterioration since the inauguration. All of this was before the president's tragic role in the Yalta Conference.

Miss Frances Perkins, a member of FDR's cabinet:

"I saw the picture (of President Roosevelt) taken on a railroad car when he made his speech of acceptance to the Democratic National Convention in Chicago. I thought it was a horrible picture which exaggerated his new leanness. I thought it had been taken with a long-range lens and had been selected for publication by his enemies in newspapers to give the impression that he was not well."*

This is a typical statement of FDR's close supporters who inwardly knew, but refused to acknowledge the fact that he had been ill during 1944. Hull, Farley, Jesse Jones and Miss Perkins were all Democrats and members of Roosevelt's cabinet. All have written accounts of his de-

*Frances Perkins, *The Roosevelt I Knew*, p. 390.

teriorating health, but no one apprised the voters.

Frances Perkins was one of the president's closest and oldest friends. She has written that, at a meeting of the cabinet the day before the fourth-term inauguration, Roosevelt's clothes looked much too big for him.

His face looked thin, his color gray, and his eyes were dull. I think everyone in the room privately had the feeling that we must not tire him. That we must end the meeting quickly. As I sat down beside him I had a sense of his enormous fatigue. He had the pallor, the deep gray color of a man who has been long ill. He looked like an invalid who had been allowed to see guests for the first time and the guests stayed too long. In a hospital, a nurse would have put her arm behind him and lowered him down onto his pillow. But he was sitting in an office chair. He supported his head with his hand as though it were too much to hold it up. His lips were blue. His hands shook . . . I rang for Mr. Stimmons, the guard, who came and pushed the president's wheelchair into his office. I whispered to him, "See that he lies down. He is tired out." I said the same thing to Grace Tully who had also noticed he was not looking well. I was frightened. I had never seen him like that. When I reached my office, my face was gray. My secretary who had known me for years asked, "What's the matter?" I closed the door and said, "Don't tell a soul. I must tell you. I can't stand it. The president looks terrible. I am afraid he is ill."

On Sunday morning I had breakfast with the Wallaces. When Henry left the room, Illo, his wife, said, "Did you take a good look at the president yesterday?" I nodded. "You know," she said, "I haven't seen him for several months. I was frightened. He looked so badly. Are you sure he is well?" I put my fingers to her lips. *We knew we must not talk about it.* This was just before he left to participate in the Yalta Conference to determine with Churchill and Stalin the future destiny of the world.

One of the cover-ups regarding the serious state of the president's health was the message given the Secret Service that "the President might go at any time," and as a result, the Secret Service agreed to increase its protection of the vice-president. This was all done in utmost secrecy and so much so that there is no record of who made the request upon the Secret Service.

Hon. James A. Farley:

Jim Farley wrote in his diary as early as 1935 that, "The President looked bad, suffering from a cold, face drawn and his reactions slow," and he felt that the strain of office was showing on him even at that early time. In 1937 Farley visited the president in his bedroom and was shocked at his appearance—his color bad, his face lined, like a man worn out. Farley was so concerned that he went to Dr. Grayson who had been Wilson's physician and had recommended McIntyre. Farley got the impression from Grayson that there was something the matter with Roosevelt's heart and that it might become serious, and urged a good doctor be flown in for consultation. Grayson agreed but felt it *should be someone who would not talk*.

Farley in *The Jim Farley Story* wrote,

From the time of his return from Teheran in December, 1943, there were disturbing reports about Roosevelt's health. Hundreds of persons, high and low, reported to me that he looked bad, his mind wandered, his hands shook, his jaws sagged and he tired easily. Almost everyone who came in had some story about the president's health, directly or indirectly, from any one of various doctors who examined him. Roosevelt looked bad in photographs and newsreels, and his voice lost much of its vitality over the radio. Members of the cabinet, senators and congressmen, members of the White House staff, various federal officials and newspapermen carried a variety of reports on the president's failing health.

Early in 1944 rumors spread throughout the country of the impairment and deterioration of the physical health of the president. For political reasons it had to be scotched. Either Vice Admiral McIntyre was carrying out orders from his superior, or he was part of a general conspiracy to hide the president's deteriorating health.

It is not in my province to investigate the mental operations and reasons for McIntyre's whitewash of a sick and dying president. It is sufficient merely to quote members of FDR's own cabinet, other associates, and outspoken members of the press.

Jim Farley knew Roosevelt personally and politically as well or better than anyone. For a long period of time he perceived the serious deterioration of his health. Writing about the Democratic National Convention, he said,

Everywhere the president's health was a major topic, though it was discussed largely in whispers at the 1944 convention. I wrote a few days afterwards, "Anyone with a grain of common sense would surely realize by the appearance of the president that he is not a well man and there is not a chance in the world for him to carry on for four years more and face the problems that a president will have before him; he just can't survive another presidential term."

The truth of the matter is, however, that he probably wanted to remain in office despite what may have been said to the contrary and that desire on his part was made easier by those around him, who thought only of themselves and their desires to remain in power. . . .

On every side I heard expressions of regret that he (Roosevelt) was not himself in the most critical days of the world's history. Had he not been physically and mentally tired at Teheran and Yalta and at home, and had America had a vigorous voice in international affairs, *statesmen of the world are agreed, and most without exception, that many of the troubles affecting the world today would not have arisen.*

What a devastating indictment. Farley even referred to the Teheran Conference that ended in December 1943, seven months before Roosevelt's nomination to a fourth term, as being the time when Roosevelt's health began to steadily decline and deteriorate.

The Duke of Windsor:

The New York *Daily News*, December 15, 1966, contained a statement by the Duke of Windsor, the former British king, about a visit to Hyde Park prior to FDR's fourth term. Winston Churchill was a guest.

When FDR was wheeled into the entrance hall to greet me I was shocked by his appearance. He had grown very thin since our last meeting and the skin of his face had taken on a strange transparency.
 I must have made an involuntary gesture of surprise which the president was quick to notice. "Ah," he exclaimed, "you find me thinner. Well the doctors wanted me to lose some weight and I feel all the better for that."
 At luncheon later on when I sat next to Mrs. Roosevelt. There was Winston in great form, growling clever things, while at the other end of the table our host sat in silence, a frail, almost feeble figure. . . . It was in that condition that FDR won and was reelected to his fourth presidential term, and went off presently for the meeting with Stalin at Yalta—*that ghastly piece of folly* by my view, which had the effect of sanctioning the entrance of Soviet power into the heart of Europe.

George M. Crocker, in his book *Roosevelt's Road to Russia*, was even more outspoken about the Yalta Conference. He said that Roosevelt was "mesmerized from the start. He presented a spectacle that only can be described as pitiful—this fading president, floating slowly out of this life, outmatched and outwitted at every point, mouthing meaningless clichés and dripping with flummery in the presence of the dictator (Stalin)."
 It has taken twenty-five years to dissipate the heavy propaganda fog that enshrouded the Yalta Conference. It is a sad and sordid story composed of camouflaged health reports, secret commitments, betrayals of our traditional friends, Poland and China, the surrender to Stalin on most of his objectives.
 The most remarkable and convincing statement re-

garding the true nature of President Roosevelt's health was made by an Englishman, Lord Moran, Churchill's distinguished physician. At the Yalta Conference when Stettinius, the secretary of state, said that the president was looking better and the voyage had apparently done him some good, Moran answered, "To a doctor's eye the president appears a very sick man. He has all the symptoms of hardening of the arteries of the brain in an advanced stage." Stettinius seemed to be shocked. "So," said Lord Moran, *"I give him only a few months to live."* He added, "But men shut their eyes when they do not want to see and the Americans here cannot bring themselves to believe that he is finished."

On February 9, Lord Moran wrote in his diary: "Everyone was shocked by his appearance and gabbled about it afterwards. The president looked old and thin and drawn. He sat looking straight ahead with his mouth open, as if he were not taking things in."

Lord Gladwyn, the only living British emissary at the Yalta Conference, issued this statement on its twenty-fifth anniversary: "I thought Roosevelt was very ill. He looked absolutely awful. We said to ourselves that he should never have come." He also stated FDR obviously tried to make up to Stalin and went too far in his Far Eastern agreements. An interpreter from our navy who on one occasion acted as FDR's personal Russian interpreter at Yalta observed that the president had no business at the conference and added, "He looked sick—he acted sick—and he talked sick."

Richard Burton, the well-known actor, put it more colorfully in a recent statement: "Were it not for the ailing and placatory Roosevelt, I think the boy from Blenheim Palace (Winston Churchill) might have won (at Yalta). He certainly would never have given an inch, and the world as we know it might never have been."

20

THE TRAGIC BETRAYAL OF FREEDOM AT YALTA

The Roosevelt delegation

Among President Roosevelt's staff at the Yalta Conference was Edward Stettinius, recently appointed secretary of state to replace Cordell Hull, who had resigned, although he, Stettinius, was hardly dry behind the ears in his new office. The Honorable James Byrnes, an able and experienced public official who was soon to become secretary of state under President Truman, was not consulted or even advised of some of FDR's major concessions.

Admiral Leahy, a top naval officer and friend of FDR, advised against making concessions to bring Stalin into the war in Manchuria. General Marshall, an ardent supporter of FDR and beholden to him for past favors, would have supported war against Patagonia if Roosevelt had urged it. Marshall later became, with dire and tragic consequences, an appeaser of the Chinese Communists.

The most important staff member was Harry Hopkins, who had little or no knowledge of foreign affairs, but played a vital part in most of the major conferences in the absence of Secretary of State Hull. Hopkins and Alger Hiss sat directly behind FDR at all the Yalta meetings and kept up a continuous exchange of notes with him. Averell Harriman, ambassador to Soviet Russia, seemed to be under the impression that Stalin was a Russian nationalist instead of a treacherous Communist leader and mass murderer. Harriman saw the light later on, but only after the barn door was open. "Chip" Bohlen, an experienced diplomat trained in the American embassy at Moscow who spoke Russian fluently, served as part-time translator at Yalta. Harriman is the only man alive, other than Alger Hiss, who has admitted before a congressional committee that he played an important part in the decisions at Yalta. Both he and Bohlen belonged to the Wilson-Roosevelt school of new internationalism.

However, President Roosevelt made the basic decisions himself and had decided most of them long before the Yalta Conference—the betrayal of Poland, the support of the proposed United Nations, the Morgenthau Plan for Germany; and when in doubt he conceded everything Joseph Stalin wanted.

The American staff played very little part in the proceedings, and Churchill and Eden did not fare much better. Churchill orated and argued at length but was voted down by FDR and Stalin and did not dare to antagonize either one vigorously. Churchill did succeed, through persistence, in getting de Gaulle and France the right to participate in one of the four spheres of military control in Germany.

Our mentally tired and physically sick president turned the Yalta Conference into the greatest Communist victory since Lenin seized control of Soviet Russia from the Kerensky regime in 1917.

The lone conqueror at the Yalta Conference was Stalin. Britain and the United States gained nothing and lost everything: The United States, a million casualties and billions of dollars in war expenditures; Britain lost half its empire, and endured huge casualties and near bankruptcy. Despite the ideals of the Atlantic Charter, the United States and Britain were responsible for the downgrading of freedom and the upgrading of totalitarian communism on a gigantic scale.

The first step of Lenin's master plan was accomplished at Yalta—the communist domination of eastern Europe. The second phase was completed when the Chinese Communists, with Stalin's support, took over China. Communism now dominates most of Asia. The next step will be to control the Suez Canal and the Red Sea, and to move into central and west Africa. The encirclement of the United States was begun by Communist seizure of Cuba, but once Russia controls western Africa, it will make the approach to South America much easier and help in the encirclement of the United States.

Of course, the Communists believe that the United States will fall like a ripe plum as soon as the Communists, fellow travelers, Socialists and radicals in America, like termites, undermine our competitive free enterprise system and substitute socialism as the dominant force in our country.

Harry Hopkins, Roosevelt's adviser at Yalta, was assailed in Congress as the Rasputin of the White House for lifting the army ban on Communists in the officers' corps and in highly confidential posts. As Walter Trohan reported in the Washington *Times Herald*, March 10, 1945: "The House Military Affairs subcommittee, investigating appointment of officers who had Communist records, was informed that the change in policy originated at the door of the number-one White House intimate."

Hopkins was the most powerful public official in the nation next to FDR, and played an important part in the Yalta Conference. Among other activities it is charged that he arranged for atomic bomb material to be surreptitiously shipped to Soviet Russia with quantities of blueprints—from Major Racey Jordan's diary. He was in charge of air cargoes to Russia and claimed that Harry Hopkins telephoned him to send secretly a shipment of uranium.

Six months after the Yalta Conference, when Stalin had already utterly ignored his commitments by communizing Poland, Czechoslovakia, Hungary and the other eastern European nations, Harry Hopkins made this incredible statement: "We know or believe Russia's interests, so far as we can anticipate them, do not afford any opportunity for a major difference with us in foreign affairs."

Germany had surrendered in May, and Stalin had dishonored his Yalta promises almost before the ink was dry. A black cloud of ghastly tyranny had descended over eastern Europe. Three or four months after the president's death, Hopkins issued this atrocious absurdity: "The Russian people" (who were enslaved and terrorized by their own government and had no experience in democracy) "think and act just like you and I do." (Author's interpolation.)

The *New York Times* on March 11, 1945, contained a brief account of a report by Earl Browder to the National Committee of the Communist Political Association that "the American people must be aroused and organized in support of the Crimea (Yalta decision) in such overwhelming numbers that the potential opposition within Congress will not dare to show itself." That was typical Communist propaganda of intimidation and fear.

If the Communists were so all-out for the Yalta Conference, there should have been the freest discussion of the proposals on their merits or demerits. We should never have been stampeded or rushed into any proposal favored by the Communists without the most careful scrutiny and deliberation.

Mr. Browder used the usual Communist tactics by charging the critics of the Yalta Conference with being Fascists or Nazis and added that this "fascism" "extends into the ranks of organized labor and liberalism." There is no wonder that Mr. Earl Browder was jubilant as a result of the Crimean Conference. A hundred million free people were forced under the yoke of communism almost immediately, and 600 million more in four years.

When James F. Byrnes mentioned Stalin's liking FDR, Secretary James Forrestal, a Democrat, answered, ". . . He (Stalin) had good reasons for liking FDR because he got out of him the Yalta agreement, anything he asked for during the war, and finally, an opportunity to push Communist propaganda into the United States and throughout the world."*

Roosevelt conceded Chinese territory including Manchuria to Stalin so that he would enter the war in the Pacific. Byrnes said, "The President did not mention it to me and the protocol was locked in his safe at the White House."

The Yalta agreements *were never submitted to the Senate for ratification*. Why? Because the concessions to Stalin in Poland, eastern Europe, and Manchuria might have aroused a great deal of opposition—even defeat.

In his memoirs, Churchill explained his dilemma in dealing with Stalin: "The United States stood on the scene of victory, master of world fortunes, but without a true and coherent design. Britain, though still powerful, could not act decisively alone. I could at this stage only warn and plead. Thus, this . . . was to me a most unhappy time. I moved amid cheering crowds with an aching heart and a mind oppressed by foreboding."

Here indeed was a paradox: The moment of victory was for the victor Churchill "a most unhappy time."

The Big Three had met at Yalta in the closing days of the European war, six months before Japan capitulated, to divide the spoils of victory and to determine how to preserve the peace of the world.

Stalin and communism won the jackpot, Britain lost most of its empire, the United States received war legacies in Korea and Vietnam, and in place of world peace a cold war began that was to continue for thirty years.

*James Forrestal diaries, p. 318.

President Roosevelt had selected his delegation—without a single Republican, Independent or well-known authority on economic and fiscal issues or on international law.

On November 22, 1943, just before the Teheran Conference Roosevelt arrived at Cairo, Egypt, and stayed at the American embassy. In the next few days he met and conferred with Generalissimo Chiang Kai-shek and his American-educated wife. He promised Chiang Kai-shek extensive reparations after the war: the return of Manchuria and the northeastern provinces, Taiwan, and military equipment for ninety Chinese divisions. All were repudiated at Yalta except the return of Taiwan.

The Four Freedoms and the Atlantic Charter granting the right of self-determination to all people and all nations, were deliberately scrapped by their creators. The people of Estonia, Lithuania, Latvia, Poland, Czechoslovakia, Hungary, Rumania, Bulgaria, Yugoslavia and China were communized by armed force and violence.

Soviet Russia and Stalin replaced Nazi Germany and Hitler with a vengeance. Russia had a much larger population than Germany's and ruthlessly employed bands of Communist quislings to carry out terroristic methods of control as terrible as Hitler's. Although Winston Churchill had called it "the unnecessary war," there were people who believed that World War II was necessary to overthrow Hitler's despotism. They found only a greater despotism—communism.

Looking back at the inescapable facts, it seems tragic that some Americans believed the end justified the means, even the involvement of the United States in war. If neutrality with regard to Hitler was branded shameful in 1941, what can possibly be said of the tragic commitments made in the name of international amity at Teheran and Yalta?

Ten minutes before President Roosevelt's death by a massive stroke, he was talking to some friends including his cousin, Miss Delano, Daisy Suckley and Lucy Rutherford when he stated without smiling, "I'm going to resign from the presidency." When asked, "What will you do?" he replied, "If I can get the job, I'll head the United Nations." This remarkable statement by the president has been given very little publicity and is not generally known by the American public. It shows that President Roosevelt had set his heart on creating the United Nations and hoped to be chosen to head it. It very largely confirms what many of Roosevelt's critics have said, that he was primarily interested in establishing the United Nations and was willing to surrender almost everything to Stalin provided he agreed to support it.

In his autobiography Jim Farley wrote, "I asked Hull whether he had seen President Roosevelt before he left for Yalta. 'Yes,' he said, 'he called on me before leaving. I tried to convince him that the time had arrived to impress on Stalin and Churchill the position of the United States and that we should maintain a definite position and not retreat an inch.' "

James F. Byrnes, former justice of the Supreme Court, U.S. senator and secretary of state, disassociated himself with some of the sordid aspects of the Yalta Conference in his book *Speaking Frankly*. He did not know of the agreement regarding slave labor. He wrote, "Had I known it, I would have urged the president to oppose the inclusion in the protocol of any provision for the use of large groups of human beings as enforced or enslaved laborers." Nor did he know about the secret agreement to give Chinese territory including Manchuria to Stalin to induce him to enter the war in the Pacific.

General MacArthur had this to say about the Yalta Conference. "Neither directly nor indirectly did I have the slightest connection with the Yalta Conference. My views on the advisability of Soviet Russia entering the war at that late date was never solicited. Neither I nor any member of my command was present at the Yalta Conference and I personally did not even know it was being held. The imminent collapse of Japan was clearly apparent. Had my views been requested with reference to Yalta, I would most emphatically have recommended against bringing the Soviets into the Pacific war at that late date. To make vital concessions for such a purpose would have seemed to me fantastic."

The Disastrous Yalta Legacies

The evidence is overwhelming that Roosevelt's Chinese concessions were made by his own decision in secret to Stalin without the knowledge of Chiang Kai-shek. His well-known Russophilism blinded him from other considerations. Mr. George M. Crocker in his excellent book, *Roosevelt's Road to Russia*, states that the claim that FDR acted under military advice has always been a sham. One of the most dishonorable features of the secret Yalta pacts was this dishonest sentence. "The heads of the three great powers had agreed that these claims of the Soviet Union shall be unquestionably fulfilled after Japan had been defeated." This meant that Roosevelt would compel Churchill to go along with him in forcing Chiang Kai-shek to acquiesce to the surrender of Manchuria, Darien and Port Arthur.

Even the faithful Robert Sherwood condemned this agreement as "the most assailable point in the entire Yalta record, because if China had refused to agree to any of the Soviets' claims presumably the United States and Britain would have been compelled to join in enforcing them." But Mr. Sherwood sought to protect Roosevelt at every turn so he said, "Roosevelt would not have agreed to that final firm commitment had it not been that the Yalta Conference was almost at an end and he was tired and anxious to avoid further argument." Sherwood's excuse that Roosevelt was tired has no merit. FDR was mentally and physically sick not only at Yalta but long before he was nominated and elected president. Sherwood avoids as the devil does holy water any reference to the pathetic and tragic health of the president.

Admiral Leahy, General Hap Arnold, General Juter and fifty top American officers signed the following petition against bringing Stalin and the Communists into the war with Japan. "If Russia enters the Asiatic war, China would certainly lose her independence, to become the Poland of Asia; Korea the Asiatic Rumania; Manchuria the Soviet Bulgaria. Whether more than a nominal China will exist, after the impact of the Russian army itself, is very doubtful. Chiang may well have to depart and a Chinese Soviet government may be installed in Nanking which we would have to recognize. . . . *Under no circumstances should we pay the Soviet Union to destroy China.* This would certainly injure the material and moral position of the United States in Asia."

This petition was presented to General Marshall, who deliberately ignored it and did not show it to President Roosevelt. He also avoided the opposition of both Nimitz and MacArthur to this belated Soviet alliance by not asking them.

Unfortunately General Marshall was consistently wrong in dealing with or advising on issues involving China. This was probably because of the advice given him by the pro-Communists in the Far Eastern Division of the state department and in official positions in China.

I am unwilling to believe that General Marshall, a Virginian, a graduate of the Virginia Military Academy, and a long time officer in the United States army was a pro-Communist. But through his long and close association with FDR, he seemed to have become an appeaser or apologist. The record is very clear. He supported Roosevelt in having Stalin enter the war in Manchuria at the eleventh hour against the advice of Admiral Leahy and General Arnold and without consulting MacArthur and Admiral Nimitz, and despite the protest of fifty-two high-ranking American officers.

Marshall later insisted that Chiang Kai-shek accept top

Communists in his government, and part of the Communist troops in his army; and on Chiang's refusal, he stopped the shipment of all arms to the nationalist army of Chiang Kai-shek. This caused its defeat. Marshall, who headed the mission to China, described this tragic act as follows: "As Chief of Staff I armed thirty-nine anti-Communist divisions. And now with a stroke of a pen, I disarmed them."

Later on as secretary of defense, Marshall testified before a senate committee on May 8, 1951, that "our purpose in Korea was to bleed the Chinese till they got tired and cried halt." Of all the cockeyed absurdities, this wins top honors for appalling military ineptitude and sheer ignorance. It must have been good news to the Chinese Communist leaders who actually needed a population reduction of 100 million of their own people who were undernourished, starving and destitute. Even today 100 million or more Chinese would be expendable in any nuclear war.

Roosevelt ignored Churchill, Byrnes, and Admiral Leahy and preferred the advice of Hopkins and Alger Hiss. MacArthur and Nimitz knew that Japan could not hold out much longer. Nimitz knew the Japanese navy had been destroyed. MacArthur knew that Japan was already trying to secure a negotiated peace almost on any terms provided their emperor were protected. If MacArthur knew it, certainly the president of the United States did also. Of course Soviet Russia knew it, as they had been asked by Japan to be the intermediary. But Stalin, for his own crafty purposes, kept silent. And in the end, FDR gave him extraordinary concessions of Chinese territories, without Chiang Kai-shek's knowledge. This was kept secret for six months.

It was the beginning of the end of the Chinese Nationalists, our greatest friends and allies in the Far East. They were finally betrayed by Stalin when a great quantity of surrendered Japanese arms were turned over by the Russians to the Communist army in Manchuria. This was how Roosevelt's Manchurian concessions to Stalin caused the liquidation of the anti-Communist army. Deprived of arms, it was quickly defeated and forced to withdraw from China to the island of Formosa (Taiwan).

Churchill emphasized he was in no way responsible for FDR's action in selling out the Republic of China. "It was regarded as an American affair . . . We were not consulted but only asked to approve."

The title of Churchill's book, *Triumph and Tragedy*, tells in a nutshell the true story of the war and of Yalta. Victory on the battlefields against Germany, Italy and Japan—these were military triumphs in the cause of freedom and democracy. But one tragedy followed the other, after the awesome and fatal decisions at Yalta. Seven hundred thousand British and American boys died fighting in that war. Yet the Yalta Conference deprived 100 million free Polish, Hungarian, Czechs, and others in the Baltic and Balkan nations, of their freedom and turned them over to become victims of totalitarian communism. Later the betrayal of China and its eventual communization was the tragedy of tragedies. The secret pact, containing the concessions forced from China, was the most shocking of all.

Chiang Kai-shek, the greatest, most courageous and consistent friend of the United States and longtime foe of Soviet communism was compelled to sign his own death warrant and that of freedom and democracy in China.

FDR's concessions giving control of Manchuria to Stalin resulted within four years in the communization of all of China. The anti-Communist forces under Chiang Kai-shek were betrayed and sacrificed to the red scourge of communism. All Asia trembled then and now awaits with dread Red China's development of nuclear weapons.

Winston Churchill was alarmed at Roosevelt's fatuous friendship for Stalin and obvious mania for helping the interests of world communism long before. On October 21, 1942, a year after we entered the war, he wrote to Anthony Eden, the British foreign secretary, "It would be a measureless disaster if Russian barbarism over-weighed the culture and independence of the ancient states of Europe."

Churchill wanted the Americans to join in an invasion of the Balkans which FDR opposed, apparently to please Stalin. Churchill's purpose was to prevent the seizure of the eastern European nations by the Red dictator. If this plan had been carried out, the Balkans, Hungary, Poland and probably Czechoslovakia would have maintained their independence as free nations.

Roosevelt was generally depicted as exceedingly friendly with the British, to such an extent that he was put on a pedestal and almost worshipped by the British public during the war. It is true that he gave England more than 35 billion dollars. *Yet, according to Prime Minister Chamberlain FDR forced Britain into the war* in which she lost many of her finest youth, most of her wealth and resources, and half of her Empire.* Chamberlain had a reputation as being an honest and honorable man whose integrity, veracity, and character were unquestioned.

History has by this time shown that the Yalta legacies include a communized eastern Europe and the enslavement of 600 million Chinese. There were other important legacies, direct and indirect: the wars in Korea and Vietnam, the communization of Cuba and Tibet, and the totalitarian socialization of Algeria, Libya, Syria and Iraq.

At one special conference between FDR and Stalin, only Harry Hopkins and Alger Hiss were present, the same Alger Hiss whom Whittaker Chambers had tried to warn our government against without success. Four years later Hiss was convicted of perjury for denying that he had supplied secret State Department documents to a Communist spy ring, and sent to prison. The same Alger Hiss testified before a congressional committee that "It is an accurate and not immodest statement to say that I helped formulate the Yalta agreements to some extent."

Friendly authors and historians of the Roosevelt regime have studiously avoided even mentioning the presence of

---

*See James Forrestal diaries, pp. 121–122.

Alger Hiss at the Yalta Conference. When they do, one would believe he was merely there to carry the secretary's briefcase. The truth is that Byrnes saw him frequently "escorted by Mr. Hopkins and Mr. Stettinius in the conference room." Secretary Stettinius wrote, "Hiss performed brilliantly throughout the Yalta Conference."

Eden was flabbergasted when he saw the secret pact agreed on by Stalin and Roosevelt. He urged Churchill to refuse to sign, but Churchill did not dare antagonize or anger either Roosevelt or Stalin on such an issue, as "the whole position of the British Empire in the Far East might be at stake."

Roosevelt was threatening to hand over Hong Kong to China. Churchill also foresaw that if Darien and Port Arthur were given to Russia, that the attempt to cut Britain out of Hong Kong would be untenable. Churchill was accompanied by his daughter, Sarah Churchill. Years later she used to stay in New York at the apartment of a close friend of mine. While reminiscing about Yalta she told my friend that after the day's conference was over, Churchill returned rather discouraged to their quarters. She spoke of how beautiful the Crimean Yalta seaside was and compared it to the Riviera, which her father loved. He replied, "It may be very beautiful, but I don't like this conference as it is dominated by a veritable devil who knows exactly what he wants and how to get it."

It will always be a moral and psychological puzzle why those of influence in the Roosevelt administration after denouncing so vehemently as wrong and evil the appeasement of Hitler before 1939, saw nothing insidious or immoral in the appeasement of Stalin.

John A. Flynn is an able historian whose intensive research gives a well-documented picture of what happened at Yalta:

Stalin got everything he wanted—everything without any exception. Churchill did not, because Roosevelt in pursuit of his vain policy sided with Stalin against Churchill. Roosevelt got nothing as we shall see. He got, of course, the United Nations. But this had already been settled on before he went to Teheran. And what is more, this was no victory because Stalin got the United Nations precisely on his own terms and in a form that enabled him to put his finger into every problem in the world and to completely frustrate the British and Americans in every effort to introduce order, peace and security.

At home, Roosevelt's red and pink collaborators and his closest consultants were busy pouring out Soviet propaganda. Harry Hopkins never tired of plugging for his friend Stalin. Henry Wallace, then vice president, was talking about encouraging a people's revolution in Europe to advance the cause of the common man. . . . All this had been instigated and urged by Roosevelt himself. And no one knew it better than Stalin.*

In a television profile of FDR fifteen years ago in which I participated, Eleanor Roosevelt pathetically stated that FDR was disappointed with Stalin just before he died and wrote him several complaining letters. This only goes to prove the fact that having appeased Stalin in almost everything and having helped to make half the world safe for communism, he finally began to realize far too late the enormity and consequences of his actions.

On the day that President Roosevelt left for Warm Springs, embittered by Stalin's refusal to abide by the agreements made at Yalta, he asked Mr. Leo T. Crowley, administrator of foreign aid, how much Lend Lease had been given to the Allies since the start of the war. Mr. Crowley replied: "Over 40 billion dollars worth." Roosevelt then asked, "How much did we give the Russians?" "About 11 billion." The president then said, "I have yet to get any concessions from Stalin," and added, "Leo, we are getting down to the tail end of the war. I do not want you to let out any more long-term contracts on Lend Lease. Further, I want you to cut off the Lend Lease the moment Germany

*John Flynn, *The Roosevelt Myth, op. cit.*, pp. 354–355.

is defeated. Don't wait for any further orders. Just cut it off the day Germany surrenders."

Evidently the president did not tell anyone else about his decision; obviously he felt that Stalin had betrayed him and had violated their agreements. These angry instructions to Mr. Crowley showed the president's determination to exact revenge, but too little and too late. Stalin had already begun to communize the captive nations. In the words so aptly expressed by John Milton: "Tears, such as angels weep, burst forth. Which, if not victory, is yet revenge."

21

FDR AND PALESTINE

On his way back from Yalta, President Roosevelt arranged for a meeting with Ibn Saud, the king of Saudi Arabia, who was very hostile to the Jews. They discussed the situation in Palestine between the Jews, Arabs and the British. A short time afterwards FDR wrote an extraordinary letter to King Ibn Saud:

Your Majesty will recall that on previous occasions I communicated to you the attitude of the American government towards Palestine and made clear our desire that no decision be taken with respect to the basic situation in that country without full consultation with both Arabs and Jews. Your Majesty will also doubtless recall that during our recent conversation I assured you that I would take no action in my capacity as chief of the executive branch of my government that might prove hostile to the Arab people.

This unnecessary and ambiguous letter catering to both sides would have aroused the Jews in America who believed in a homeland for the Jews in Palestine. If President Roosevelt had lived a few months longer it would have been embarrassing politically.

I introduced the Fish Resolution in the House of Representatives in 1922, advocating and supporting a cultural,

While 6 Million Died

A chronicle of American apathy by Arthur D. Morse

The breathtaking story of how America ducked chance after chance to save the Jews.

religious and historic homeland in Palestine for the Jews which was adopted by the Congress and signed by President Harding. As a result of this resolution hundreds of millions of American dollars went to Palestine to turn the wasted and arid soil from Dan to Beersheba into a land of milk and honey.

Four years after President Roosevelt's letter to Ibn Saud, the Jews proclaimed and established a free and independent state of Israel. Ted Berkman, author of *Sabra*, the best book on the Six-Day War, inscribed my copy: "For Hamilton Fish, maker of history and lifetime friend of Jewry, without whom the Sabra dream could never have been achieved. New York, April 1969."

After twenty-seven years and three wars, through the tireless and active efforts of Secretary of State Henry Kissinger, supported by President Nixon, peace was established between Israel and the surrounding Arab nations. But even now it is not assured. Peace, peace but there is no peace, and once again the vultures of war are hovering over Israel and the Arab nations. If the Israelis are provided with sufficient modern arms, unlike the South Vietnamese, they will defend the existence of their state.

There is no question that Stalin double-crossed FDR at Yalta and FDR found it out just before his death and protested in writing. There is no question but that FDR played footsie with the Arabs, and that the Jews in America found it out just before his death, too late even to protest.

I introduced in Congress in the early part of 1943 a resolution denouncing Hitler for his inhuman racial policies and for killing millions of Jews in gas chambers in Poland and Germany. For some inconceivable reason, the State Department claimed they had no knowledge of the atrocities and thereby prevented adoption of my resolution calling upon all the nations in the world to protest the barbarous liquidation of the Jews. Every nation in Europe knew by that time of the brutal extermination of the European Jews but for some unknown and unexplained reason, FDR's State Department actually opposed my resolution.

Ben Hecht in his autobiography said that "President Roosevelt's failure to raise one of his humanitarian fingers to prevent the extermination of the Jews, his many sullen statements about the Jewish situation, and his spiritual anesthesia to the greatest genocide in history" was beyond comprehension. He added, "I was informed by David Niles, FDR's chief secretary and a Jew, that Roosevelt would not make a speech or issue a statement denouncing the German extermination of the Jews."

One has to admire Ben Hecht not only for his courage but for his prescience and foreknowledge of events. He was completing a one-act show entitled *Call the Next Case* in which Franklin Roosevelt was summoned before the bar of history to state what he had done to save the Jews of Europe. The jury trying the case consisted of twelve dead Jews from German crematoriums. Just as Hecht was finishing his script at the Beverly Hills Hotel, he heard the radio announcement that Roosevelt was dead.

In retrospect I have become an admirer of Ben Hecht because he had the vision, foresight and the courage to insist that President Roosevelt make a definite moral appeal to world humanity and to all nations, neutral and otherwise, to demand that the Nazi government (Hitler) should stop its extermination policy of the Jews or suffer the moral obloquy of the entire world and be responsible after Germany's defeat to criminal prosecution. If such a definitive announcement had been made from the White House, it might well have stopped the megalomaniac Hitler or at least brought home the truth to the German and Polish people, most of whom probably knew little of Hitler's extermination policy.

Ever since I left Congress in 1945, thirty years ago, I have considered writing a book outlining my record in Congress against racism, religious intolerance, bigotry and persecution. However I kept putting it off as I disliked the idea of defending myself against the slurs and arrows of Communists, radicals and misguided partisans who sought in every way to twist and distort my record in Congress in behalf of civil rights, equal opportunity and justice for all minorities, black, white and particularly in behalf of those of the House of Abraham.

I admit it is distasteful for me, as I believe I have done more for the Jewish people than any single person not of their own race. Many years ago I played football at Harvard and learned that the best defense was a good offense, but at the same time I was so offended by the totally false smear attacks made by Communists, radicals, and their partisan friends, that I kept putting off presenting the facts and the truth, not only to the seven million Jews in America, but to all the American people. After all, I am 87 years of age, certainly not a candidate for any office; and I feel that the time has come before I pass on to greener pastures to make my record against all forms of class and religious hatred, intolerance and racial injustices and persecution crystal-clear. I do this not merely to uphold and maintain my own record in the state legislature for three years, Congress for twenty-five years, and since then, but to let the Jewish people know the plain truth without reservations.

As author of the American Palestine Resolution, sometimes called the American Balfour Resolution, which was signed by President Harding in 1922, I now leave my political legacy, long overdue.

The Soviet Union under Stalin and his successors have turned their backs on the Communist promises of freedom for millions of Jews in Russia from the harsh oppression under the czars. The ugly head of anti-Semitism has once again been raised in eastern Europe and in the Soviet Union. Both Jews and Zionists have been oppressed and discriminated against. Both Stalin and Hitler were violently anti-Semitic and both were terroristic megalomaniacs.

The worship of God is doomed in Soviet Russia, whether it is the God of the Jews, of the Christians, or of the Moslems.

While Six Million Died, a chronicle of American apathy by Arthur D. Morse, says on page one that "In January 1944, President Roosevelt was shown the startling conclusions of a secret memorandum, its title, 'Acquiescence of This Government in the Murder of the Jews.'

"The untold and shocking story behind this report, never before described in full, exposes the appalling apathy and callousness of our government, particularly the state department in the face of Nazi genocide."

The following is quoted from page 34: "While the Allied declaration was being considered, Representative Hamilton Fish, Jr., of New York telephoned the State Department and inquired about reports of mass murder and whether the State Department had any suggestions for thwarting the Nazis. Fish was an isolationist, but he had been moved by a letter to the *New York Times* from Pierre Van Paasen. Van Paasen, a journalist who had observed the Nazis at first hand, had written: 'To be silent in this hour when thousands of unarmed, innocent Jewish human beings are murdered each day, is not only a betrayal of elementary human solidarity, it is tantamount to giving the bloodthirsty Gestapo *carte blanche* to continue and speed its ghastly program of extermination.'

"Fish's call to the State Department was transferred to Reams. When asked about Van Paasen's statement, the man in charge of 'Jewish questions' replied that the matter was under consideration and that the reports of the Nazi killings were unconfirmed."

Also quoted from page 95: "Among the more than four million Jews in the United States there was of course great apprehension; there was also paralyzing disagreement about what to do. Sporadic rallies were held across the nation. The largest meeting of 1933 occurred at Madison Square Garden in New York. An audience of twenty thousand within the Garden and thirty-five thousand outside heard former Governor Alfred E. Smith and Senator Robert F. Wagner of New York excoriate the Nazis' racist policies.

"The White House maintained a discreet silence, neither applauding nor criticizing these expressions of public sentiment. But congressional opinion seemed in the main to support the views of Representative Hamilton Fish,

Jr., of New York. Fish defended the right of Jewish groups to protest the violence done to American Jews in Germany but stressed that 'It is of no concern to America what form of government is set up in Germany or in any other nation.' "

Note—I was never an isolationist, but with 85 percent of the American people I was a noninterventionist regarding foreign wars unless America were attacked.

I prefer to report what others who knew me have said, rather than to indulge in any self-congratulation. On January 6, 1938, Congressman Sirovich, speaking in the House of Representatives, said: "I congratulate the distinguished member of Congress from the State of New York, Hamilton Fish, following in the footsteps of his father who also served in Congress, as well as the magnificent contribution of his grandfather, one of the most eminent Americans in our history, upon the altar of humanity."

December 10, 1942

Dear Congressman:

I read in the Congressional Record, page 969, your speech and your letter sent to the Secretary of State in regard to the Jewish pogroms by the Nazis. God bless you. It was you who helped put through the Congress the Palestine Resolution based on the Balfour Declaration. If you recollect, the Jewish people in Middletown, N.Y., gave you a banquet and a Jewish Bible. I was then the rabbi and had the pleasure to preside.

I read your letter before the meeting of the Rabbinical Association of Boston. It was also becoming a colonel of a colored regiment during the First World War to speak so beautifully of the only out-going Negro Congressman. I wish we had more of your type in Congress, and the future of America would be assured.

Thanking you, I assure you these words come from the bottom of my heart.

Rabbi Bick, one of your former constituents

To the editor of the Newburgh *News*:

Of late there has been much printed about the wanton murder against the Jews in Hitlerized Europe. I am particularly impressed with the public statement by my longtime friend, Hon. Hamilton Fish, that whatever can be done to curtail wholesale elimination of these defenseless people should be undertaken at once. Colonel Fish, through his long public career, has been a champion of minorities. I feel his assistance as an official in Washington will be of great importance. Already two million Jews have been eradicated and five million more remain in the death holes of concentration camps fearing death in gas ovens or shooting. The young and the old fall dead in graves which they had dug, and there is no organized protest in the United States.

       Seymour S. Cohen, President
       Newburgh Jewish Community Council

22

A FRIENDLY CHINA BECOMES A COMMUNIST EMPIRE

*Proof of the tragic betrayal of
anti-Communist China*

History tells us that we won great and glorious victories, despite the hundreds of thousands of lives of American youth lost in Europe and the Far East, despite the wounded, disabled, blinded and shell-shocked.

Historians tell us that we went to war to preserve freedom and democracy against the military aggressions of the totalitarian Axis powers. (They tell us that our war sacrifices in blood and treasure were to preserve and maintain peace throughout the world.)

But they do not tell us how we lost the peace and our war objectives at the Yalta Conference in January 1945. Within four years of the total defeat of Germany and Japan, the Communists seized and controlled China. FDR's and Marshall's ghastly blunders will plague and endanger our own security for generations and may engulf us in a far more bloody and disastrous nuclear war.

The fruits of victory handed over to Stalin by FDR at Yalta turned into Communist scorpions that undermined and jeopardized our future more gravely than anything since the founding of our republic 200 years ago. Within five years the U.S. was obliged to send 360,000 American soldiers to defend South Korea from Communist military aggression. Thirty-eight thousand American boys were killed fighting in a country 9,000 miles away.

This was another of the Yalta legacies. It was followed by war in Vietnam against Communist aggression ten years later. A peace with honor was finally agreed to providing for the freedom and independence of South Vietnam, at great cost in blood and treasure, the release of our prisoners, and the recall of our troops. But when our soldiers were withdrawn the North Vietnamese began a new war of aggression, ignoring the peace terms they had signed—the usual Communist tactics.

The tragic momentum of Communist aggression is on the march in all of Southeast Asia. South Vietnam was speedily overwhelmed and the red flag of communism may soon wave over Laos, Malaya, Thailand, Burma and Indonesia.

One must resurrect our ghastly blunders and tragic betrayal of Chiang Kai-shek and our traditional Chinese friends and wartime allies to understand the present situation in Red China, Taiwan, Korea and Vietnam.

Why was China, that for eight years had heroically held out against the Japanese armed forces, after victory had been won at the expense of millions of Chinese lives, betrayed and sacrificed to the red scourge of communism and to Stalin, the bloody Soviet butcher?

The surrender of friendly China to communism was a crime against humanity and the free nations of the world. Today Red China is in a position to foment the spread of revolution and terroristic communism throughout the world by force and violence. China supplied the Communist troops in Vietnam and Cambodia with military equipment to kill American soldiers, as she did years ago in Korea.

In the 1940s the *Saturday Evening Post, Colliers* and other influential American magazines were flooded with articles glorifying the Chinese Communists as agrarian reformers. During 1943–49 the *Saturday Evening Post* published over fifty articles which promoted the Communist line. With the fall of China, the second step of Lenin's plan for world conquest was practically accomplished.

The pro-Communist appeasers in China and in our State Department sought to destroy the anti-Communist forces in China by building up and glorifying the Red Chinese. They succeeded in poisoning the mind of Secretary of State Marshall.

Admiral Leahy in his book observed that after General Stilwell's insults had forced Chiang Kai-shek to demand his recall as the price for remaining in cooperative wartime relations with America, Marshall made "repeated efforts to induce the president to retain Vinegar Joe regardless of Chiang's objections." Leahy observed that FDR had to send "direct and positive orders to Marshall before Stilwell was at long last called home."

Miss Agnes Smedley, a recreant American, was a Russian spy throughout her long career in China. I quote from Freda Utley's book, *China Story*, a scholarly and temperate account of the Acheson, Lattimore, Hiss, Lauchlin Currie, Harry Dexter White, Wallace and Marshall group and their accomplices who converted the Chinese civil war in 1945–49 into a Chinese Communist victory.

"Agnes Smedley captivated Vinegar Joe Davies, the American consul at Hankow, who was also a great admirer of Agnes Smedley, whom he called 'one' of the pure at heart'. He used to invite us to excellent dinners at the American consulate at which he expressed both his admiration and affection for Agnes . . . He, Davies, became a very potent influence in the department of state, furthering the cause of Chinese communism."*

Congresswoman Edith Rogers of Massachusetts exposed the attempt in the Aid to China bill to provide for the training and equipping of the Chinese Communists.

*Freda Utley, *China Story* (New York: Constructive Action, 1951).

She demanded to know who had written the bill and was finally told by Dean Acheson that it was done by the State, War and Navy Coordinating Committee. She found on investigation that there was no such committee but there was a State Department Coordinating Committee with Dean Acheson as chairman. Among its members, said Mrs. Rogers, were Alger Hiss and John Carter Vincent. Mr. Hiss also was listed as a director of the Office of Special Political Affairs. Mr. Vincent was listed as director of the Office of Far Eastern Affairs. "I think," said Mrs. Rogers, "my question was pertinent then and that it is pertinent today in the light of the tragedy we are undergoing now in Korea." Mrs. Rogers demanded to know what assurances we had that the Chinese would not use our arms against us. Mr. Acheson replied, "I think we can rest assured that the Chinese will not do that." But they certainly did, shortly afterwards, by sending 250,000 of their armed forces into Korea to fight our troops there.

A consistent Roosevelt apologist, Sumner Welles, in his book, *Seven Decisions Which Shaped History*, claimed that Roosevelt would never have permitted his appointees in China

to browbeat Chiang Kai-shek as General Marshall did in trying to bring representatives of the Chinese Communist Party into his cabinet. It is in fact a strange anomaly that the United States government, within a year after Yalta urged Prime Minister De Gasperi of Italy to oust the Communists who were then in the Italian Government.

De Gasperi's decision to take that step was in the highest degree salutary. It was probably the chief reason why a successful coup d'état in Italy that year was prevented. Yet in the autumn of that year General Marshall, as President Truman's special representative in China, was informing Chiang Kai-shek that "all American assistance would be withdrawn unless he broadened his government by appointing Communists to his cabinet."

History makes crystal clear that the Acheson-Marshall-Lattimore-Wallace group helped to betray our anti-Communist allies into the hands of our Communist enemies. To avoid charges of partisanship, I quote from a speech delivered on January 30, 1949, by John F. Kennedy, then a member of Congress during the administration of Harry S. Truman. This is what the future Democratic president had to say:

Our policy in China has reaped the whirlwind. The continued insistence that aid would not be forthcoming unless a coalition government with the Communists was formed, was a crippling blow to the Nationalist government. So concerned were our diplomats and their advisers, the Lattimores and the Fairbanks, with the imperfections of the diplomatic system in China after twenty years of war and the tales of corruption in high places, that *they lost sight of our tremendous stake in a non-communist China.*

There were those who claimed and still claim that Chinese communism was not really communism at all but an advanced agrarian reform government which did not take directions from Moscow.

This is the tragic story of China whose freedom we once fought to preserve.

What our young men have saved, our diplomats and our president have frittered away.

Generals MacArthur, Wedemeyer, Hurley and Chennault were the most active, fearless and outspoken critics of our disastrous China policy. They all had firsthand experience in China; all opposed the Chinese Communists and the terrible abandonment of Chiang Kai-shek and the anti-Communist forces in China. The record proves that the shocking betrayal of Chiang Kai-shek resulted in the communization of China. Few Americans will refute this statement now. Yet one month after the conquest of China by the Communists, Secretary of State Dean Acheson declared in a speech before the National Press Club, "What we conclude, I believe there is a new day which has dawned in Asia and we do not think that any part of Asia is lost to the free world." But he lived to repudiate his advice and to apologize to the American people.

Secretary of State John Hay's Open Door policy in China was adhered to by every Democratic and Republican president for seventy years until Dean Acheson assumed command of our foreign policy. Simply stated, our longtime foreign policy was to maintain a free, friendly China. This protected our Pacific backdoor. Neither the Democrats nor the Republicans of this nation ever voted to change our recognized and successful Chinese foreign policy.

General MacArthur said, *"It is my own personal opinion that the greatest political mistake we made in a hundred years in the Pacific was in allowing the Communists to grow in power in China. . . . I believe we will pay for it for a century."* (Russell Committee Hearings, May 3, 1951.)

Chiang Kai-shek was put up against the wall by President Roosevelt and told to agree to our terms—in effect, "if you do we will be nice to you and let you stay in China as the nominal ruler; if not, the Communists will take over." Chiang Kai-shek was coerced by FDR into turning Manchuria, Darien and Port Arthur over to Stalin. After FDR's death Stalin demanded that Chiang Kai-shek swap horses, turn against the U.S. and align himself and China with Communist Russia. On Chiang's refusal, the Russian army commander in Manchuria turned all the captured Japanese arms over to the Chinese Communist army who were mostly in Manchuria at that time. To pile disaster upon disaster, General Marshall refused to permit any more American arms to be sent to Chiang unless he complied with his request to bring the Communists into his government and into his army. General MacArthur characterized this as trying to make oil and water mix.

FDR betrayed China at the Yalta Conference and Marshall was responsible for disarming the thirty-nine friendly Chinese divisions of Chiang Kai-shek.

Marshall's disarmament policy and Stalin's armament of the Chinese Communists caused a tragic demoralization among our friends, the anti-Communist forces, and their inevitable defeat. It meant the communization of an entire nation of 600 million (now 700 million) people. China has become an enemy of freedom. It is growing steadily in military and industrial strength and is doing its utmost to perfect nuclear weapons. In a few years it will be one of the most militaristic nations in the world, more powerful than England, France or Germany, and a dangerous threat to world peace.

When the anti-Communist forces were defeated in China in 1949 they retired to Formosa. As of today, there are roughly 500,000 friendly anti-Communist Chinese soldiers on the island of Formosa. These soldiers, together with the South Korean army, constitute a military force of a million men in the Pacific area.

In 1944, after lunch with Ambassador Patrick Hurley who had just returned from China, James Forrestal wrote in his diary, "He (Hurley) said a good many of the professional staff had not merely been of no help but a definite hindrance to him. He said that many of the American newspaper correspondents were communistically inclined, as well as many of the people in the state department who he said felt no obligation to the United States except to draw their pay."

Furthermore, Walter Trohan, the *Chicago Tribune* veteran Washington correspondent, reported that an editor of the New York *Herald Tribune*, which bought the diary from the Forrestal estate, told him before publication that the original diary, which he had seen, was rough on Marshall. This is an eyewitness report on the deletions that protected Marshall. Even Mr. Miles, who edited Forrestal's diary, admitted deleting numerous parts of it, particularly those reflecting on well-known characters and high officials in the FDR administration. This was the same game of covering up for friends of the administration that apparently was done in the Watergate fiasco.

General Marshall's idea of continuing American casualties in Korea to bleed the Chinese was almost irrational. Their population was three or four times greater than ours. China had a very serious overpopulation problem and still has. It may lead within a few years to a war with Soviet Russia for living space in Siberia. Marshall's advice about the use of Stalin's armed forces in Manchuria was in line with his consistently bad advice and appeasement record which resulted in the loss of all of China to the Communists.

In *Triumph and Tragedy* Churchill emphasized he was in no way responsible for Roosevelt's action in selling out the Republic of China.

FDR made famous the words, ". . . again and again and again . . . I promise that your sons will not be sent to fight in foreign wars." The question is why, why, why did Roosevelt break his sacred pledge upon which he was elected as a third-term president? And why after helping to win the war did he lose the peace to Stalin and the Communists? Why did FDR, mentally sick and physically deteriorating at the Yalta Conference, ignore Churchill, Eden and Byrnes, and prefer the advice of Harry Hopkins and Alger Hiss?

There have been at least a hundred books written favorable to FDR and his policies, foreign and domestic, 1937–1945. The Roosevelt myth, supported by overwhelming propaganda, prevailed for a generation, blotting out the other side of the coin, revealed by the lessons of history. Even today not more than one percent of the American people know how we were tricked into World War II. Isn't it about time that the American people are allowed to judge history for themselves on the basis of something other than propaganda, myths and cover-ups, and discover the other side of the coin?

23

FDR'S ATTEMPTS TO USURP THE POWER OF CONGRESS TO DECLARE WAR

Why America must rediscover constitutional government

John Bassett Moore, one of our greatest authorities on international law, former judge of the World Court and counselor in the Department of State under Woodrow Wilson, wrote me a letter which was incorporated on March 1, 1937, into the minority report to accompany HJ Resolution 242:

You are correct in saying that so far as concerns the proposed surrender by Congress of its exclusive Constitutional power to declare war, it in no respect differs from the measure introduced a year ago to empower the president in his uncontrolled discretion, to engage in war and carry it on without the prior declaration which our fundamental law requires. To seek to save appearances by using in the title a phrase such as "to maintain neutrality of the United States" or "to promote peace" is at best a form of self-deception of the United States, of the most elusive and unsubstantial kind. No one who wishes unlimited power to make war, could ask for more than the authority, in his own discretion to impose and revoke and to modify and adjust embargoes upon our foreign commerce. Therefore to commit to the Executive power at his discretion to adopt and persecute measures that naturally lead to war, is virtually to transfer to him the power to make war, so that the formal declaration by Congress of the existence of the state of war, would become an essentially perfunctory act.

This statement by Judge Moore is of historic interest because it shows that President Roosevelt as far back as 1936 was trying to usurp the Constitutional war powers of the Congress by means of new legislation. The minority report concluded as follows:

We are opposed to granting enormous and unwarranted discretionary power to the president in the . . . proposed permanent neutrality bill. The Congress should grant a minimum of discretionary power to the president, as it is generally passed on to subordinates in the department of state who enjoy having their finger in every foreign pie and are more apt to involve us in war than to pull out a plum. If we are to have a war in the future, it must be in defense of the United States, and not in defense of the war profiteers, munition makers, or through discretionary powers in the hands of the president or the state department or in the interest of any foreign nation.
    Respectfully submitted, Hamilton Fish, Joseph W. Martin, Sr., Edith N. Rogers, Leo E. Allen, George A. Dondero.

As we now know, the effort of the president to usurp the war powers of Congress beginning in 1936 continued for five years, and culminated in FDR's drastic war ultimatum to Japan without the knowledge or consent of Congress in 1941.

The Congress, supported by the noninterventionists, had over the years succeeded in blocking the determination of President Roosevelt, his prowar cabinet, and the international press and bankers, to get the United States into war. Not one percent of the American people know today that Roosevelt served a war ultimatum on Japan ten days before Pearl Harbor. The facts were covered up by experts.

This is my message to the majority of the American people who were opposed to our entrance into another foreign war: that if their representatives in Congress and in the Senate, backed by public opinion, had not made a knock-down, drag-out fight against every attempt of Roosevelt to involve us in war, he would have taken us into war six months or a year or more before. If he had succeeded in involving us in war before June 22, 1941, I emphasize again and again, Hitler would never have attacked Stalin and invaded Soviet Russia where the German army lost most of its army, artillery, tanks, airplanes, equipment and oil. If that German army had been intact with all its equipment, the United States could never have landed troops in France or Africa, and the war would have probably gone on for many years and ended in exhaustion and stalemate with millions of American casualties.

FDR stated publicly: "I repeat again that I stand on the platform of our party." Three months later on December 29, 1940, he stated publicly: "There is no demand for sending any expeditionary force outside of our own borders. There is no intention of any member of our government to send such a force. You can therefore nail any talk about sending armies to Europe *as deliberate untruths.*"

A few months later he sent American troops to occupy Iceland, prepared to defend it against any attack by Nazi forces. There is no question but that Iceland was outside of the American hemisphere and that his ordering troops there was in violation of the Democratic national platform and of his direct and explicit promise made on October 30, 1940, not to send troops to foreign lands. This was done without the knowledge or consent of the Congress. It was clearly usurping the powers of Congress. If any president, Republican or Democrat, can send American troops outside of the American hemisphere *without the consent of Congress*, then it amounts to undermining and destroying the Constitutional power of Congress to declare war.

Later on, President Roosevelt ordered a convoy for

ships, issued shoot-at-sight orders *without the consent of Congress*, and finally sent the war ultimatum to Japan that goaded and forced Japan to fight.

The restoration of the war powers to Congress is a nonpartisan issue as it affects the lives of the American people. It is all the more important in this age of nuclear weapons to restore these powers to Congress and restrict the president's usurpation of them. Unless it is done, some militant war-minded future president could, without the knowledge of Congress, involve us in a total war of destruction.

The Constitutional right of the Congress to declare war has largely been disregarded or usurped by recent presidents. It now becomes the clear duty of the Congress to restore its own rights. In other words, the sole right of Congress to declare war should be reaffirmed, safeguarded and made crystal clear to all future presidents. This means curbing the powers of the president to involve us in war by dangerous maneuvers and unneutral acts. This can only be accomplished by restoring to Congress its legitimate and rightful power and at the same time by preventing the tendency of concentrating totalitarian powers in the executive, in time of peace, to name aggressor nations, to define war zones, to commit obviously unneutral acts such as the transfer of warships to belligerents, give shoot-at-sight orders, police actions and proclamations of emergencies without consulting Congress or the Foreign Relations Committee of the Senate and the Foreign Affairs Committee of the House. *No President should have the right to promise or imply participation in any way in war without consulting Congress.*

The argument that Congress may not be in session is specious; Congress is in session most of the year, and can today be reconvened within twenty-four hours. Furthermore, in case of a major attack such as by nuclear missiles, the president could automatically declare war and is especially authorized to do so.

To permit one individual to be the sole arbiter of war or peace is un-American, opposed to every principle of democracy, the Constitutional rights of Congress and of a government of, by, and for the people. It is in its essence, military dictatorship, part and parcel of the Divine Right of Kings which the founders of our nation fought against in our war for independence.

It is precisely what we opposed in the despotism and tyranny of Hitler, Mussolini and Stalin. There should be a full scale debate in Congress to curb the powers of the president to issue executive orders in the place of treaties and to make secret commitments that may involve us in future wars. The existing procedure is nothing less than one-man rule.

Looking back, one sees that the firm and constant determination of the American people to keep out of war, until the Japanese attack on Pearl Harbor, was an extraordinary example of democracy in action. The American people, regardless of partisanship, disillusioned by the results of World War I, refused to be influenced by the avalanche of prowar propaganda that swept over the country.

Public opinion was so powerful that all the efforts of the president, cabinet and international press to involve us again in a foreign war were of no avail.

The Congress in 1973 passed, over the president's veto, legislation designed to curb the powers of the president to involve the American people in war without the approval and consent of the Congress. I have been urging such action for many years but the legislation was not strong enough and can still be circumvented by a militant president. Peace in a nuclear age must be maintained unless we are attacked. If not, the American people are living in a fool's paradise.

James Madison, the mastermind and spirit of the Constitution of the United States and one of the founders of our republic, said:

In no part of the Constitution is more wisdom to be found than in the clause which confines the question of war or peace to the Legislature, and not to the Executive Department. The trust and temptation would be too great for any one man. War is in fact the true menace of Executive aggrandisement. In war, a physical force is to be created; and it is the Executive will, which is to direct it. In war the public treasures are to be unlocked; and it is the Executive hand which is to dispense them.

Hence it has drawn into an axiom that the Executive is the Department of power most *distinguished by its propensity to war*; hence it is the practice of all states in proportion as they are free to disarm this propensity of its influence.*

Madison's statement of wisdom and caution is, if anything, even more relevant to government in our nuclear age.

---

*James Madison, letter to William Cabell Rivers.

CONCLUSION

The vast Roosevelt propaganda mills were gradually silenced after his death, but due to the fantastic volume of propaganda, many Americans had been deluded into believing that FDR had restored our economic, industrial, and free enterprise system; reduced unemployment, made up with de Gaulle, and had won a great victory for freedom and democracy. These are the fictions of the propaganda myth. He did not restore prosperity or employment. After seven years of the New Deal, the American Federation of Labor said that there were twelve million unemployed wage earners. He increased the national debt of 19 billion, to 250 billion dollars, and raised the federal budget from four to forty billion. He was the greatest spender in American history, the grandfather of present-day inflation and of today's heavy burden upon wage earners and business from both taxation and inflation. He tricked the American people into a war which was won by the sacrifices and bravery of our armed forces, with 300,000 killed, 700,000 wounded.

But the war was tragically lost when a sick, ailing and dying President at Yalta surrendered a large part of the free and democratic world to Stalin, to be communized. These new "People's Republics" became the avowed enemy of freedom, democracy and religion, an awesome menace to the lives of all Americans and the very existence of the United States in this nuclear age.

Three months after FDR's fourth-term inauguration, two months after the betrayal of freedom and democracy at Yalta, and one month before the end of the war with Germany, President Roosevelt died of a massive stroke at Warm Springs, Georgia, April 12, 1945.

Constant war propaganda affected the minds of many of the leaders in both the Allied and Axis nations. Pope Pius XII stood like a rock in a war-torn world for the sacred principles of peace and charity, and against man's inhumanity to man. The following are reports of a radio address of Pope Pius XII, recorded by the Associated and United Press at Vatican City on May 9, 1945.

The pope expressed gratitude today for the conclusion of the war in Europe and offered a prayer for a just end to the "bloody struggle still underway in the East." In a broadcast to the world he said that

the European war had left in its wake the greatest "material and moral ruin" in the history of mankind. "Cries of gratitude break forth ardently," he said, "in hailing the end of hostilities. They rise from the depths of our hearts towards the Lord Father of Mercy. But gigantic difficulties confront the world in preparing for a truthful and lasting peace." He asserted that those who have fallen in the war would say: "may they arise from our bones and from our tombs, workers and builders for a new and better Europe—a new and better world based on the principle of equality of rights of all nations, great and small, and weak and strong. If the world wants to gain peace it is necessary that lies and rancor disappear and be replaced with truth and charity."

During the Bicentennial, we should reaffirm our faith in our democratic processes and constitutional government. If we let down our emigration barriers and the Communists tore down the Iron Curtain, half the captive nations and many Russians would try to enter the United States. Our Constitution is the greatest charter of human liberty ever devised by the mind of man. It provides for our liberties as free citizens and, as Al Smith said, for the liberties of our racial and religious minorities. We Americans, Democrats, Republicans and Independents, do not propose to yield one iota of our freedom for foreign forms of tyranny or police states.

Appendix I

ROOSEVELT'S FOREIGN POLICIES, 1933–1941

Extracts from the president's war message to Congress, December 8, 1941

The United States was at peace with that nation (Japan) and, *at the solicitation of Japan, was still in conversation with its government* and its emperor looking toward the maintenance of peace in the Pacific. (Wrong—only a proforma meeting with the Japanese ambassadors, but no communications with the emperor and his foreign or prime ministers.) Instead, one hour after Japanese air squadrons had commenced bombing in Ohau, the Japanese ambassador to the United States and his colleague delivered to the secretary of state a formal reply to a recent American message. *Even though this reply stated that it seemed useless to continue diplomatic negotiations, it contained no threat or a hint of war or armed attack.*

This statement is completely erroneous and false because the night before, at 6 o'clock, President Roosevelt read secret decoded parts of the Japanese reply to Harry Hopkins, and, in the hearing of other people, said, "This means war." Therefore, approximately eighteen hours before his message to Congress, the president knew that it was a threat or a hint of war or armed attack and did nothing about it, which was the second step in the biggest cover-up in the history of the United States, involving the loss of 300,000 Americans killed and 700,000 wounded and a cost of 500 billion dollars. (The beginning of America's greatest cover-up was ten days before, when the drastic war ultimatum was presented to the Japanese government to get out of Vietnam, China and Manchuria with all their armed forces. This left Japan like cornered rats, with no alternative except to fight or commit suicide.) All this was done without the knowledge or consent of Congress or of the American people and in violation of the Constitution.

Appendix II

THE FORRESTAL DIARIES

August 25, 1944, Cabinet meeting

The Secretary of the Treasury, Henry Morgenthau, Jr., came in with the president, with whom he had lunched. The president said he had been talking with the Secretary of the Treasury on the general question of the control of Germany after the war. He said he had just heard about a paper prepared by the Army and that he was not at all satisfied with the severity of the measures proposed. He said that the Germans should have simply a subsistence level of food. As he put it, soup kitchens would be ample to sustain life. Otherwise, they should be stripped clean and should not have a level of subsistance above the lowest level of the people they have conquered.

The Forrestal Diaries, page 11:

Brynes recalled that the president proposed his program for Germany at the Cabinet meeting after having lunch with Morgenthau. It came as a shock to Hull (Cordell Hull, Secretary of State) and Stimson when he named Morgenthau head of the committee to deal with German matters. At this same lunch he read a number of excerpts from the proposed army directive indictating his disapproval and scorn of the soft policy towards Germany. Brynes recalled that Hull did not go to the subsequent Quebec Conference and that Morgenthau did; and at that meeting he got Roosevelt's and Churchill's signatures to his conception of the treatment of Germany. Brynes said that Hull was so angry when he got this message that he expressed a desire to resign. The assistant secretary of war, John J. McCloy, told me on September 18, 1944, that the secretary of the treasury, Mr. Morgenthau, had formulated a program of the most severe character in dealing with Germany after its collapse. He said the secretary of war was in violent disagreement and that the president had decided to go along with Morgenthau. In general the program, according to Mr. McCloy, called for the conscious destruction of the economy in Germany and the encouragement of a state of impoverishment and disorder. He said he felt the army's role in any program would be most difficult because the army, by training and instinct, would naturally turn to the recreation of order as soon as possible, whereas under this program they apparently were to encourage the opposite.

Governor Earl arrived in Istanbul in the spring of 1943. He told me one morning there was a knock on his hotel room door. He opened it and there stood a broad-shouldered, medium-sized man in civilian clothes who requested an informal conference. He presented himself as Admiral Wilhelm Canaris, head of the German Secret Service. The gist of his conversation was, there were many sensible German people who loved their fatherland and who greatly disliked Adolf Hitler, feeling that Hitler was leading their nation down a destructive path. Admiral Canaris continued, saying that the unconditional surrender policy recently announced by Roosevelt and Churchill at Casablanca was something the German generals could not swallow. He said, however, if President Roosevelt would merely indicate he would accept an honorable surrender from the German army to the American forces, such an event could be arranged. That the real enemy of western civilization (Soviet Communism) could then be stopped. The German army, if so directed, would move to the eastern front and stop the Communist army's march into eastern Europe. The Soviets' main objective was to establish themselves as the supreme power in Europe.

The governor remarked that at first he was staggered, but was extremely cautious of his reaction to the admiral and to the startling proposal.

Then followed a meeting with the German ambassador Fritz von Papen, a devout Roman Catholic and strongly anti-Hitler in his feelings. The governor told me that he soon became convinced of the sincerity manifested by the anti-Nazi Germans. Becoming further informed concerning the hidden designs of the Soviet forces, he promptly dispatched a coded message to FDR in Washington via the diplomatic pouch reporting the whole matter. He then waited for the requested prompt reply. None came. Thirty days later, as agreed, Admiral Canaris phoned him and asked, "Have you any news?" The governor replied, "I am waiting for news but have none today."

Appendix III

INTERVIEW BETWEEN CURTIS B. DALL AND FORMER GOVERNOR GEORGE EARL OF PENNSYLVANIA REGARDING SECRET EFFORTS OF HIGH GERMAN OFFICERS AND OFFICIALS TO SURRENDER EIGHTEEN MONTHS BEFORE THE END OF THE WAR

Colonel Curtis B. Dall, the author of *FDR, My Exploited Father-in-Law*, very kindly gave me permission to use parts of his interview with former Governor George Earl of Pennsylvania, a close friend of President Roosevelt and his appointee as minister to Austria and minister to Bulgaria. In 1943 Earl was the special envoy of the president as naval attaché to neutral Istanbul (Constantinople), Turkey, to keep the White House informed of what was going on in the Balkans and in Germany.

Colonel Dall lunched with Earl many years after the war. The latter opened the conversation by saying, "Dall, I told your father-in-law, FDR, when I was his naval attaché in Istanbul, how we could greatly shorten World War II. The governor then proceeded to unfold an amazing story:

The same question was again posed to Governor Earl by Baron von Lersner, who headed the Orient Society: If the anti-Nazi forces in Germany delivered the German army to the American forces, could they then count on allied cooperation in keeping the Soviets out of central Europe? Hence, if Roosevelt would merely agree to an "honorable surrender," von Lersner stated, even if Hitler was not killed by his group, he would be handed to the Americans. Furthermore, the Soviet army could be held in check and contained in suitable areas.

Again, the governor said, he dispatched an urgent coded message to the White House, pleading with President Franklin Roosevelt to explore what the anti-Nazis had to offer. Still no reply came back to him!

Then followed another meeting with von Lersner, who came up with an added plan to surround Hitler's remote eastern military headquarters, then move the German army to the eastern front until a ceasefire could be arranged.

Governor Earl said he then prepared and sent a most urgent message to Roosevelt in Washington, not only via the diplomatic pouch but through Army-Navy channels, this time to make sure the important message got through to FDR. He said he felt that FDR and his top advisers were under the spell of Joe Stalin, or that he, Roosevelt, mistakenly felt that he could "charm" Stalin.

A plane had been readied in Istanbul, he said; upon receipt of the hoped-for favorable reply from Roosevelt Governor Earl was to fly to an undisclosed spot in Germany, there to receive more details leading to surrender terms to be sent at once to the White House for further action. The plane near Istanbul awaited the next step—and it waited and waited.

The governor said he was getting more and more discouraged and frustrated when no reply came from Washington in response to his urgent messages.

Finally, in effect, a purported answer did come. It was that he should take up with the field commander in Europe any proposals for a negotiated peace. Could any procedure have been more impractical or tragic?

Governor Earl continued, "I was shocked, greatly disheartened, and felt my usefulness was about over. So I returned to the U.S.A., came back home, and World War II proceeded along its scheduled course until the Soviets sat astride Europe."

He then added, after a while, "However, I decided to make known some of my views and observations about our so-called allies, the Soviets, so as to wake up the American people about what was really going on. I contacted the president about it, but he reacted strongly and specifically forbade me to make my views known to the public. Then, upon my requesting active duty in the Navy, I was ordered to Samoa in the distant South Pacific. There my extensive experience with the double-faced Soviets and our lost opportunity to stop needless carnage, to prevent a great Soviet victory in Europe would not make any impression on the friendly Samoans."

Here is a truthful account by former Governor Earl of Pennsylvania, a friend and supporter of FDR, as to how he conveyed to President Roosevelt, eighteen months before the end of the war, a direct offer from the German army to surrender to the American army and kill Hitler or turn him over to American control. In return the German army offered to fight to prevent Stalin and the Communists from taking over the free and independent eastern European nations and bringing communism into central Europe. What a tragedy!

The freedom and democracy for which we fought was destroyed in eastern Europe. FDR refused to accept a black-out of Nazism, the protection of Poland and eastern European nations from Communist domination, and to save the lives of scores of thousands of American, British and French soldiers and enormous additional war costs.

The American public has probably never heard of Governor Earl's repeated attempts to end the war against Germany through the surrender of the German army and the trial and execution of Hitler by our armed forces.

If Roosevelt had accepted this capitulation, practically on his own terms, it would have been the end of Hitler and Nazism. Freedom and democracy would have been restored to Czechoslovakia, Poland, Hungary and other nations. It is enough to make the angels weep.

If the offer of the German army to surrender unconditionally, to kill Hitler or turn him over to the American authorities a year and a half before the end of the war had been accepted by FDR, it would have saved the lives of millions of Jews who had been seized throughout Europe and sent to concentration camps and death in the gas chambers of Poland and Germany and the lives of many thousands of brave young American soldiers.

Appendix IV

TRIBUTES TO GENERAL DOUGLAS MacARTHUR, A GREAT AMERICAN

"He was one of the world's outstanding military commanders. He was also a statesman for peace. The world is a finer place for his having lived in it, and for the standards of courage and character he set. Truly, his watchword was 'Duty, Honor, Country.' He was a truly great man, a great general, and a great patriot."—Herbert Hoover

"General Douglas MacArthur...has given of himself with exceptional strength and valor and will be remembered as one of the great military men in our history."—Harry S. Truman

"In the hearts of his countrymen and in the pages of history his courageous presence among us and his valiant deeds for us will never die. At a time of increasing complexity, where ancient virtues are obscured by the rush of events and knowledge, his life has reminded us that the enduring strength of America rests on its capacity for such simple qualities of integrity and loyalty; honor and duty."—Lyndon Baines Johnson

MacArthur as chief of staff and General Pershing, 1933. (Acme Photo)

"He fought a wonderful campaign in the Pacific. In my opinion he was the best soldier produced by the United States during the Hitler war."—Field Marshall Viscount Montgomery

"I cannot forget the great achievement of the general in rebuilding our nation out of the ashes of defeat. Out of stringent food shortages, out of the confusion of our political, economic and social systems, and out of the insecurity of men's hearts, *MacArthur laid the foundation for a new Japan which became the source of our nation's prosperity today.*"—Former Japanese Prime Minister Shigeru Yoshida

"[He was] a great soldier, a man of remarkable talents and personality. [He has] an assured place in the history of Australia."—Sir Robert Menzies, Prime Minister of Australia.

Appendix V

STATEMENT BY HERMAN H. DINSMORE

Statement by Herman H. Dinsmore, who served for thirty-four years on the *New York Times*, nine years as editor of the International Edition, in a book entitled *The Bleeding of America*, published in 1974: "Did you know that the Japanese 'surprise' attack on Pearl Harbor was not a surprise at all but that the Japanese had been lured in with a sacrifice of more than 3,300 American lives and over 1,200 wounded?"

On page 102 of Mr. Dinsmore's book, he says:
There is now a wealth of evidence that the Japanese were drawn into making the attack, with the risk of the great loss of American lives and American fighting capability—eight battleships knocked out of action, three cruisers likewise, four destroyers damaged, two beyond repair, a seaplane tender and a repair ship damaged, a target ship sunk, and 177 American planes destroyed. The Japanese lost 48 planes and three worthless midget submarines. The Japanese were lured to Pearl Harbor while the American commanders there were kept in ignorance of the strategy. That is a fact now established beyond question. But the public as a whole, still does not know it.

Mr. Dinsmore was assistant foreign editor of the *New York Times*, a position which required a tremendous amount of reading of all foreign news. He stated that at first he could not believe the worst about a president of the United States. The idea that a president of the United States would do such a thing was revolting and repugnant to him.

BIBLIOGRAPHY

The following list of books from the author's library were used in writing *FDR: The Other Side of the Coin*. The complete bibliography also includes considerable material from newspapers, magazines and the *Congressional Record*.

The author, desiring to have this book published in the early part of our Bicentennial year, has been obliged to omit a number of footnotes which he hopes to have time to insert in the new editions. He is in the process of having three other books published. His first book *New York State, the Battleground of the Revolutionary War* was published in 1975. The three other books are *The American People Are Living on a Nuclear Volcano*, *The Manifesto on Communism by Marx and Engels is a Hoax on American Wage Earners*, and *Lafayette in America During the Revolutionary War*.

Baruch, Bernard M. *The Public Years*. New York: Holt, Rinehart & Winston, 1960.

Beard, Charles A. *American Foreign Policy in the Making, 1932–1940*. New Haven, Conn.: Yale University Press, 1946.

——. *President Roosevelt and the Coming of the War, 1941*. New Haven, Conn.: Yale University Press, 1948.

Beck, Col. Jozef. *Final Report*. New York: Robert Speller & Sons, 1957.

Bergamini, David. *Japan's Imperial Conspiracy*. New York: William Morrow & Co., 1972.

Bishop, Jim. *FDR's Last Year*. New York: William Morrow & Co., 1974.

Burns, James MacGregor. *Roosevelt: The Soldier of Freedom*. New York: Harcourt, Brace, Jovanovich, 1970.

Byrnes, James F. *Speaking Frankly*. New York: Harper & Bros., 1947.

Castle, Eugene W. *Billions, Blunders, and Baloney*. New York: Devin-Adair Co., 1955.

Chamberlain, William H. *America's Second Crusade*. Chicago: Henry Regenery Co., 1950.

———. *The European Cockpit*. New York: Macmillan Co., 1947.

Churchill, Winston S. *The End of the Beginning*. Boston: Little, Brown & Co., 1943.

——— *The Gathering Storm*. Boston: Houghton Mifflin Co., 1948.

——— *The Hinge of Fate*. Boston: Houghton Mifflin Co., 1950.

Ciechanowski, Jan. *Defeat in Victory*. Garden City, N.Y.: Doubleday & Co., 1947.

Congdon, Don, ed. *Combat: World War II*. Vol. 1, *European Theater*. New York: Dell Books, 1958.

Congressional Directory, 78th Congress, 1st Sess., May 1943. Washington, D.C.

Dall, Curtis B. *FDR: My Exploited Father-in-Law*. Action Associates, 1970.

Dennis, Lawrence. *A Trial on Trial*. National Civil Rights Committee.

Dies, Martin, *Martin Dies' Story*. New York: Bookmailer, 1973.

———. *The Trojan Horse in America*. New York: Dodd, Mead & Co., 1940.

Eisenhower, Dwight D. *Eisenhower's Own Story of the War*. New York: Arco Publishing Co., 1946.

Farley, James A. *Jim Farley's Story*. London: Whittlesey House, 1948; New York: McGraw Hill Co., 1948.

Farr, Finis. *FDR*. New Rochelle, N.Y.: Arlington House, 1972.

Flynn, John T. *As We Go Marching*. Garden City, N.Y.: Doubleday & Co., 1944.

——— *Country Squire in the White House*. Garden City, N.Y.: Doubleday & Co., 1940.

——— *The Final Secret of Pearl Harbor*. New York: J. T. Flynn, 1945.

——— *The Lattimore Story*. New York: Devin-Adair Co., 1953.

——— *The Roosevelt Myth*. New York: Devin-Adair Co., 1948.

——— *The Smear Terror*. New York: John T. Flynn, 1947.

——— *While You Slept*. New York: Devin-Adair Co., 1957.

Forrestal, James. *The Forrestal Diaries*. New York: Viking Press, 1951.

Geddes, Donald P., ed. *Franklin Delano Roosevelt, a Memorial*. New York: Pocket Books, 1945.

Gilbert, John L., ed. *The New Era in American Foreign Policy*. New York: St. Martin's Press, 1973.

Grattan, C. Hartley. *The Deadly Parallel*. Harrisburg, Pa.: Stackpole Books, 1939.

Gunther, John. *The Riddle of MacArthur*. New York: Harper & Bros., 1950.

Hauptaengl, Ernst. *Unheard Witness*. Philadelphia: J.B. Lippincott Co.

Hoover, Herbert. *America's First Crusade*. New York: Charles Scribner's Sons, 1942.

Horne, Alistair. *To Lose a Battle: France 1940*. Boston: Little, Brown & Co., 1969.

Hull, Cordell. *Memoirs of Cordell Hull*. New York: Macmillan Co., 1948.

Hunt, Frazier. *The Untold Story of Douglas MacArthur*. New York: New American Library, 1964.

Ickes, Harold L. *The Autobiography of a Curmudgeon*. New York: Reynal & Hitchcock, 1943.

———. *The Secret Diary of Harold Ickes*, 2 vols. New York: Simon & Schuster, 1953.

Johnson, George. *Eleanor Roosevelt*. New York: Monarch Press, 1962.

Kluckhohn, Frank L. *America: Listen!* New York: Monarch Press, 1961.

Knox, Frank. *We Planned It That Way*. New York: Longmans, Green & Co., 1938.

Lane, Arthur Bliss. *I Saw Poland Betrayed*. Indianapolis, Ind.: Bobbs-Merrill Co., 1948.

Lash, Joseph P. *Eleanor and Franklin*. New York: W.W. Norton & Co., 1971.

Lasky, Victor. *JFK: The Man and the Myth*. New York: Macmillan Co., 1963.

Lindley, Ernest K. *Franklin D. Roosevelt*. Blue Ribbon, 1931.

Little, Arthur. *From Harlem to the Rhine*. New York: Covia-Friede, 1936.

Loewenheim, F.; Langley, H.; and Jonas, M., eds. *Roosevelt and Churchill: Their Secret Wartime Correspondence*. New York: Saturday Review Press, 1975.

Lord, Walter. *Day of Infamy*. New York: Bantam Books, 1970.

Ludwig, Emil. *Roosevelt: A Study in Fortune and Power*. New York: Viking Press, 1938.

Lundberg, Ferdinand. *Imperial Hearst*. 1936.

Lyons, Eugene. *Our Unknown Ex-President*. Garden City, N.Y.: Doubleday & Co., 1948.

MacArthur, Douglas. *MacArthur's Address to Congress*. Chicago: Rand McNally & Co.

McCarthy, Sen. Joseph R. *America's First Retreat From Victory*. New York: Devin-Adair Co., 1951.

Moley, Raymond. *After Seven Years*. New York: Harper & Bros., 1939.

Morgenstern, George. *Pearl Harbor*. New York: Devin-Adair Co., 1947.

Moses, Robert. *A Tribute to Governor Smith*. New York: Simon & Schuster, 1962.

National Committee of Americans of Polish Descent. *Death at Katyn*. New York, 1944.

Perkins, Frances. *The Roosevelt I Knew*. New York: Viking Press, 1946.

Pettengill, Samuel B. *Smoke Screen*. Nashville, Tenn.: Southern Publishers, 1940.

Pratt, John M. *Revitalizing a Nation*. Heritage Foundation, 1952.

Republican National Committee. *The Roosevelt Record in Red*. Washington, D.C., 1940.

Robey, Ralph. *Roosevelt versus Recovery*. New York: Harper & Bros., 1934.

Roosevelt, Eleanor. *This Is My Story*. Garden City, N.Y.: Doubleday & Co., 1939.

Roosevelt, Elliott. *As He Saw It*. New York: Duell, Sloan & Pearce, 1946.

Roosevelt, Elliott and Brough, James. *An Untold Story: The Roosevelts of Hyde Park*. New York: G.P. Putnam's Sons, 1973.

Roosevelt, Franklin D. *Roosevelt's Foreign Policy 1933–1941*. (Franklin D. Roosevelt's Unedited Speeches and Messages.) New York: Wilfred Funk, 1942.

———. *Public Papers and Addresses, 1928–1940*, 8 vols. New York: Random House.

Schwarz, Dr. Paul. *This Man Ribbentrop*. New York: Julian Messner, 1943.

Sherwood, Robert E. *Roosevelt and Hopkins*. New York: Harper & Bros., 1948.

Shirer, William L. *Berlin Diary*. New York: Alfred Knopf, 1941.

Shulman, Milton. *Defeat in the West*. New York: E.P. Dutton & Co., 1948.

Stettinius, E.R. *Lend-Lease*. New York: Macmillan Co., 1944.

———. *Roosevelt and the Russians*. London: Jonathan Cape, 1950.

Stimson, Henry L., and Bundy, McGeorge. *On Active Service in Peace and War*. New York: Harper & Bros., 1947.

Sweeny, Charles. *Pearl Harbor*. Privately printed, 1946.

Tansill, Charles C. *Back Door to War. The Roosevelt Foreign Policy, 1933–1941*. Chicago: Henry Regenery Co., 1952.

Taylor, Robert L. *Winston Churchill*. New York: Pocket Books, 1965.

Theobald, Rear Adm. Robert A. *The Final Secret of Pearl Harbor*. New York: Devin-Adair Co., 1954.

Thompson, Walter H. *Assignment: Churchill*. New York: Popular Library, 1961.

U.S. Department of State. *United States Relations with China*. Washington, D.C., 1949.

Utley, Freda. *Last Chance in China*. Indianapolis, Ind.: Bobbs-Merrill Co., 1947.

Van Tyne, Claude H. *The American Revolution*. New York: Harper & Bros., 1905.

Viorst, Milton. *Hostile Allies: FDR and Charles de Gaulle*. New York: Macmillan Co., 1965.

Warburg, James P. *Hell Bent for Election*. Garden City, N.Y.: Doubleday, Doran Co., 1936.

Warner, Emily Smith, and Daniel, Hawthorne. *The Happy Warrior*. Garden City, N.Y.: Doubleday & Co., 1956.

Whalen, Richard J. *The Founding Father: The Story of Joseph P. Kennedy*. New York: New American Library, 1966.

Zevin, Ben D., ed. *Nothing To Fear: Selected Addresses of Franklin Delano Roosevelt*. Boston: Houghton-Mifflin Co., 1946.

INDEX

Acheson, Dean, 7, 32, 163–167, 170, 219–221
Allen, Robert, 45, 47
Atlantic Charter, 44, 50, 66, 125–129, 157, 190

Barkley, Alben W., 80
Barton, Bruce, 34
Baruch, Bernard, 81, 85
Beck, Josef, 86, 100, 102–103, 107–110
Biddle, Anthony, 110, 118
Bohlen, Charles, 116, 194
Bonnet, Georges, 59, 61–63, 82, 88, 99, 106–107, 109
Brewster, Senator, 154, 156
Browder, Earl, 39, 196
Bullitt, William, 45, 47, 59, 61–62, 76, 82, 106–107, 110, 114–115
Burns, James MacGregor, 34
Burton, Richard, 192
Byrnes, James, 67, 193, 197, 199

Catledge, Turner, 11
Chamberlain, Neville, 46–47, 53, 74, 76–77, 97–98, 101, 104, 106–107, 110, 204
Chamberlain, William H., 120
Chiang Kai-shek, 135, 138, 165, 190, 200–202, 217, 219–221
Churchill, Randolph, 176
Churchill, Winston, 11, 40, 44, 48, 50–52, 54–58, 60–61, 63, 67–70, 78, 110, 115–116, 119, 126–127, 129, 131, 138, 141, 157, 170, 174–179, 187, 191, 194, 197, 203–205, 223

Ciechanowski, Jan, 117–118
Clark, Bennett, 27, 34, 179
Clark, Gen. Mark, 170
Coolidge, Calvin, 20
Cochran, Tommy, 1
Crowley, Leo T., 206–207
Currie, Lauchlin, 6, 66, 131, 138, 165

Daladier, Premier, 59, 62, 99, 110
Dall, Col. Curtis B., 233
Danzig, Poland, 17–18, 32, 41, 75–76, 86, 92–93, 98–105, 108–109, 114, 177, 180
Davies, Joseph, 33, 218
Davis, Elmer, 13
de Gaulle, Charles, 34, 44, 52, 54–56, 59–61, 67–69
De Valera, President, 81
Dewey, Thomas E., 26, 34
Dies, Martin, 34, 37, 42
Duke of Windsor, 191

Eden, Anthony, 55, 67, 110, 115, 203, 205
Eisenhower, Dwight D., 2, 90

Farley, James A., 2, 11, 185, 189–190, 199
Ferguson, Senator, 154, 156
Flynn, Edward J., 2
Flynn, John, 11, 205
Forrestal, James V., 76, 107, 197, 222

George, Lloyd, 75, 104, 179
Giraud, Gen. Henri, 69
Gladwyn, Lord, 192

253

Grayson, Admiral, 183, 189
Greene, Theodore Francis, 80
Greene, William, 26
Grew, Joseph, 134, 147

Haakon, King, 92
Halifax, Lord, 81, 98, 109
Halsey, Admiral, 132, 152, 158
Hambro, Mr., 96
Harriman, Averell, 21, 32, 119, 194
Hecht, Ben, 211
Henderson, Nevile, 98, 109
High, Stanley, 1
Hillman, Sidney, 6–7, 33
Hirohito, Emperor, 134
Hiss, Alger, 6–7, 40, 67, 120–121, 193, 204–205, 219, 223
Hitler, Adolph, 11–12, 21. 32–34, 41, 46, 53. 62, 75, 76, 78, 87–88, 96, 98, 101–105, 108–110, 115, 210
Hoover, Herbert, 2, 27, 96, 111, 172
Hopkins, Harry, 6–7, 11, 21, 26, 31, 33, 40, 67, 119–121, 146, 150, 185, 193, 195–196, 204–206, 223
Howe, Louis, 1–2
Hull, Cordell, 46–47, 67, 75, 90, 132, 136–139, 141–144, 146, 148, 150–151, 161, 175, 184–185, 193, 199
Hurley, Patrick, 222

Ickes, Harold, 17, 21. 33, 46
Interparliamentary Union Conference, 79, 84, 91–92

Johnson, Hiram, 9
Johnson, Hugh S., 12
Jones, Jesse, 3, 17, 184

Kennedy, John F., 2, 22, 220
Kennedy, Joseph, 46, 62, 72–78, 101, 107, 114
Kenoye, Prince, 134
Kimmel, Admiral, 9, 132, 138, 148, 150–154, 156, 158, 162
Knox, Henry, 21–22, 39, 132, 136, 139, 143, 146, 148–152
Krock, Arthur, 13–14, 133–134
Kurusu, Saburo, 137

LaChambre, Guy, 82
LaFollette, Robert M., 27–28
Laird, Melvin, 41
Lattimore, Owen, 131, 135, 138, 165
Leahy, Admiral, 193, 201, 218
Lend Lease, 56, 70, 206
Lewis, John L., 12, 27
Lindbergh, Col. Charles, 34, 62
Lippman, Walter, 11, 129
Long, Huey, 12, 34–35
Lothian, Lord, 108–109
Ludlow, Louis, 26
Lukasiewicz, Ambassador, 114

McCarran, Pat, 34
McCormack, Col. Robert, 34
McIntyre, V/Adm. Ross T., 182, 183, 185, 189, 190
McNeider, Hanford, 27
MacArthur, Gen. Douglas, 163, 165–173, 187, 199, 202, 221, 240, 242
MacLeish, Archibald, 13
Marshall, Gen. George, 7, 90, 132–133, 136, 139, 143, 146, 148–152, 158, 163, 165, 170, 193, 201–202, 218–219, 221–223
Martin, Joseph, 34, 169, 174
Mikolajczyk, 119
Mineta, Norman, 140
Moffat, J. Pierpont, 76
Moley, Ray, 1
Molotov, 119, 128
Montgomery, Field Marshall Viscount, 172
Moore, John Bassett, 224–225
Moran, Lord, 192
Morgenthau, Henry, 21, 73–74, 185
Morgenthau Plan, 52, 194
Moses, Robert, 34
Mruk, Joseph, 117
Mussolini, 51, 53, 95–96, 98

NRA, 3, 12
New Deal, 7–10, 12, 14, 17, 19, 22, 230
Niemcewicz, Count Julian, 113–114
Nimitz, Adm. Chester, 166, 202
Nixon, Richard, 43
Nomuro, Ambassador, 132, 136–138,

143, 161
Nye, Senator, 34, 133

O'Malley, Sir Owen, 123

Pearl Harbor, 10, 33, 131, 133, 135, 139, 143, 146, 149, 152–159, 162
Pearson, Drew, 45, 47
Perkins, Miss Frances, 1, 14, 187–188
Pilsudski, Marshall, 102–103
Potocki, Jerzy, 105–107, 114, 117

Rayburn, Sam, 26
Reconstruction Finance Corp., 17
Reynaud, Premier, 59–62
Reynolds, Robert, 25, 34, 155
Richardson, Admiral J. O., 156–157, 160
Roberts Commission, 147, 152, 154–155
Roberts, Owen, 152
Rockefeller, Nelson, 26
Rogers, Edith, 218–219
Roosevelt, Eleanor, 7, 186, 206
Roosevelt, Elliott, 68
Roosevelt, Franklin
  ghost-writers, 1
  lust for power, 17, 38, 181, 183
  personal association with author, 3, 6–7, 34–35, 158
  ultimatum to Japan, 8, 10, 12, 28, 31, 40–41
Roosevelt, Theodore, 2, 55
Rosenman, Sam, 1
Rozmarek, Charles, 118

Sallett, Richard, 83, 91
Saud, King Ibn, 208
Schlesinger, Arthur M., Jr., 171
Sherwood, Robert, 1, 19–20, 31, 39, 126, 200
Short, General, 8, 132, 138, 148–154. 156
Short, Dewey, 162
Simon, Sir John, 78
Smedley, Agnes, 218
Smith, Alfred E., 3, 34, 39–40
Spellman, Francis Cardinal, 64–65, 67, 69–70
Stalin, Joseph, 7–8, 11–12, 17, 27, 33, 40–44, 48, 50, 52–53, 56–58, 65–66, 69–71, 76, 78, 103, 116, 120, 123, 194, 197, 206
Stark, Admiral, 132, 137, 139, 143, 146, 148–152, 158–159, 162
Stettinus, Edward, 185, 192–193, 205
Stimson, Henry L., 21–22, 29, 131–132, 136, 139–142, 144, 146, 148–152, 157, 160

Taft, Sen. Robert, 174, 179
Teheran Conference, 43, 48, 51, 54, 64–65, 117, 181, 190
Theobald, Adm. Robert A., 151–152, 158
Thomas, Norman, 8, 27
Trohan, Walter, 195, 222
Truman, Harry, 27, 33, 90, 115, 163, 168–169, 179
Tugwell, Rexford Guy, 6
Tully, Grace, 183, 188
Tydings, Senator, 34

United Nations, 17, 119, 199, 206

Vandenberg, Arthur, 174, 176, 179
Van Fleet. Gen. James, 171
Van Paasen, Pierre, 213
Vincent, Carl, 36
Vincent, John Carter, 165, 219
von Ribbentrop, Joachim, 79, 81, 83–89, 91–92, 101

Wallace, Henry, 6–7, 21, 26, 33, 165, 188, 206
Walsh, David, 34, 155, 158
Warburg, James D., 9
Warren, Earl, 122
Washington Post. 19, 25
Welles, Sumner, 46, 67, 126, 129, 185, 219
Wheeler, Burton, 34, 179
White, Harry Dexter, 6–7, 66, 165
Wiley, Alexander, 80
Willkie, Wendell, 30
Wilson, Woodrow, 2, 105
Wood, Gen. Robert, 27
Woodrum, Clifton, 26

Yalta Conference, 23, 38, 40–41, 48, 51–52, 54–57, 120–121, 129–130, 190–199, 203